Impact of GLOBALISATION ON EDUCATION

Learning to Live Together

Impact of GLOBALISATION ON EDUCATION

Learning to Live Together

Indira Madhukar

AUTHORSPRESS

Worldwide Circulation through Authorspress Global Network
First Published 2003
Reprinted 2004, 2006
Reprinted 2007
by Authorspress

E-35/103, Jawahar Park
Laxmi Nagar, Delhi-110092

e-mail: authorspress@yahoo.com

Typeset in NewCenturySchlbk by Chitra Computers

Impact of Globalisation on Education: Learning to Live Together
ISBN 81-7273-113-2

Printed in India at Tarun Offset, Delhi.

Preface

The phenomenon of globalisation is considered as the most widespread trends in our century has ever witnessed. It has resulted from the worldwide integration of economic and financial sectors. Globalisation contributes to a wide diffusion of ideas and values mobilising international attention to universalistic issues and challenges. In this context of a changing world, the central role played by education to favour social and professional integration appears to be hugely reinforced. Even countries under endemic conflict with their neighbours, or having suffered from decades of discrimination, are revising their teaching of history and geography to learn to live together.

Globalisation has permitted technical progress in the communications field which enables users to access and exchange information at any time and from any place in the world, which has largely facilitated the speeding-up of production, as well as the sharing of goods, services, capital flows—and also ideas. The multiplication of sources of information (newspapers, radio, television, the web, CD-ROMs and other multimedia materials, etc.) and the fast evolution of knowledge, in particular, in the fields of science and technology, imply not only the need to update educational content regularly, but also to review the design of curricula and the teaching of subjects in an interdisciplinary manner.

The new information and communication technologies could lead to a uniform computer culture without a human face spreading around the world. They allow instantaneous exchange and sharing of the information and knowledge and enhance our diverse learning processes and accelerate the formation of learning communities. They can open up spaces for learning to be more creative and generative, and the focus of the learning process shifts from teaching to self-directed learning, and from learning as a one-time event to learning as a lifelong process. On the other hand, they could create a sense of 'global village'. A village where people chose to share across geopolitical, social and cultural boundaries while proudly preserving their own identity. And not just preserving it, we enhance our culture and our identity when we share it with others and when we share theirs.

The rapid evolution of today's societies requires new skills from individuals. These were summarised in a report published by UNESCO in 1996 as follows: 'learning to know, learning to do, learning to live together and learning to be.' They call for the redefinition of educational programmes on a competency-based approach: this implies that from now on, curricula should focus on students attaining a stated number of clearly defined skills or competencies at the end of each stage and level of school education.

The 21st century calls for a wider vision of education which breaks down the traditional distinction between initial education and continuing education. What we now call our 'knowledge societies' require all of us to update our knowledge and skills regularly throughout life. Only in this way we can cope confidently with technological change and the social and economic transformations of our communities.

Today, globalisation is progressing rapidly in all fields of human activity, from terrorism to business and from culture to what we eat. Of course terror and hatred still exist, and there is a great gap between the technologically advanced and economically affluent countries and the least developed countries. However, there is also the hope for peaceful and harmonious relationship among peoples, who now have so many ways to share their experience, knowledge and skills with each other.

The book is an attempt to present the implications and challenges raised by globalisation in the sphere of education. Focusing on the principle of teaching/learning to live together, it provides different means of introducing learning to live together in educational content and the problems that this may entail. It is hoped that this book will help the policy planners and academics and educators to develop a sound and effective system of education results in the continuous development of the young generation's potentialities, which strengthen their skills and fostering positive interests, attitudes and values to cope up with the challenges raised by globalisation, thereby by enabling them to live together.

Indira Madhukar

Contents

1

Introduction

The phenomenon of globalisation is considered as the most widespread trend our century has ever witnessed. It has resulted from the worldwide integration of economic and financial sectors. The current trend towards globalisation will create the necessary infrastructure for individuals and nations to interact with each other and mutually benefit from such a process. A globalised world is one in which political, economic, cultural, social and educational events become more and more multidirectional but yet interconnected.

The trend of globalisation has existed historically since the development of international trade. However, it can be considered, to a certain extent, as a more recent phenomenon, since over the past few years it has experienced a high acceleration, due to the following factors are given below:

— *Geopolitical changes*: the erosion of the power of nation states, in a context of transfer of sovereignty from governments to regional entities, and the development of multinational corporations have contributed to a dramatic increase in trans-border exchanges.

— *A dominant ideology of regulation by market forces*: the end of the regulation of financial and economic markets, following, in particular, the setting up of the Bretton Woods system, the General Agreement on Trade and Tarrif (GATT), finally, the expansion of the free-market ideology after the collapse of the Soviet Bloc, has greatly contributed to the interpenetration of national economies;

— *Fast and significant technological progress*: technical progress in the communications field has permitted users to access and exchange information at any time and from any place in the world, which has largely facilitated the speeding-up of production, as well as the sharing of goods, services, capital flows—and also ideas.

— The aim of *increasing return on capital investment*, added to the possibility of locating the units of production of goods and services almost anywhere in the world, have also contributed to uniting or globalising our planet.

Among the main implications of the phenomenon of globalisation, one can mention:

— The emergence of learning societies due to the multiplication of sources of information and communication;

— the transformation of the nature of work with, in particular, the need for more flexibility and mobility, the importance of communication skills, the necessity for teamwork, the increasing use of new technologies, etc.;

— the progression of social exclusion—a large part of the world's population does not participate in this process.

In this context of a changing world, the central role played by education to favour social and professional integration appears to be hugely reinforced.

EDUCATION CHALLENGES RAIS ED BY GLOBALISATION

The educational challenges raised by globalisation are a multitude. We may mention the following as examples:

— *The need to rethink the delivery of content, integrating new sources of information*: The multiplication of sources of information (newspapers, radio, television, the web,

CDROMs and other multimedia materials, etc.) and the fast evolution of knowledge, in particular, in the fields of science and technology, imply not only the need to update educational content regularly, but also to review the design of curricula and the teaching of subjects in an interdisciplinary manner. This also raises the need for better co-operation with 'information brokers'—such as science museums—that can play the role of intermediaries between 'knowledge producers' (universities) and 'knowledge consumers' (pupils/students).

— *The need to favour the development of skills alongside knowledge*: The fast evolution of today's societies—and, more specifically, of labour markets— requires new skills from individuals. These were summarised in a report published by UNESCO in 1996 as follows: learning to know, learning to do, learning to live together and learning to be. They call for the redefinition of educational programmes on a competency-based approach: this implies that from now on, curricula should focus on students attaining a stated number of clearly defined skills or competencies at the end of each stage and level of school education. This, of course, should have consequences on teaching/learning methods, student assessment procedures and certification.

— *The need to adapt curricula to the needs of different sociocultural groups, and to maintain the national and social cohesion of the country*: The phenomenon of globalisation has helped to widen the gap between those who globalise, and those who are globalised—or left out—of the process at the local, national, regional and international levels. This raises the problem for public authorities of how to maintain the cohesion of a country. As a result, there are implications for education, since the situation and the sociocultural background of learners are seldom taken into consideration when conceiving and implementing curricula. Trying to cope with this situation means not only having to refer to the national identity or promote the concept of citizenship, but also having to include the teaching of peaceful coexistence in educational content.

Teaching to live together is synonymous with developing an understanding of other people and an appreciation of interdependence in a spirit of respect for the values of pluralism, mutual understanding and peace'. There are several ways of introducing this concept into educational content. The three main strategies are given below:

— By defining new scopes for 'old disciplines' (history and geography, foreign languages, etc.) a study led by the University of Geneva, under the leadership of the IBE, has shown that traditional subjects, such as history and geography, can contribute, to a great extent, to teaching about living together. It thus categorised three different ways of teaching geography.

The role played by geography in learning to live together

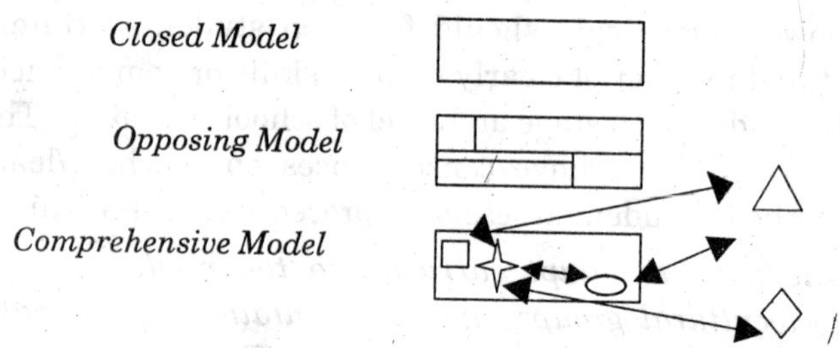

In the case of the 'closed model', a country is presented as a homogenous space, delimited by its borders. The 'opposing model' takes into account the existence of several overlapping entities (geographical, administrative, economic, linguistic, etc.) in the national territory. The 'comprehensive model' puts forward the existence of various entities, both inside and outside the national territory, and their mutual interactions. The only model favouring learning to live together is obviously the comprehensive one, which brings together different geographical scales to permit an understanding of the continuity from the local to the global, and which allows not only the concept of identity to develop, but also those of otherness, interdependency and universality.

— *By introducing new subjects (i.e. education towards active citizenship, environmental issues, etc.) in curricula:* The widespread concern for global issues, such as population control, urbanisation, environment, consumption, citizenship, etc., favours their integration in educational programmes. The example of the project entitled 'Educating towards active citizenship', launched by Quebec (Canada) in 1998, shows that the introduction of these new concepts demands a review of curriculum design by adopting a comprehensive approach, developing more participatory teaching/learning methods and working in partnership with out-of-school actors so as to enable students to put what they have learned into practice.

— *By promoting social consensus on a common core of values:* The teaching of specific values, such as the acceptance of diversity, fairness, tolerance, etc., can help in learning to live together. Australia has developed an innovative project in this area. A 'charter of values', including a list of values, has thus been set up. Each Australian state has the possibility of selecting values from the list: the state of Queensland, for instance, has agreed to teach in its schools, among other things, the values of compassion, equality, respect for human rights and respect and the search for truth.

Nevertheless, a few warming can be issued about the introduction of teaching to live together in curricula. They are summarised in table 1.

The development of new teaching/learning methods appears to be fundamental in obtaining a significant change in learners' behaviours. An article published in the *Journal of vocational education and training* gives a good illustration of the importance of the pedagogy used students from the Hong

Kong Polytechnic University were failing to integrate into the food and management sector, although they had been trained to do so.

Table 1: Risks and remedies of teaching about living together

Risks	*Remedies*
The 'Panicapproach	Rigorous planning of the development of curricula.
Over-loading of curricula	Focus on the basics Review the balance between subjects Inter-disciplinarity
Accumulation of a fragmented knowledge	Bridges between general education and the world of work
Limited impact on learners behaviour	Modern teaching/learning methods

This was partly due to the irrelevancy of the teaching methods used, which did not help them feel sufficiently confident to communicate in English with foreigners, who were to be their main customers.

TEACHERS ADAPT THEIR TEACHING METHODS

Teachers are the key actors if any actual reform of educational programmes is to take place. Several policies can be followed in order to help them adapt their teaching methods, three of which are presented hereafter:

— *To help them develop new skills through initial and in-service training (involvement in teamwork, etc.).*

The most obvious strategy consists of renewing their initial training through in-service courses designed to integrate new subjects that will be taught in an interdisciplinary way, at the same time familiarising them with participatory and student-centred approaches. Regular in-service training should help teachers to update their knowledge and share their experience with others.

— *To modify the design of textbooks to allow them to be used differently*: In order to modify their teaching methods, teachers should be given the opportunity to use newly-designed educational materials. A report published by the French Ministry of National Education contains recommendations to review the design and use of textbooks. It suggests, in particular, that textbooks should be defined as 'a reference tool', summarising the main concepts which children should acquire. They should not to be too long, nor contain too many pictures, quotations, etc. This would enable teachers to organise their course autonomously, referring to textbooks, but using other materials as well—in particular, multimedia sources—to illustrate their presentation as they want.

— *To make new evaluation means available to teachers, defined together with different actors*: In order to be ready to adopt 'competency-based' curricula, teachers should be provided with new evaluation tools. The example of the United States' General Educational Development Testing (called GED Testing) can give a few ideas on this point. In its 2000 version, it includes a series of tests aimed at evaluating the capacity of students on information processing and at assessing their communication skills. A cross-disciplinary test also makes it possible to see if students are able to solve a global problem, by making use of what they have learned in different subjects.

— *By giving them the possibility of resorting to non-formal educational resources (science museums, etc.)*: The creation of innovative science museums.

Favouring a 'sense of ownership' towards the curriculum on the part of teachers should be looked at as a key factor for change. Two main strategies can be explored in this area:

— *To involve teachers in the development of curricula:* Innovative experiments have been conducted in Sub-Saharan Africa in order to enable teachers to take part actively in the setting-up of educational programmes. Curriculum conferences have thus been organised to allow teachers to decide how prescribed curriculum guidelines should be put into practice. These conferences have proved to be successful, helping teachers to feel involved and, as a result, responsible for what they teach.

— *To favour school-based curricula:* an example from Scotland illustrates another way of associating teachers with the development of educational programmes. For a while, Scottish teachers have been authorised to select, adapt and develop, at school level, the limited guidelines provided to them by the government. They have had, for instance, no textbooks available to help them. This experience was said not only to favour a sense of ownership of curricula among teachers, but also to help improve the relevance of what was taught, by adapting it both to local and school needs.

A selected number were chosen to be discussed during the sub-regional course on curriculum development, namely:

— The relevance of new trends in the teaching of science, social science and humanities to the challenges of globalisation and the principle of living together.

— Decentralisation of curriculum development to local or school level.

— Integrated and interdisciplinary approaches in curriculum reform.

— The adaptation of teacher training to curriculum change.

— The potentials and challenges of information and communication technologies in the adaptation of curricula.

— Non-school science resources and collaboration between formal and non-formal educational institutions.

— The need for vocationalising curricula.

ROUND-TABLE DEBATE

Four resource persons participated in the round-table debate, which was then followed by group discussions on issues relating to the three broad subject areas examined: humanities, science and social science.

The full text of the presentation on the humanities is included below.

Humanities

The human child is born to learn. The learning process begins at birth and continues throughout life. The human capacity to learn is best demonstrated by the child's ability to learn a first language. Bombarded with ungrammatical, incomplete and mutilated baby talk, nevertheless the child learns to speak his/her mother-tongue perfectly by the age of four or five.

In this way, the child is able to control his or her total environment—social, emotional, and psychological—through language. A child is even able to learn more than one language—two, sometimes more—if the social environment so requires.

Very few of us realise or appreciate that 'normal' children perform a miracle in mastering their mother-tongue so quickly, and can learn more than one language if they are exposed to more languages. We can appreciate this miracle when we see the problems that adults have in trying to learn a 'new' language. By age four or so, every child has learned to speak the mother-tongue or home language perfectly; understands what others say, and makes himself/herself understood. By this age, the child is able to use the language creatively and may be likened to a 'born' poet. The only difference between the child and the adult is in the range of vocabulary that a child controls. And, of course, the child has yet to learn to read and write.

When children enter school they are already accomplished users of the mother-tongue or the home language. But the school often ignores this linguistic competence of the child, since a uniform standard form of language is 'taught' to all children. Often this standard language is so different from the child's home language that the child has problems comprehending it—as well as the school itself. It is bad enough when the child's home language is simply a social or regional dialect of the standard school language. The problem is compounded when the school language is totally different from the home language of the child.

In many bi- or multilingual countries, children have to start school using a language that is entirely different from their mother tongue. When this happens the child not only feels lost, but is traumatised. In such a situation, linguistically the child becomes an infant again, while still actually being an accomplished user of the mother-tongue.

The situation is even more complex, because the schoolteacher believes that the child has to be taught basic language skills—listening and speaking, followed by reading and writing—in a language that the child does not actually understand in the first place. Very soon, the teacher becomes convinced that the child will not be able to learn the school language efficiently and writes him/ her off as a poor learner. In the absence of basic vocabulary, grammatical intuition and communication skills, the child will not able to take on the other school subjects either.

In some school systems this complex problem is bypassed by a simple strategy whereby the teacher trains the child to memorise facts and standard responses which can be reproduced during examinations. And this is passed off as formal learning. The child learns to don two personalities: one of limited competence in the school, and another of fluent communication at home. Unfortunately, in such bi- or multilingual settings the school language, which can be regional, pan-national or international, often enjoys social prestige and leads to economic advantage. Consequently, the child gradually learns to favour the prestigious 'other' tongue in preference to the mother-tongue. As a result, by the time they complete their formal education children end up as linguistic cripples, having poor competence in the other language, and having allowed their mother tongue to atrophy through disuse.

The place and function of language in school ought to be very different from this situation, especially in bi- and multilingual school systems. Language education in school must primarily aim at sharpening the linguistic skills that children bring with them. Primary education Round-table: The relevance of new trends in the teaching of science, social science and humanities to the challenge of globalisation and the principle of learning to live together should essentially be focused on language education, because at this stage children need to build on the linguistic abilities that they have already acquired. If the child is functioning in a monolingual setting, he/she has to transit gradually from the oral mode of communication to the written mode, which can take four or five years of formal primary school.

During this period, children should not only acquire basic literacy skills, but should be allowed to build on their intuition in the mother-tongue. Children should be made aware of the immense power of language and the potential that they already possess to use that language creatively. Children have to build on their lexical resources, experiment with descriptive devices, and learn to reflect on their environment—physical, social, psychological and emotional. On the other hand, if the child has to acquire a new language in school, the school should build on the child's existing skills in the mother-tongue when learning the new language.

Although languages appear to be different from each other, there are crucial underlying similarities in the manner in which human languages are organised. The structures of the mother-tongue can be exploited to teach a second and even a third language. All young children have a natural ability to learn other languages quickly, provided they perceive them as essential for day-to- day communication. What young children do not understand is why they should learn a new language, which is obviously not needed for communication. If left to themselves, children would learn a new language only if it hastened their integration into a milieu.

The motivation to learn a language for instrumental purposes comes at a later stage. However, the school curriculum can be designed so that young children can become motivated to learn a second language that will be useful to them later in life.

In order to plan and implement a creative language curriculum, it is necessary to understand how children learn languages. It is necessary to map the communicative strategies that children naturally employ and to build on these so that they internalise their expanding experiences in school. The language curriculum should be to enlarge the child's vocabulary in the mother-tongue and link it to the language used in school.

If the school language is different from the mother-tongue, the curriculum should allow the child to use the mother-tongue vocabulary as a basis for learning the lexicon of the language used in school. The enriching of the child's vocabulary can be achieved in various creative ways. Ensure that children perceive the linguistic/cultural categories that their mother tongue employs for looking at the real world. This is significant, especially in bilingual and multilingual settings.

Different cultures categorise reality in different ways. Colour terms, relational terms and spatio-temporal relationships are perceived differently by different cultures, and these differences are reflected in the languages. For children to acquire intuition in a second or third language, it is crucial that they should apprehend the linguistic/cultural categories of a language. Equip children with adequate descriptive devices so that they can describe their experiences and their environment. In the current school curricula, children are seldom encouraged to give expression to their thoughts, perceptions, feelings or emotions. Instead, they are given samples of excellent writing by well-known authors that they are required to emulate. This results in a reluctance on the part of the children to experiment with language. In bilingual and multilingual settings, children can be guided to discover how different languages employ descriptive devices. It is possible for a child to enrich his/her linguistic repertoire by personally comparing two or more languages.

Enable the child to reflect on his/ her reality in the mother-tongue and the other tongue(s). Children learn to ask 'why?' at a very early age. Unfortunately, the school often drills out this natural inquisitiveness in the child. This happens when children are expected to conform to the standard norm, and are not allowed to be different from each other. Language education is inadequate if children do not learn to reflect and work out, on their own, equations such as 'X ... therefore Y', 'if not X ... then what?', and many more. Reflection is the ultimate goal of language education. A language curriculum that enables and supports the child's natural capacity to learn can be designed, provided the school system sees the child as the focus of education. Education is clearly unsatisfactory if it consists merely of learning information and superficial facts.

A language teacher has a major role to play in enabling the child to become an excellent communicator. In fact, all teachers are language teachers, no matter what subject(s) they may teach. Each discipline uses the resources of language to impart knowledge. Therefore it is incumbent on every teacher to become aware of the vast potential of a language. Language teachers need to be trained to transact the language curriculum creatively. They must understand that the four fundamental skills of listening, speaking, reading and writing are merely teaching devices, and not ends in themselves. The goal of language education is to enlarge the natural resources of the mother-tongue that the child brings to school.

The teacher's job is to ensure that children are provided with sufficient opportunities to practice and sharpen their natural skills. One way of ensuring that this happens is to encourage children to read on their own. Reading stimulates the imagination. Reading enables each child to create magnificent images in the mind, an ability that can be severely impaired by the more modern practice of watching television images created by some other person. The teacher must also be a learner and observe what the child is capable of doing. The teacher must continuously enlarge his/her capacity to enthuse children to use their natural language skills in order to understand the world. In the present information age, the vast reservoir of human knowledge is available in a dominant international language. It is not surprising, therefore, that many school systems find it both necessary and profitable to teach an international language. Currently, the most profitable global language is English. However, it is important to be alive to the dangers of adopting an international language at the cost of indigenous languages. While English may assist in the process of globalisation, neglect of local and national languages may result in their marginalisation. And, of course, the impact of such neglect on human cultures the world over cannot even be imagined or calculated.

Science

There are two principal new trends in the teaching of science are the opening up of schools to society and an increasing recognition of the importance of developing scientific methodology and ways of thinking among students. For the past twenty years the school has grown to recognise the need to keep up with changes taking place in society. This trend can be observed through the evolution of the subjects in the curriculum, the participation of different actors from the wider community in the classroom, and the increasing use in the classroom of technical tools used in the world of work, in particular information and communication technologies. There are seven characteristics of this new trend may be identified:

— *The end of isolation between school and the rest of the society*: If the school is to prepare a larger number of pupils for adult life more effectively, the education system must be less isolated from the rest of the society. This end of isolation is characterised not only by the evolution of the teaching tools available in school, but by all the following points.

— *The increasing incorporation of global and interdisciplinary topics into the curriculum:* To understand the effects of science and technology on society, it is necessary to teach these subjects in an interdisciplinary manner, relating specific themes to the broader subject and showing their relevance to other disciplines in the curriculum.

— *Vocational education and lifelong learning*: One of the new demands on the school is adequate preparation of pupils for the world of work. The right balance has to be found between general education and the vocational preparation for working life. There needs to be better knowledge of the job market, its structure and organisation, and the training required to enter it.

— *Citizenship education:* Another new role for schools is to prepare children to assume their responsibilities as citizens. This should involve not only learning about the organisation of society and the role of its institutions, but should also provide models of democratic behaviour, foster rigorous moral attitudes and generate debates on subjects of general interest. All of these concerns are relevant to the effective teaching of science and technology.

— *The new function of non-school organisations:* To help schools assume their new role, diverse non-school organisations can be solicited: the media, museums, libraries, trade unions, businesses and industries can all help schools in this new mission.

— *Basic knowledge versus 'up-to-date' contents*: The vast amount of available knowledge creates the problem of what to include in the science and technology curriculum and what to leave out. Fundamental knowledge is essential, but it is also necessary to be familiar with the latest developments in science in order to understand the society we live in. These developments often differ from basic knowledge in that they are evolving and our understanding of them is constantly being modified. Therefore we need an increasing quantity of knowledge. One of the solutions (but not the only one) would be to determine what basic knowledge is required, as well as the principal new developments to be taught in the classroom. In addition, students must be taught the skills of research, inquiry and interpretation so that they may continue learning and expanding their knowledge beyond the classroom and beyond the school.

The second main trend for teaching science is the importance of training in scientific attitudes and the ability to relate these to the real world around us. Today, it is vital to acquire a general and scientific education at school, but also crucial to have the skills and rigorous attitudes required for research and lifelong learning. Seven aspects of this scientific behaviour can be identified:

— *Skills of observation, analysis, comparison and classification:* These intellectual skills are as important as acquiring and owning knowledge. Developing them demands rigour and objectivity.
— *Carrying out experiments to understand and respect reality:* Experimental activity is one of the most important approaches in science. Starting from a question, students have to be taught to state a hypothesis, to establish the experimental protocol to confirm or invalidate the hypothesis and, armed with the outcome, to progress from this new temporary understanding of reality to another question.
— *Documentary research*: Developing information research skills is essential to learning science. Students must be taught universal research methods, including the selection of appropriate keywords and the identification of suitable

sources and resources. This method can draw on books, documents and newspapers, but also on the huge quantity of information available on the Internet.

— *Developing critical thinking skills:* One important attitude to be developed in conjunction with documentary research is the training of a critical mind. Pupils must be taught to check and assess all the information they encounter, compare it with other sources, and weigh up the probability of truth in each. This behaviour is not only useful in documentary research, but also during any activity in which information is being transmitted: debates, meetings, radio, television, etc.

— *Active learning and collaborative learning*: For all the types of activities described above, the pupils have to be active learners and participants in the process. The advantage in working in small groups is that it makes possible the sharing of intellectual resources and supports each other's learning.

— *Developing a pedagogy of the project:* The global dimension of a project, with the involvement of all pupils throughout its development is a vital means of giving pupils a sense of ownership, of meaningful participation in the learning process.

— *Starting from the pupils' representations/initial knowledge as the starting point for differentiated learning:* It is essential to take into account the differences among pupils' initial representations of science and technology and the diversity of their learning styles. It is very important to adapt the learning process to the initial conceptions of individual pupils and assess the evolution of their representations at the end of the lesson. This presentation clearly underlines the urgent need to change traditional approaches to teaching, and to pay attention to the selection and use of instructional materials, and to the organisation of the class. For these changes to be carried out in schools, innovation and reform in teacher education are vital.

Focusing on the recent curriculum reform in Norway, the speaker discussed how subject syllabi in the social sciences, humanities and religious/moral education can support general education especially in the light of the principle of learning to live together. A major concern of curriculum development should be how the various subject areas can support general education for lifelong learning. The curriculum should ideally be seen as a document not just for schools and teachers, but for, and belonging to, society. The ultimate aim of curriculum development should be the achievement of education for all in a unified system, which at the same time acknowledges and caters to difference and diversity. A major preoccupation is how to develop a balanced curriculum while avoiding overload. How does one decide what to exclude? One way of coping with the excessive amount of knowledge is to develop and foster a spirit of inquiry in the student which will permit him/her to go on learning throughout life.

The best approach is to first assist pupils to discover the reality around them and then to expand their inquiry to the wider, global environment. The development of research skills should be an integral part of the core curriculum. The curriculum should focus on the all-round development of the individual. Students should be taught to see themselves as both citizens of their own country and of the world. It is a prerequisite for a truly democratic society that its members are familiar with, and support, certain democratic values. Each new generation needs to learn the value of participation, and to uphold the democratic rules that govern various sectors of the society.

Social studies are intended to prepare pupils for different tasks in society by equipping them with knowledge, confidence in their own values, and the desire to undertake tasks for the common good. These aims must be achieved in close co-operation with the wider society outside school. The social studies disciplines show how people, through their interaction with nature and with each other, have developed different kinds of social life and forms of society.

Developing considered attitudes to society past and present is an important aim of social studies. The methods used in social studies must provide the pupils with an opportunity to gain insight into the subject matter, relevant skills and the ability to co-operate with others, as well as preparing them for action. Their work must stimulate their curiosity and ability to ask questions. Pupils must be given scope to learn to conduct arguments, to exercise critical analysis, to work independently, and to experience how to organise work in co-operation with others. Throughout schooling, social studies are based on close contacts and co-operation between schools and their local communities. Active participation in school affairs through pupil council and other co-operative bodies makes school work in a wider sense of the term an important feature of training in social studies.

In the social studies syllabus, objectives and areas of study are arranged and presented under the disciplines history, geography and society. 'History' covers the chronological dimension, discusses different views of people and different forms of society through the years, and considers the driving forces behind social development. 'Geography' deals with space and changes in space, and the localisation and distribution on the Earth's surface of natural and man-made phenomena and processes. Geography discusses and explains society as it appears at the intersection between people and nature, and surveys the world's living conditions, ways of life and standards of living. 'Society' deals with politics and socialisation and shows why society needs laws and rules, organisation and government in order to function.

Society studies human interplay and conflict, and discusses the rights and obligations, the influences and challenges that individuals encounter as participants in various communities. At the primary stage, social studies to a large extent form integrated parts of broad interdisciplinary areas. Later on, these three disciplines emerge more clearly as separate units, but social studies should aim throughout to combine history, geography and society into an overall picture.

In Norway, the study of this subject is intended to give the pupils a thorough insight into the State religion and what the Christian view of life implies, as well as familiarity with other world religions and philosophies. The subject is to be approached openly and contribute to insight, respect and dialogue across the boundaries between faiths and philosophies, and promote understanding and tolerance in religious and moral questions. The subject mediates knowledge of a faith—the classroom is not intended to be a place for the preaching of any particular faith. It must respect each pupil's identity in terms of his or her faith, while at the same time furthering dialogue within a shared culture. In order to meet other faiths and views of life with understanding, one needs to be able to place them in a context that is already familiar.

The subject thus has various functions in basic schooling: to transmit a tradition, to maintain a sense of identity, and to build bridges which advance insight and dialogue. It is natural to have links between the religious and aesthetic heritage, for instance by giving emphasis to graphic arts, architecture, music, drama and literary texts. At the lower secondary stage, the pupils are better able to adopt a critical approach to both the teaching material and divergant opinions, and understand both metaphors and symbols.

Discussions, lectures, and excursions all offer relevant approaches to the subject. More weight is given at this stage to comparing various features of religions and philosophies. In view of its aesthetic dimension, this subject invites cooperation with art and crafts, music and drama, adding variety and raising pupils' levels of activity. What pupils learn about religion and philosophy also brings them into contact with social circumstances and literature, so that an interdisciplinary approach with social studies and mother-tongue instruction is relevant. The human view of nature, and developments in cosmology, research and science, have also depended on religious outlook; co-operation can also be envisaged with natural sciences and technology.

2

Basic Learning Needs

Basic Learning Needs derives from the World Declaration on Education for All, adopted by the World Conference on Education for All, which brought together representatives of governments, international and bilateral development agencies, and non-governmental organisations. Based on the best collective knowledge and the commitment of these partners, the Framework is intended as a reference and guide for national governments, international organisations, bilateral aid agencies, non-governmental organisations (NGOs), and all those committed to the goal of Education for All in formulating their own plans of action for implementing the World Declaration. It describes three broad levels of concerted action:

— direct action within individual countries,
— co-operation among groups of countries sharing certain characteristics and concerns, and
— multilateral and bilateral co-operation in the world community.

Individual countries and groups of countries, as well as international, regional and national organisations, may use the Framework to develop their own specific plans of action and programmes in line with their particular objectives, mandates and constituencies. This indeed has been the case in the ten-year experience of the UNESCO Major Project on Education for

Latin America and the Caribbean. Further examples of such related initiatives are the UNESCO Plan of Action for the Eradication of Illiteracy by the Year 2000, adopted by the UNESCO General Conference at its 25th session (1989); the ISESCO Special Programme (1990); the current review by the World Bank of its policy for primary education; and USAID's programme for Advancing Basic Education and Literacy.

Policies and programmes are consistent with this Framework, efforts throughout the world to meet basic learning needs will converge and facilitate co-operation. While countries have many common concerns in meeting the basic learning needs of their populations, these concerns do, of course, vary in nature and intensity from country to country depending on the actual status of basic education as well as the cultural and socio-economic context.

Globally by the year 2000, if enrolment rates remain at current levels, there will be more than 160 million children without access to primary schooling simply because of population growth. In much of sub-Saharan Africa and in many low income countries elsewhere, the provision of universal primary education for rapidly growing numbers of children remains a long-term challenge. Despite progress in promoting adult literacy, most of these same countries still have high illiteracy rates, while the numbers of functionally illiterate adults continue to grow and constitute a major social problem in much of Asia and the Arab States, as well as in Europe and North America.

Many people are denied equal access on grounds of race, gender, language, disability, ethnic origin, or political convictions. In addition, high drop-out rates and poor learning achievement are commonly recognised problems throughout the world. These very general characterisations illustrate the need for decisive action on a large scale, with clear goals and targets.

GOALS AND TARGETS

The ultimate goal affirmed by the World Declaration on Education for All is to meet the basic learning needs of all children, youth, and adults. The long-term effort to attain that goal can be maintained more effectively if intermediate goals are established and progress toward these goals is measured. Appropriate authorities at the national and subnational levels may establish such intermediate goals, taking into account the objectives of the Declaration as well as overall national development goals and priorities. Intermediate goals can usefully be formulated as specific targets within national and subnational plans for educational development. Such targets are:

1. specify expected attainments and outcomes in reference to terminal performance specifications within an appropriate time-frame,
2. specify priority categories (e. g. the poor, the disabled), and
3. are formulated in terms such that progress toward them can be observed and measured. These targets represent a "floor" (but not a "ceiling") for the continued development of education programmes and services.

Time-bound targets convey a sense of urgency and serve as a reference against which indices of implementation and accomplishment can be compared. As societal conditions change, plans and targets can be reviewed and updated. Where basic education efforts must be focussed to meet the needs of specific social groups or population categories, linking targets to such priority categories of learners can help to maintain the attention of planners, practitioners and evaluators on meeting the needs of these learners. Observable and measurable targets assist in the objective evaluation of progress.

Targets need not be based solely on current trends and resources. Initial targets can reflect a realistic appraisal of the possibilities presented by the Declaration to mobilise additional human, organisational, and financial capacities within a cooperative commitment to human development. Countries with low literacy and school enrolment rates, and very limited national resources, will need to make hard choices in establishing national targets within a realistic timeframe. Countries may wish to set their own targets for the 1990s in terms of the following proposed dimensions:

1. Expansion of early childhood care and developmental activities, including family and community interventions, especially for poor, disadvantaged and disabled children;
2. Universal access to, and completion of, primary education (or whatever higher level of education is considered as "basic") by the year 2000;
3. Improvement in learning achievement such that an agreed percentage of an appropriate age cohort (e. g. 80% of 14 year-olds) attains or surpasses a defined level of necessary learning achievement;
4. Reduction of the adult illiteracy rate to, say, one-half its 1990 level by the year 2000, with sufficient emphasis on female literacy to significantly reduce the current disparity between male and female illiteracy rates;
5. Expansion of provisions of basic education and training in other essential skills required by youth and adults, with programme effectiveness assessed in terms of behavioural changes and impacts on health, employment and productivity;
6. Increased acquisition by individuals and families of the knowledge, skills and values required for better living and sound and sustainable development, made available through all education channels including the mass media, other forms of modern and traditional communication, and social action, with effectiveness assessed in terms of behavioural change.

Levels of performance in the above should be established, when possible. These should be consistent with the focus of basic education both on universalisation of access and on learning acquisition, as joint and inseparable concerns. In all cases, the performance targets should include equity by gender. However, setting levels of performance and of the proportions of participants who are expected to reach these levels in specific basic education programmes must be an autonomous task of individual countries.

PRINCIPLES OF ACTION

The first step consists in identifying, preferably through an active participatory process involving groups and the community, the traditional learning systems which exist in the society, and the actual demand for basic education services, whether expressed in terms of formal schooling or non-formal education programmes. Addressing the basic learning needs of all means: early childhood care and development opportunities; relevant, quality primary schooling or equivalent out-of-school education for children; and literacy, basic knowledge and life skills training for youth and adults. It also means capitalising on the use of traditional and modern information media and technologies to educate the public on matters of social concern and to support basic education activities.

These complementary components of basic education need to be designed to ensure equitable access, sustained participation, and effective learning achievement. Meeting basic learning needs also involves action to enhance the family and community environments for learning and to correlate basic education and the larger socio-economic context. The complementarity and synergistic effects of related human resources investments in population, health and nutrition should be recognised.

Because basic learning needs are complex and diverse, meeting them requires multisectoral strategies and action which are integral to overall development efforts. Many partners must join with the education authorities, teachers, and other educational personnel in developing basic education if it is to be seen, once again, as the responsibility of the entire society. This implies the active involvement of a wide range of partners are:

— families, teachers, communities, private enterprises (including those involved in information and communication), government and non-governmental organisations, institutions, etc.

— in planning, managing and evaluating the many forms of basic education. Current practices and institutional arrangements for delivering basic education, and the existing mechanisms for co-operation in this regard, should be carefully evaluated before new institutions or mechanisms are created. Rehabilitating dilapidated schools and improving the training and working conditions of teachers and literacy workers, building on existing learning schemes, are likely to bring greater and more immediate returns on investment than attempts to start afresh.

Great potential lies in possible joint actions with non-governmental organisations on all levels. These autonomous bodies, while advocating independent and critical public views, might play roles in monitoring, research, training and material production for the sake of non-formal and life-long educational processes.

The primary purpose of bilateral and multilateral co-operation should appear in a true spirit of partnership—it should not be to transplant familiar models, but to help develop the endogenous capacities of national authorities and their in country partners to meet basic learning needs effectively.

Action and resources should be used to strengthen essential features of basic education services, focusing on managerial and analytical capacities, which can stimulate further developments. International co-operation and funding can be particularly valuable in supporting major reforms or sectoral adjustments, and in helping to develop and test innovative approaches to teaching and management, where new approaches need to be tried and/or extraordinary levels of expenditure are involved and where knowledge of relevant experiences elsewhere can often be useful.

International co-operation should give priority to the countries currently least able to meet the basic learning needs of their populations. It should also help countries redress their internal disparities in educational opportunity. Because two-thirds of illiterate adults and out-of-school children are female, wherever such inequities exist, a most urgent priority is to improve access to education for girls and women, and to remove every obstacle that hampers their active participation.

PRIORITY ACTION AT NATIONAL LEVEL

Progress in meeting the basic learning needs of all will depend ultimately on the actions taken within individual countries. While regional and international co-operation and financial assistance can support and facilitate such actions, government authorities, communities and their several in country partners are the key agents for improvement, and national governments have the main responsibility for coordinating the effective use of internal and external resources. Given the diversity of countries situations, capacities and development plans and goals, this Framework can only suggest certain areas that merit priority attention. Each country will determine for itself what specific actions beyond current efforts may be necessary in each of the following areas.

To achieve the targets set for itself, each country is encouraged to develop or update comprehensive and long-term plans of action (from local to national levels) to meet the learning needs it has defined as "basic". Within the context of existing education-sector and general development plans and strategies, a plan of action for basic education for all will necessarily be multisectoral, to guide activities in the sectors involved (e. g. education, information, communications/ media, labour, agriculture, health). Models of strategic planning, by definition, vary. However, most of them involve constant adjustments among objectives, resources, actions, and constraints. At the national level, objectives are normally couched in broad terms and central government resources are also determined, while actions are taken at the local level. Thus, local plans in the same national setting will naturally differ not only in scope but in content. National and subnational frameworks and local plans should allow for varying conditions and circumstances. These might, therefore, specify:

— studies for the evaluation of existing systems (analysis of problems, failures and successes):
— the basic learning needs to be met, including cognitive skills, values, attitudes, as well as subject knowledge;
— the languages to be used in education
— means to promote the demand for, and broadscale participation in, basic education;
— modalities to mobilise family and local community support;
— targets and specific objectives;
— the required capital and recurrent resources, duly costed, as well as possible measures for cost effectiveness;
— indicators and procedures to be used to monitor progress in reaching the targets;
— priorities for using resources and for developing services and programmes over time;

— the priority groups that require special measures;
— the kinds of expertise required to implement the plan;
— institutional and administrative arrangements needed;
— modalities for ensuring information sharing among formal and other basic education programmes; and
— an implementation strategy and timetable.

A multisectoral plan of action implies adjustments to sectoral policies so that sectors interact in a mutually supportive and beneficial manner in line with the country's overall development goals. Action to meet basic learning needs should be an integral part of a country's national and subnational development strategies, which should reflect the priority given to human development.

Legislative and other measures may be needed to promote and facilitate co-operation among the various partners involved. Advocacy and public information about basic education are important in creating a supportive policy environment at national, subnational and local levels. Four specific steps that merit attention are:

1. initiation of national and subnational level activities to create a broad, public recommitment to the goal of education for all;
2. reduction of inefficiency in the public sector and exploitative practices in the private sector;
3. provision of improved training for public administrators and of incentives to retain qualified women and men in public service; and
4. provision of measures to encourage wider participation in the design and implementation of basic education programmes.

The preconditions for educational quality, equity and efficiency, are set in the early childhood years, making attention to early childhood care and development essential to the achievement of basic education goals. Basic education must correspond to actual needs, interests, and problems of the participants in the learning process. The relevance of curricula could be enhanced by linking literacy and numeracy skills and scientific concepts with learners concerns and earlier experiences, for example, nutrition, health, and work.

While many needs vary considerably within and among countries, and therefore much of a curriculum should be sensitive to local conditions, there are also many universal needs and shared concerns which should be addressed in education curricula and in educational messages. Issues such as protecting the environment, achieving a balance between population and resources, slowing the spread of AIDS, and preventing drug abuse are everyone's issues.

Specific strategies addressed to improve the conditions of schooling may focus on: learners and the learning process, personnel (teachers, administrators, others), curriculum and learning assessment, materials and physical facilities. Such strategies should be conducted in an integrated manner; their design, management, and evaluation should take into account the acquisition of knowledge and problem-solving skills as well as the social, cultural, and ethical dimensions of human development.

Depending on the outcomes desired, teachers have to be trained accordingly, whilst benefiting from in-service programmes as well as other incentives of opportunity which put a premium on the achievement of these outcomes; curriculum and assessment must reflect a variety of criteria while materials and conceivably buildings and facilities as well must be adapted along the same lines. In some countries, the strategy may include ways to improve conditions for teaching and learning such that absenteeism is reduced and learning time increased. In order to meet the educational needs of groups not covered by formal schooling, appropriate strategies are needed for non-formal education. These include but go far beyond the aspects described above, but may also give special attention to the need for coordination with other forms of education, to the support of all interested partners, to sustained financial resources and to full community participation. An example for such an approach applied to literacy can be found in UNESCO's Plan of Action for the Eradication of Illiteracy by the Year 2000.

Other strategies still may rely on the media to meet the broader education needs of the entire community. Such strategies need to be linked to formal education, non-formal education or a combination of both. The use of the communications media holds a tremendous potential to educate the public and to share important information among those who need to know. Expanding access to basic education of satisfactory quality is an effective way to improve equity. Ensuring that girls and women stay involved in basic education activities until they have attained at least the agreed necessary level of learning, can be encouraged through special measures designed, wherever possible, in consultation with them. Similar approaches are necessary to expand learning opportunities for various disadvantaged groups.

Efficiency in basic education does not mean providing education at the lowest cost, but rather the most effective use of all resources (human, organisational, and financial) to produce the desired levels of access and of necessary learning achievement. The foregoing considerations of relevance, quality, and equity are not alternatives to efficiency but represent the specific conditions within which efficiency should be attained. For some programmes, efficiency will require more, not fewer, resources. However, if existing resources can be used by more learners or if the same learning targets can be reached at a lower cost per learner, then the capacity of basic education to meet the targets of access and achievement for presently underserved groups can be increased.

Many kinds of expertise and skills will be needed to carry out these initiatives. Managerial and supervisory personnel, as well as planners, school architects, teacher educators, curriculum developers, researchers, analysts, etc., are important for any strategy to improve basic education, but many countries do not provide specialised training to prepare them for their responsibilities; this is especially true in literacy and other out-of-school basic education activities.

A broadening of outlook toward basic education will be a crucial prerequisite to the effective co-ordination of efforts among these many participants, and strengthening and developing capacities for planning and management at regional and local levels with a greater sharing of responsibilities will be necessary in many countries. Pre- and in-service training programmes for key personnel should be initiated, or strengthened where they do exist. Such training can be particularly useful in introducing administrative reforms and innovative management and supervisory techniques.

The technical services and mechanisms to collect, process and analyse data pertaining to basic education can be improved in all countries. This is an urgent task in many countries that have little reliable information and/or research on the basic learning needs of their people and on existing basic education activities. A country's information and knowledge base is vital in preparing and implementing a plan of action.

One major implication of the focus on learning acquisition is that systems have to be developed and improved to assess the performance of individual learners and delivery mechanisms. Process and outcome assessment data should serve as the core of a management information system for basic education.

The quality and delivery of basic education can be enhanced through the judicious use of instructional technologies. Where such technologies are not now widely used, their introduction will require the selection and/or development of suitable technologies, acquisition of the necessary equipment and operating systems, and the recruitment or training of teachers and other educational personnel to work with them. The definition of a suitable technology varies by societal characteristics and will change rapidly over time as new technologies (educational radio and television, computers, and various audio-visual instructional devices) become less expensive and more adaptable to a range of environments. The use of modern technology can also improve the management of basic education. Each country may reexamine periodically its present and potential technological capacity in relation to its basic educational needs and resources.

New possibilities are emerging which already show a powerful impact on meeting basic learning needs, and it is clear that the educational potential of these new possibilities has barely been tapped. These new possibilities exist largely as a result of two converging forces, both recent by-products of the general development process. First, the quantity of information available in the world—much of it relevant to survival and basic well-being—is exponentially greater than that available only a few years ago, and the rate of its growth is accelerating.

A synergistic effect occurs when important information is coupled with a second modern advance—the new capacity to communicate among the people of the world. The opportunity exists to harness this force and use it positively, consciously, and with design, in order to contribute to meeting defined learning needs.

In designing the plan of action and creating a supportive policy environment for promoting basic education, maximum use of opportunities should be considered to expand existing collaborations and to bring together new partners: e.g., family and community organisations, non-governmental and other voluntary associations, teachers' unions, other professional groups, employers, the media, political parties, co-operatives, universities, research institutions, religious bodies, as well as education authorities and other government departments and services (labour, agriculture, health, information, commerce, industry, defence, etc.). The human and organisational resources these domestic partners represent need to be effectively mobilised to play their parts in implementing the plan of action. Partnerships at the community level and at the intermediate and national levels should be encouraged; they can help harmonise activities, utilise resources more effectively, and mobilise additional financial and human resources where necessary.

Governments and their partners can analyse the current allocation and use of financial and other resources for education and training in different sectors to determine if additional support for basic education can be obtained by:

— improving efficiency,
— mobilising additional sources of funding within and outside the government budget, and
— allocating funds within existing education and training budgets, taking into account efficiency and equity concerns. Countries where the total fiscal support for education is low need to explore the possibility of reallocating some public funds used for other purposes to basic education.

Assessing the resources actually or potentially available for basic education and comparing them to the budget estimates underlying the plan of action, can help identify possible inadequacies of resources that may affect the scheduling of planned activities over time or may require choices to be made. Countries that require external assistance to meet the basic learning needs of their people can use the resource assessment and plan of action as a basis for discussions with their international partners and for coordinating external funding.

The individual learners themselves constitute a vital human resource that needs to be mobilised. The demand for, and participation in, learning opportunities cannot simply be assumed, but must be actively encouraged. Potential learners need to see that the benefits of basic education activities exceed the costs the participants must bear, such as earnings foregone and reduced time available for community and household activities and for leisure. Women and girls especially may be deterred from taking full advantage of basic education opportunities because of reasons specific to individual cultures.

Such barriers to participation may be overcome through the use of incentives and by programmes adapted to the local context and seen by the learners, their families and communities to be "productive activities". Also, learners tend to benefit more from education when they are partners in the instructional process, rather than treated simply as "inputs" or "beneficiaries". Attention to the issues of demand and participation will help assure that the learners' personal capacities are mobilised for education.

Family resources, including time and mutual support, are vital for the success of basic education activities. Families can be offered incentives and assistance to ensure that their resources are invested to enable all family members to benefit as fully and equitably as possible from basic education opportunities.

The preeminent role of teachers as well as of other educational personnel in providing quality basic education needs to be recognised and developed to optimise their contribution. This must entail measures to respect teachers' trade union rights and professional freedoms, and to improve their working conditions and status, notably in respect to their recruitment, initial and in-service training, remuneration and career development possibilities, as well as to allow teachers to fulfill their aspirations, social obligations, and ethical responsibilities.

In partnerships with school and community workers, libraries need to become a vital link in providing educational resources for all learners—pre-school through adulthood—in school and non-school settings. There is therefore a need to recognise libraries as invaluable information resources.

Community associations, co-operatives, religious bodies, and other non-governmental organisations also play important roles in supporting and in providing basic education. Their experience, expertise, energy and direct relationships with various constituencies are valuable resources for identifying and meeting basic learning needs. Their active involvement in partnerships for basic education should be promoted through policies and mechanisms that strengthen their capacities and recognise their autonomy.

PRIORITY ACTION AT REGIONAL LEVEL

Basic learning needs must be met through collaborative action within each country, but there are many forms of co-operation between countries with similar conditions and concerns that could, and do, assist in this endeavour. Regions have already developed plans. By exchanging information and experience, pooling expertise, sharing facilities, and undertaking joint activities, several countries, working together, can increase their resource base and lower costs to their mutual benefit.

Such arrangements are often set up among neighboring countries (sub-regional), among all countries in a major geo-cultural region, or among countries sharing a common language or having cultural and commercial relations. Regional and international organisations often play an important role in facilitating such co-operation between countries. In the following discussion, all such arrangements are included in the term "regional". In general, existing regional partnerships will need to be strengthened and provided with the resources necessary for their effective functioning in helping countries meet the basic learning needs of their populations.

Various regional mechanisms, both intergovernmental and nongovernmental, promote co-operation in education and training, health, agricultural development, research and information, communications, and in other fields relevant to meeting basic learning needs. Such mechanisms can be further developed in response to the evolving needs of their constituents. Among several possible examples are the four regional programmes established through UNESCO in the 1980s to support national efforts to achieve universal primary education and eliminate adult illiteracy:

— Major Project in the Field of Education in Latin America and the Caribbean;
— Regional Programme for the Eradication of Illiteracy in Africa;
— Asia-Pacific Programme of Education for All (APPEAL);
— Regional Programme for the Universalisation and Renewal of Primary Education and the Eradication of Illiteracy in the Arab States by the Year 2000 (ARABUPEAL).

In addition to the technical and policy consultations organised in connection with these programmes, other existing mechanisms can be used for consulting on policy issues in basic education. The conferences of ministers of education organised by UNESCO and by several regional organisations, the regular sessions of the regional commissions of the United Nations, and certain trans-regional conferences organised by the Commonwealth Secretariat, CONFEMEN (standing conference of ministers of education of francophone countries), the Organisation of Economic Co-operation and Development (OECD), and the Islamic Educational, Scientific and Cultural Organisation (ISESCO), could be used for this purpose as needs arise.

In addition, numerous conferences and meetings organised by non-governmental bodies provide opportunities for professionals to share information and views on technical and policy issues. The conveners of these various conferences and meetings may consider ways of extending participation, where appropriate, to include representatives of other constituencies engaged in meeting basic learning needs. Full advantage should be taken of opportunities to share media messages or programmes that can be exchanged among countries or collaboratively developed, especially where language and cultural similarities extend beyond political boundaries.

There are many possible joint activities among countries in support of national efforts to implement action plans for basic education. Joint activities should be designed to exploit economies of scale and the comparative advantages of participating countries. Six areas where this form of regional collaboration seems particularly appropriate are:

— training of key personnel, such as planners, managers, teacher educators, researchers, etc. ;
— efforts to improve information collection and analysis;
— research;
— production of educational materials;
— use of communication media to meet basic learning needs; and
— management and use of distance education services.

Here, too, there are several existing mechanisms that could be utilised to foster such activities, including UNESCO's International Institute of Educational Planning and its networks of trainees and research as well as IBE's information network and the Unesco Institute for Education, the five networks for educational innovation operating under UNESCO's auspices, the research and review advisory groups (RRAGs) associated with the International Development Research Centre, the Commonwealth of Learning, the Asian Cultural Center for UNESCO, the participatory network established by the International Council for Adult Education, and the International Association for the Evaluation of Educational Achievement, which links major national research institutions in some 35 countries.

Certain multilateral and bilateral development agencies that have accumulated valuable experience in one or more of these areas might be interested in participating in joint activities. The five United Nations regional commissions could provide further support to such regional collaboration, especially by mobilising policymakers to take appropriate action.

PRIORITY ACTION AT WORLD LEVEL

The world community has a well-established record of co-operation in education and development. However, international funding for education stagnated during the early 1980s; at the same time, many countries have been handicapped by growing debt burdens and economic relationships that channel their financial and human resources to wealthier countries. Because concern about the issues in basic education is shared by industrialised and developing countries alike, international co-operation can provide valuable support for national efforts and regional actions to implement the expanded vision of basic Education for All.

Time, energy, and funding directed to basic education are perhaps the most profound investment in people and in the future of a country which can be made; there is a clear need and strong moral and economic argument for international solidarity to provide technical co-operation and financial assistance to countries that lack the resources to meet the basic learning needs of their populations.

Meeting basic learning needs constitutes a common and universal human responsibility. The prospects for meeting basic learning needs around the world are determined in part by the dynamics of international relations and trade. With the current relaxation of tensions and the decreasing number of armed conflicts, there are now real possibilities to reduce the tremendous waste of military spending and shift those resources into socially useful areas, including basic education.

The urgent task of meeting basic learning needs may require such a reallocation between sectors, and the world community and individual governments need to plan this conversion of resources for peaceful uses with courage and vision, and in a thoughtful and careful manner. Similarly, international measures to reduce or eliminate current imbalances in trade relations and to reduce debt burdens must be taken to enable many low-income countries to rebuild their own economies, releasing and retaining human and financial resources needed for development and for providing basic education to their populations. Structural adjustment policies should protect appropriate funding levels for education.

International support should be provided, on request, to countries seeking to develop the national capacities needed for planning and managing basic education programmes and services. Ultimate responsibility rests within each nation to design and manage its own programmes to meet the learning needs of all its population. International support could include training and institutional development in data collection, analysis and research, technological innovation, and educational methodologies.

Management information systems and other modern management methods could also be introduced, with an emphasis on low and middle level managers. These capabilities will be even more in demand to support quality improvements in primary education and to introduce innovative out-of-school programmes. In addition to direct support to countries and institutions, international assistance can also be usefully channelled to support the activities of international, regional and other inter-country structures that organise joint research, training and information exchanges.

The latter should be based on, and supported by, existing institutions and programmes, if need be improved and strengthened, rather than on the establishment of new structures. Support will be especially valuable for technical cooperation among developing countries, among whom both circumstances and resources available to respond to circumstances are often similar.

Meeting the basic learning needs of all people in all countries is obviously a long-term undertaking. This Framework provides guidelines for preparing national and subnational plans of action for the development of basic education through a long-term commitment of governments and their national partners to work together to reach the targets and achieve the objectives they set for themselves. International agencies and institutions, many of which are sponsors, co-sponsors, and associate sponsors of the World Conference on Education for All, should actively seek to plan together and sustain their long-term support for the kinds of national and regional actions outlined in the preceding sections. In particular, the core sponsors of the Education for All initiative (UNDP, UNESCO, UNICEF, World Bank) affirm their commitments to supporting the priority areas for international action presented below and to making appropriate arrangements for meeting the objectives of Education for All, each acting within its mandate, special responsibilities, and decisions of its governing bodies. Given that UNESCO is the UN agency with a particular responsibility for education, it will give priority to implementing the Framework for Action and to facilitating provision of services needed for reinforced international co-ordination and co-operation.

Increased international funding is needed to help the less developed countries implement their own autonomous plans of action in line with the expanded vision of basic Education for All. Genuine partnerships characterised by co-operation and joint long-term commitments will accomplish more and provide the basis for a substantial increase in overall funding for this important sub-sector of education. Upon governments' request, multilateral and bilateral agencies should focus on supporting priority actions, particularly at the country level in areas such as the following:

1. *The design or updating of national and subnational multisectoral plans of action*, which will need to be elaborated very early in the 1990s. Both financial and technical assistance are needed by many developing countries, particularly in collecting and analysing data, as well as in organising domestic consultations.
2. *National efforts and related inter-country co-operation to attain a satisfactory level of quality and relevance in primary education:* Experiences involving the participation of families, local communities, and non-governmental organisations in increasing the relevance and improving the quality of education could profitably be shared among countries.
3. *The provision of universal primary education in the economically poorer countries:* International funding agencies should consider negotiating arrangements to provide long-term support, on a case-by-case basis, to help countries move toward universal primary education according to their timetable. The external agencies should examine current assistance practices in order to find ways of effectively assisting basic education programmes which do not require capital and technology-intensive assistance, but often need longer-term budgetary support. In this context, greater attention should be given to criteria for development co-operation in education to include more than mere economic considerations.
4. *Programmes designed to meet the basic learning needs of disadvantaged groups, out-of-school youth, and adults with little or no access to basic learning opportunities.* All partners can share their experience and expertise in designing and implementing innovative measures and activities, and focus their funding for basic education on specific categories and groups (e.g., women, the rural poor, the disabled) to improve significantly the learning opportunities and conditions available for them.

5. *Education programmes for women and girls:* These programmes should be designed to eliminate the social and cultural barriers which have discouraged or even excluded women and girls from benefits of regular education programmes, as well as to promote equal opportunities in all aspects of their lives.
6. *Education programmes for refugees:* The programmes run by such organisations as the United Nations High Commission for Refugees (UNHCR) and the United Nations Relief and Works Agency for Palestine (UNRWA) need more substantial and reliable long-term financial support for this recognised international responsibility. Where countries of refuge need international financial and technical assistance to cope with the basic needs of refugees, including their learning needs, the international community can help to share this burden through increased cooperation. The world community will also endeavour to ensure that people under occupation or displaced by war and other calamities continue to have access to basic education programmes that preserve their cultural identity.
7. *Basic education programmes of all kinds in countries with high rates of illiteracy (as in sub-Saharan Africa) and with large illiterate populations (as in South Asia):* Substantial assistance will be needed to reduce significantly the world's large number of illiterate adults.
8. *Capacity building for research and planning and the experimentation of small-scale innovations:* The success of Education for All actions will ultimately be determined by the capacity of each country to design and implement programs that reflect national conditions. A strengthened knowledge base nourished by research findings and the lessons of experiments and innovations as well as the availablity of competent educational planners will be essential in this respect.

The coordination of external funding for education is an area of shared responsibility at country level, in which host governments need to take the lead to ensure the efficient use of resources in accordance with their priorities. Development funding agencies should explore innovative and more flexible modalities of co-operation in consultation with the governments and institutions with which they work and co-operate in regional initiatives, such as the Task Force of Donors to African Education. Other forums need to be developed in which funding agencies and developing countries can collaborate in the design of inter-country projects and discuss general issues relating to financial assistance.

Existing channels of communication and forums for consultation among the many partners involved in meeting basic learning needs should be fully utilised in the 1990s to maintain and extend the international consensus underlying this Framework for Action. Some channels and forums, such as the biannual International Conference on Education, operate globally, while others focus on particular regions or groups of countries or categories of partners. Insofar as possible, organisers should seek to coordinate these consultations and share results. Moreover, in order to maintain and expand the Education for All initiative, the international community will need to make appropriate arrangements, which will ensure co-operation among the interested agencies using the existing mechanisms insofar as possible:

— to continue advocacy of basic Education for All, building on the momentum generated by the World Conference;

— to facilitate sharing information on the progress made in achieving basic education targets set by countries for themselves and on the resources and organisational requirements for successful initiatives;

— to encourage new partners to join this global endeavour; and;

— to ensure that all partners are fully aware of the importance of maintaining strong support for basic education.

REFERENCES

Aggarwal, J.C., *Education Policy in India, 1992, Retrospect and Prospect*, New Delhi, Shipra Publications, 1992.

Birzea, C., 1996, Education in a World in Transition: between Post-communism and Post-modernism. In *Prospects, vol 26, no. 4,1996*. p. 673-681.

Dakar Framework for Action: Education for All: *Meeting Our Collective Commitments*. Text adopted by the World Education forum, Dakar, Senegal, 26-28 April 2000.

Education and Development, National Commission on Education 1966, Government of India, New Delhi, 1968.

Education for All: Achieving the goal : The Amman Affirmation. Mid-Decade Meeting of the International Consultative Forum on Education for All, Amman, Jordan, 1996.

EFA 2000 Assessment (2000) *Draft Country Report*: Japan http://www2.unesco.org/wef/countryreports/japan/contents.html.

EFA 2000 Assessment (2000) *Country report* :Namibia.

Education for All Year 2000 Assessment:*Statistical Document* (2000). Paris: UNESCO, International Consultative Forumon Education for All.

Framework for Action—Meeting Basic Learning Needs: Guidelines for Implementing the World Declaration on Education for All. Jomtien, Thailand, 5-9. March 1990.

Himes. J., Colbert, V., and Mendez, R.G., 1994, *Child Labour and Basic Education in Latin America and the Caribbean: A Proposed UNICEF Initiative, Florence*, United nations Children's Fund Innocenti Research Centre.

Kolucki, Barbara, New Focus for A Safe and Enhanced Learning Environment Report for United Nations Children's Fund, 1999.

Krogh, T. (1999) *Feasibility study on the creation* of an International Academy for Education *and Democracy*. Copenhagen: Ministry of Education.

O'Gara, Chloe et al, *Qualities of Caring: Good Practices in Infact and Toddier Group Care*, Washington, D.C., Education Section, World Bank/Academy for Education Development, 1999.

Sixth All India Educational Survey / NCERT.

UNICEF, 1999, *Progress, Challenges and Future Strategies in Basic Education.*

Vasantha R. Patri, *Education in India: Programmes and Policies*, Authorspress, New Delhi, 2000.

World Declaration on Education for All: *Meeting Basic learning needs*, World Conference for Education for All, Jomtien, Thailand, 5-9 March 1990.

3

World Declaration on Education For All

More than 40 years ago, the nations of the world, speaking through the Universal Declaration of Human Rights, asserted that "everyone has a right to education". Despite notable efforts by countries around the globe to ensure the right to education for all, the following realities persist:

— More than 100 million children, including at least 60 million girls, have no access to primary schooling;

— More than 960 million adults, two-thirds of whom are women, are illiterate, and functional illiteracy is a significant problem in all countries, industrialised and developing;

— More than one-third of the world's adults have no access to the printed knowledge, new skills and technologies that could improve the quality of their lives and help them shape, and adapt to, social and cultural change; and

— More than 100 million children and countless adults fail to complete basic education programmes; millions more satisfy the attendance requirements but do not acquire essential knowledge and skills;

At the same time, the world faces daunting problems: notably mounting debt burdens, the threat of economic stagnation and decline, rapid population growth, widening economic disparities among and within nations, war, occupation, civil strife, violent crime, the preventable deaths of millions of children and widespread environmental degradation. These problems constrain efforts to meet basic learning needs, while the lack of basic education among a significant proportion of the population prevents societies from addressing such problems with strength and purpose.

These problems have led to major setbacks in basic education in the 1980s in many of the least developed countries. In some other countries, economic growth has been available to finance education expansion, but even so, many millions remain in poverty and unschooled or illiterate. In certain industrialised countries too, cutbacks in government expenditure over the 1980s have led to the deterioration of education.

Yet the world is also at the threshold of a new century, with all its promise and possibilities. Today, there is genuine progress toward peaceful detente and greater cooperation among nations. Today, the essential rights and capacities of women are being realised.

Today, there are many useful scientific and cultural developments. Today, the sheer quantity of information available in the world—much of it relevant to survival and basic well-being—is exponentially greater than that available only a few years ago, and the rate of its growth is accelerating. This includes information about obtaining more life-enhancing knowledge—or learning how to learn. A synergistic effect occurs when important information is coupled with another modern advance—our new capacity to communicate.

These new forces, when combined with the cumulative experience of reform, innovation, research and the remarkable educational progress of many countries, make the goal of basic education for all—for the first time in history—an attainable goal.

Therefore, we participants in the World Conference on Education for All, assembled in Jomtien, Thailand, from 5 to 9 March, 1990:

— Recalling that education is a fundamental right for all people, women and men, of all ages, throughout our world;
— Understanding that education can help ensure a safer, healthier, more prosperous and environmentally sound world, while simultaneously contributing to social, economic, and cultural progress, tolerance, and international cooperation;
— Knowing that education is an indispensable key to, though not a sufficient condition for, personal and social improvement;
— Recognising that traditional knowledge and indigenous cultural heritage have a value and validity in their own right and a capacity to both define and promote development;
— Acknowledging that, overall, the current provision of education is seriously deficient and that it must be made more relevant and qualitatively improved, and made universally available;
— Recognising that sound basic education is fundamental to the strengthening of higher levels of education and of scientific and technological literacy and capacity and thus to self-reliant development; and
— Recognising the necessity to give to present and coming generations an expanded vision of, and a renewed commitment to, basic education to address the scale and complexity of the challenge; proclaim the following:

EDUCATION FOR ALL: THE PURPOSE

Every person—child, youth and adult—shall be able to benefit from educational opportunities designed to meet their basic learning needs. These needs comprise both essential learning tools (such as literacy, oral expression, numeracy, and problem solving) and the basic learning content (such as knowledge, skills, values, and attitudes) required by human beings to be able to survive, to develop their full capacities, to live and work in dignity, to participate fully in development, to improve the quality of their lives, to make informed decisions, and to continue learning. The scope of basic learning needs and how they should be met varies with individual countries and cultures, and inevitably, changes with the passage of time.

The satisfaction of these needs empowers individuals in any society and confers upon them a responsibility to respect and build upon their collective cultural, linguistic and spiritual heritage, to promote the education of others, to further the cause of social justice, to achieve environmental protection, to be tolerant towards social, political and religious systems which differ from their own, ensuring that commonly accepted humanistic values and human rights are upheld, and to work for international peace and solidarity in an interdependent world.

Another and no less fundamental aim of educational development is the transmission and enrichment of common cultural and moral values. It is in these values that the individual and society find their identity and worth.

Basic education is more than an end in itself. It is the foundation for lifelong learning and human development on which countries may build, systematically, further levels and types of education and training.

To serve the basic learning needs of all requires more than a recommitment to basic education as it now exists. What is needed is an "expanded vision" that surpasses present resource levels, institutional structures, curricula, and conventional delivery systems while building on the best in current practices. New possibilities exist today which result from the convergence of the increase in information and the unprecedented capacity to communicate. We must seise them with creativity and a determination for increased effectiveness.

Basic education should be provided to all children, youth and adults. To this end, basic education services of quality should be expanded and consistent measures must be taken to reduce disparities.

For basic education to be equitable, all children, youth and adults must be given the opportunity to achieve and maintain an acceptable level of learning.

The most urgent priority is to ensure access to, and improve the quality of, education for girls and women, and to remove every obstacle that hampers their active participation. All gender stereotyping in education should be eliminated.

An active commitment must be made to removing educational disparities. Underserved groups: the poor; street and working children; rural and remote populations; nomads and migrant workers; indigenous peoples; ethnic, racial, and linguistic minorities; refugees; those displaced by war; and people under occupation, should not suffer any discrimination in access to learning opportunities.

The learning needs of the disabled demand special attention. Steps need to be taken to provide equal access to education to every category of disabled persons as an integral part of the education system.

Whether or not expanded educational opportunities will translate into meaningful development—for an individual or for society—depends ultimately on whether people actually learn as a result of those opportunities, i.e., whether they incorporate useful knowledge, reasoning ability, skills, and values. The focus of basic education must, therefore, be on actual learning acquisition and outcome, rather than exclusively upon enrolment, continued participation in organised programmes and completion of certification requirements. Active and participatory approaches are particularly valuable in assuring learning acquisition and allowing learners to reach their fullest potential. It is, therefore, necessary to define acceptable levels of learning acquisition for educational programmes and to improve and apply systems of assessing learning achievement.

The diversity, complexity, and changing nature of basic learning needs of children, youth and adults necessitates broadening and constantly redefining the scope of basic education to include the following components:

Learning begins at birth: This calls for early childhood care and initial education. These can be provided through arrangements involving families, communities, or institutional programmes, as appropriate.

The main delivery system for the basic education of children outside the family is primary schooling: Primary education must be universal, ensure that the basic learning needs of all children are satisfied, and take into account the culture, needs, and opportunities of the community. Supplementary alternative programmes can help meet the basic learning needs of children with limited or no access to formal schooling, provided that they share the same standards of learning applied to schools, and are adequately supported.

The basic learning needs of youth and adults are diverse and should be met through a variety of delivery systems: Literacy programmes are indispensable because literacy is a necessary skill in itself and the foundation of other life skills. Literacy in the mother-tongue strengthens cultural identity and heritage. Other needs can be served by: skills training, apprenticeships, and formal and non-formal education programmes in health, nutrition, population, agricultural techniques, the environment, science, technology, family life, including fertility awareness, and other societal issues.

All available instruments and channels of information, communications, and social action could be used to help convey essential knowledge and inform and educate people on social issues. In addition to the traditional means, libraries, television, radio and other media can be mobilised to realise their potential towards meeting basic education needs of all.

These components should constitute an integrated system—complementary, mutually reinforcing, and of comparable standards, and they should contribute to creating and developing possibilities for lifelong learning.

Learning does not take place in isolation. Societies, therefore, must ensure that all learners receive the nutrition, health care, and general physical and emotional support they need in order to participate actively in and benefit from their education. Knowledge and skills that will enhance the learning environment of children should be integrated into community learning programmes for adults. The education of children and their parents or other caretakers is mutually supportive and this interaction should be used to create, for all, a learning environment of vibrancy and warmth.

National, regional, and local educational authorities have a unique obligation to provide basic education for all, but they cannot be expected to supply every human, financial or organisational requirement for this task. New and revitalised partnerships at all levels will be necessary: partnerships among all sub-sectors and forms of education, recognising the special role of teachers and that of administrators and other educational personnel; partnerships between education and other government departments, including planning, finance, labour, communications, and other social sectors; partnerships between government and non-governmental organisations, the private sector, local communities, religious groups, and families. The recognition of the vital role of both families and teachers is particularly important. In this context, the terms and conditions of service of teachers and their status, which constitute a determining factor in the implementation of education for all, must be urgently improved in all countries in line with the joint ILO/ UNESCO Recommendation Concerning the Status of Teachers. Genuine partnerships contribute to the planning, implementing, managing and evaluating of basic education programmes. When we speak of "an expanded vision and a renewed commitment", partnerships are at the heart of it.

Supportive policies in the social, cultural, and economic sectors are required in order to realise the full provision and utitlisation of basic education for individual and societal improvement. The provision of basic education for all depends on political commitment and political will backed by appropriate fiscal measures and reinforced by educational policy reforms and institutional strengthening. Suitable economic, trade, labour, employment and health policies will enhance learners' incentives and contributions to societal development.

Societies should also insure a strong intellectual and scientific environment for basic education. This implies improving higher education and developing scientific research. Close contact with contemporary technological and scientific knowledge should be possible at every level of education.

If the basic learning needs of all are to be met through a much broader scope of action than in the past, it will be essential to mobilise existing and new financial and human resources, public, private and voluntary. All of society has a contribution to make, recognising that time, energy and funding directed to basic education are perhaps the most profound investment in people and in the future of a country which can be made.

Enlarged public-sector support means drawing on the resources of all the government agencies responsible for human development, through increased absolute and proportional allocations to basic education services with the clear recognition of competing claims on national resources of which education is an important one, but not the only one. Serious attention to improving the efficiency of existing educational resources and programmes will not only produce more, it can also be expected to attract new resources. The urgent task of meeting basic learning needs may require a reallocation between sectors, as, for example, a transfer from military to educational expenditure. Above all, special protection for basic education will be required in countries undergoing structural adjustment and facing severe external debt burdens. Today, more than ever, education must be seen as a fundamental dimension of any social, cultural, and economic design.

Meeting basic learning needs constitutes a common and universal human responsibility. It requires international solidarity and equitable and fair economic relations in order to redress existing economic disparities. All nations have valuable knowledge and experiences to share for designing effective educational policies and programmes.

Substantial and long-term increases in resources for basic education will be needed. The world community, including intergovernmental agencies and institutions, has an urgent responsibility to alleviate the constraints that prevent some countries from achieving the goal of education for all. It will mean the adoption of measures that augment the national budgets of the poorest countries or serve to relieve heavy debt burdens. Creditors and debtors must seek innovative and equitable formulae to resolve these burdens, since the capacity of many developing countries to respond effectively to education and other basic needs will be greatly helped by finding solutions to the debt problem.

Basic learning needs of adults and children must be addressed wherever they exist. Least developed and low-income countries have special needs which require priority in international support for basic education in the 1990s.

All nations must also work together to resolve conflicts and strife, to end military occupations, and to settle displaced populations, or to facilitate their return to their countries of origin, and ensure that their basic learning needs are met. Only a stable and peaceful environment can create the conditions in which every human being, child and adult alike, may benefit from the goals of this Declaration.

We, the participants in the World Conference on Education for All, reaffirm the right of all people to education. This is the foundation of our determination, singly and together, to ensure education for all. We commit ourselves to act cooperatively through our own spheres of responsibility, taking all necessary steps to achieve the goals of education for all. Together we call on governments, concerned organisations and individuals to join in this urgent undertaking. The basic learning needs of all can and must be met. There can be no more meaningful way to begin the International Literacy Year, to move forward the goals of the United Nations Decade of Disabled Persons (1983-92), the World Decade for Cultural Development (1988-97), the Fourth United Nations Development Decade (1991-2000), of the Convention on the Elimination of Discrimination against Women and the Forward Looking Strategies for the Advancement of Women, and of the Convention on the Rights of the Child. There has never been a more propitious time to commit ourselves to providing basic learning opportunities for all the people of the world.

REFERENCES

Dakar Framework for Action: Education for All: *Meeting Our Collective Commitments.* Text adopted by the World Education forum, Dakar, Senegal, 26-28 April 2000.

Education for All: Achieving the goal : The Amman Affirmation. Mid-Decade Meeting of the International Consultative Forum on Education for All, Amman, Jordan, 1996.

EFA 2000 Assessment (2000) *Draft Country Report*: Japan http://www2.unesco.org/wef/countryreports/japan/contents.html.

EFA 2000 Assessment (2000) *Country report* :Namibia.

Education for All Year 2000 Assessment:*Statistical Document* (2000). Paris: UNESCO, International Consultative Forumon Education for All.

Haggis, S.M. (1991) *Education For All :Purpose and context.* Roundtable themes I. Paris: UNESCO.

Towards education for all (1993) The Ministry of Education for Namibia.

4

Global Initiatives on Globalisation

The World Education Forum (Dakar, April 2000) reaffirmed the vision of the World Declaration on Education for All (EFA) that all children, young people and adults have the human right to benefit from an education that will meet their basic learning needs in the best and fullest sense of the term (World Education Forum, 2000). The Forum collectively committed itself to attaining the following goals:

i) expanding and improving comprehensive early childhood care and education, especially for the most vulnerable and disadvantaged children.

ii) ensuring that by 2015 all children, particularly girls, children in difficult circumstances and those belonging to ethnic minorities, have access to and complete, free and compulsory primary education of good quality.

iii) ensuring that the learning needs of all young people and adults are met through equitable access to appropriate learning and life-skills programmes.

iv) achieving a 50 per cent improvement in levels of adult literacy by 2015, especially for women, and equitable access to basic and continuing education for all adults.

v) eliminating gender disparities in primary and secondary education by 2005, and achieving gender equality in education by 2015, with a focus on ensuring girls' full and equal access to and achievement in basic education of good quality.

vi) improving all aspects of the quality of education and ensuring excellence of all so that recognised and measurable learning outcomes are achieved by all, especially in literacy, numeracy and essential life skills.

In addition to the six goals, the Forum identified a number of particularly critical themes, for example HIV/AIDS, teachers and quality of education, education in situations of emergency and crisis, and Information Technology (IT), as needing immediate attention and action.

Governments have an obligation to ensure that EFA goals and targets are reached and sustained. This can most effectively be done through broad-based partnerships within countries, supported by cooperation with regional and international agencies and institutions. The international community is called upon to launch with immediate effect a global initiative aimed at "formulating the strategies and mobilising the resources needed to provide effective support to national efforts".

Which has been developed in an interactive process with representatives of all EFA partners, interprets the nature of this initiative and presents their consolidated understanding of the six options (or elements) outlined in the Framework:

a) increasing external finance for education, in particular basic education;

b) ensuring greater predictability in the flow of external assistance;

c) providing earlier, more extensive and broader debt relief and/or debt cancellation for poverty reduction, with a strong commitment to basic education;

An important outcome of the consultation process was that the global initiative must be understood in a wider development, rather than a narrow, financial sense. While directing itself towards the Education for All goals and targets, the global initiative must ensure support for overall development and poverty alleviation, and contribute to establishing an enabling environment where needed in the countries in the South. Support for education rests on political will and must be understood in a macro financial and political context with human and institutional capacity-building as critical components. Political will and financial resources are critical for the achievement of the EFA goals in the context of wider development.

Other important resources are professional and technical assistance, knowledge and information, and communication. The success of the global initiative depends, amongst others, on the application of general principles for international development cooperation announced, for example, in the European Union (EU) code of conduct. This includes an active dialogue built on trust in the negotiation between partner countries and partner agencies, on transparency and accountability as mutually accepted principles, and on participatory and inclusive planning and implementation of EFA whose progress must be effectively coordinated and monitored.

With respect to financing, the initiative must reinforce not only resource mobilisation, but also its effective utilisation and management. Increased financial resources are, thus, expected to be mobilised both through increased allocations and through efficiency measures in its utilisation and management. The actual mix of the six elements would vary depending on the particular national context which may require additional or alternative options as well, for example the use of IT to improve the delivery of education.

The contribution of development partners is complementary to that of national governments who bear the main responsibility for advancing and/or achieving the EFA goals. While being global in scope, the success of the initiative rests particularly on its capacity to respond to specific country needs as determined by the complexity of understanding EFA in a wider development context.

EDUCATION FOR HUMAN DEVELOPMENT

The EFA goals underline the long-existing and prevailing concerns of the international community that have been expressed in numerous declarations and conventions since the Universal Declaration of Human Rights in 1948 stipulated free education for all—a goal reaffirmed in the Convention on the Rights of the Child in 1989. Two of the EFA goals, universal primary education by 2015 and elimination of gender disparity in primary and secondary education by 2005, also form part of the recognised international development targets that aim at global poverty reduction through strategies for health and the environment in addition to those for education. Proposed at the World Summit for Social Development in Copenhagen in 1995, these targets were agreed by the Development Assistance Committee (DAC) of the Organisation for Economic Co-operation and Development (OECD) in 1996. They were reaffirmed in the United Nations Millennium Declaration in 2000.

The EFA goals highlight the downside of globalisation, namely marginalisation and exclusion of certain population groups, countries and regions that have persisted, even grown more extensive, despite the numerous international declarations and conventions issued since the Second World War in support of free education for all, equity, social development and poverty reduction.

According to the Dakar Framework, more than 113 million children have no access to primary education, 880 million adults are illiterate, gender discrimination continues to permeate education systems, and the quality of learning and acquisition of human values and skills fall far short of the aspirations and needs of individuals and societies (World Education Forum, 2000). Furthermore, disruptive conditions related to, for example, persistent civil wars and the HIV/AIDS pandemic, call for radical rethinking of, or at least a much wider range of approaches to, the teaching and learning process. They also highlight the relevance of the Dakar focus themes and the need to find diversified solutions for countries in different circumstances, including those in emergency, crisis or post-conflict situations.

The plea of the late 1980s for structural adjustment with a human face or the need to protect the vulnerable while promoting growth thus continues to be valid. Furthermore, there continues to be a strong contrast between official government support for the international declarations and their implementation, despite relative consistency in the thinking on the necessity and benefits of education for development.

Investment in human and social capital are now widely accepted as means of creating sustainable development, achieving poverty reduction and reducing inequalities within and among nations, and of enhancing personal development and quality of life. The synergy between education and improved health, higher productivity, innovation, increased political participation and empowerment is comparatively well established, although many of the precise mechanisms still have to be more clearly understood because of differences in outcomes in different contexts. Significantly, education is the critical force in creating tolerance, respect for diversity and peaceful understanding—a purpose which has gained even more significance in light of recent developments on the world scene.

Education is also central to the current, pervasive emphasis to establish a mutually reinforcing relationship between macro-economic stability and structural reform on one hand, and growth and reduction of poverty and inequality on the other. This is reflected in the outcomes of top-level meetings, such as those of the G8 countries in Cologne in 1999 and in Genoa in 2001 and of the G7 education ministers in Tokyo in 2000 at which investment in lifelong learning, education and skills was placed at the core of the development of future information-based societies. "Education and skills are indispensable to achieving economic success, civic responsibility and social cohesion", as stated in the 1999 Cologne charter.

The leaders in Okinawa also called on international financial institutions, in partnership with developing countries, to focus on education in their poverty reduction strategies and to provide greater assistance for countries with sound education strategies. "These strategies should maximise the potential benefits of IT in this area through distance learning wherever possible and other effective means," the leaders stressed. This theme was underlined again at the Genoa meeting in 2001 when the G8 countries also reaffirmed their "commitment to help countries meet the Dakar Framework for Action goal of universal primary education by 2015".

Thus, while education's central role in development efforts is undisputed and backed by high-level political commitment in the case of Education for All, not all EFA goals seem to carry the same weight. The wider development targets and millennium goals supported by the statements of the G8 countries do not address the expanded basic education concept of the World Declaration on Education for All (World Conference on Education for All, 1990) and the focus of the Dakar Framework for Action. In particular, the development targets for universal primary education and gender equality neglect the strong emphasis of the Dakar goals on the quality of education. It is essential that attention be paid to the expanded concept of basic education and to all six Dakar goals. These must be interpreted comprehensively in the context of support for intermediary and higher-level education in order to achieve holistic development processes.

Particularly significant is the fact that the initiative is not to be understood as a global fund, as originally announced by the Global Campaign for Education at the World Education Forum in Dakar in 2000. The initiative goes beyond financing of EFA to interpreting the principles and specific mechanisms for international cooperation as related to all of the stipulated six elements and their use in achieving EFA. Providing adequate financial resources is but one of the strategies.

The Global Campaign for Education is now emphasising the importance of the initiative as a ledger and mechanism to monitor fulfilment of commitments both by national governments and by development partners related to such aspects as the formulation and implementation of EFA plans, identification of resource gaps, and brokering and channelling of financing. The World Bank (and UNDP) have also, in accordance with the Dakar Framework for Action, linked the global initiative to the fulfilment of the commitment to fund viable national EFA plans in the context of an overall poverty reduction framework, specifically the World Bank Poverty Reduction Strategy Papers (PRSP), the Enhanced Heavily Indebted Poor Countries (HIPC) Initiative and the Comprehensive Development Framework (CDF).

According to the Bank (and UNDP), implementing the initiative would require massive partnerships based on a division of labour and identification of tasks in light of the comparative advantage of all partners. In the view of the Bank (and UNDP), this should rest on a three-pronged strategy aiming at:

1) reaching consensus on policy and technical issues recognised as barriers to development of basic education, especially in HIPC;
2) undertaking key non-lending activities to help countries identify gaps, financial or others, hindering the achievement of EFA; and
3) developing an implementation strategy aimed at increasing the effectiveness of international assistance. The World Bank is currently examining the practical implications of establishing a global financial mechanism for EFA.

According to these suggestions, the nature of the global initiative is rather understood as a mechanism for short-term support, in particular to strengthen incentives for governments to prepare and implement plans, and for comprehensive policy dialogue. According to the Bank (and UNDP), particular attention should be paid to reaching consensus on the definition of a national plan, criteria for countries to join the initiative, mobilisation of extra financial resources and ensuring regular, transparent monitoring of subsequent policy dialogue and action.

This focus can be regarded as justifiable in light of the first, time-bound goal in the Dakar Framework for Action, namely that countries must produce national EFA action plans by 2002, either through modification of existing national education plans in accordance with the Dakar goals or through development of new ones. As interpreted in this paper, this would, however, limit the wider development perspectives that support for education and the Dakar goals are intended to serve and restrict the understanding of resources which are here understood as financial, human, material and non-material in nature. Finally, while deployment of resources must be strategically targeted, the principle for the global initiative, as interpreted here, is to assist in creating the preconditions necessary for as many countries as possible to join it and to apply the initiative in accordance with diversified needs.

THE FINANCIAL CHALLENGE OF ACHIEVING EDUCATION FOR ALL

There are ongoing efforts in the World Bank, UNESCO and other organisations to estimate the financial resources needed to achieve Education for All. They include attempts both at establishing a global financing goal and at identifying resource gaps at the country level. In line with the international development targets, current calculations have focused on estimating the financial resource gap to meet the goal of universal primary education by 2015. Because of the difficulty of measuring qualitative aspects of universal primary education and of the lack of focus on the other five EFA goals, highlighting the difficulty of the concept of a global funding gap.

According to the World Bank, current funding for education budgets in developing countries originates predominantly from national governments (97 per cent) while the international community provides only 3 per cent of the total, of which 1.5 per cent represents World Bank funding (World Bank, 2000a). Other calculations indicate that up to 10 per cent of total funding comes from the international community. This proportion can be even higher (by some estimated at 40 per cent) in specific countries. In general, funding from the international community is considered to play a critical, catalytic and supportive role.

Set in the context of education's critical multi-purpose role in societal and personal development, the relative proportion of total education funding in developing countries provided by the international community is small. The highest figure estimated to reach UPE by 2015 represents less than 0.3 per cent of the total GNP of the developing countries, 0.06 per cent of the total GNP of developed countries and 0.05 per cent of the world's GNP (UNESCO, 2001). While enhanced national resource mobilisation, utilisation and management is critical, the international community must comply with its stated commitment to concerted action that will lead to increased support for national EFA efforts along the lines of the Dakar Framework for Action. Such efforts are particularly important in light of recent international developments. They must be well integrated with other international efforts to reduce poverty and global, regional and national inequalities.

The six elements for resource mobilisation and efficiency measures identified for the global initiative in the Dakar Framework (increasing external finance; greater predictability in the flow of external assistance; earlier, more extensive and broader debt relief; effective donor coordination; sector-wide approaches; and monitoring) must be understood and applied as a function of the different institutional and structural contexts and constraints at the national level that would determine the specific approaches and strategies adopted by development partners and national governments.

In this respect, macro-economic and sectoral reform must be linked in order to ensure a supportive environment that would enable the education system to function efficiently and effectively as a development tool. Reform efforts must include policy reform to enhance locally generated resources for education and other development purposes through, for example, more effective fiscal instruments, appropriate taxation and taxation incentives, enhanced private sector contributions and budgetary re-allocations, and the attraction of additional private international capital flows, concessional resources and improved measures for debt relief.

All resources and expenditures must be treated within a common budgetary framework. Simultaneous policy reform of the education sector must aim at cost-shifting and cost-sharing. Cost-sharing should be undertaken without adverse effects for the poor and without enhancing gender, rural/urban, regional and other inequalities, thus implying at the same time the elimination of direct and indirect user fees at the basic level. The efficiency and effectiveness of the teaching-learning processes must be heightened through locally adapted solutions, including the use of new information technologies. This also includes the adoption of sector-wide approaches to educational development and improving aid conditionalities.

Support for EFA must form part of other education sector support and of the core elements of a government's budget. EFA must be linked within sector frameworks with poverty reduction and development strategies. This means coherence among national Education for All action plans, education sector plans, development strategies and other policy frameworks, such as the Common Country Assessments (CCA), the United Nations Development Assistance Framework (UNDAF), CDF, PRSPs and the HIPC Initiative.

International and national resource mobilisation must, thus, be complementary and well targeted in pursuit of holistic national development processes. Such mobilisation depends on high-level political commitment of both national governments and international agencies. Global and national redistribution of resources through, for example, improved trade conditions or budgetary re-allocations might be particularly instrumental in filling the estimated funding gap both in the short and the long term.

In the current context of increased international security measures, it will be particularly important not only to protect education and wider social sector spending, but to invest at a level that can guarantee their critical functions for poverty reduction, sustainable development and international peace and solidarity. Further development and implementation of the global initiative must, therefore, continue to involve all EFA partners and must form part of the thinking on financing and development in organisations. The EFA partners are, therefore, faced with several challenges.

— They should radically increase support for basic education and for overall international development assistance. This has become even more crucial in the currently difficult international security situation. Increased financing must be ccompanied by greater predictability in the flow of external assistance and maximum reliance on all available and possible new funding sources, including debt relief and/or debt cancellation for basic education.

— They must ensure that increased financial flows, ODA as well as private financing, act as a catalyst for national resource mobilisation and sustainable development with due attention to the critical role of basic education. This would require targeting of resources and setting conditionalities in view of differential needs in specific regions and countries.

— They should strengthen policy coherence and coordination of EFA efforts nationally and internationally, adopt sector-wide approaches and strengthen partnerships with all EFA actors. This will ensure that the various international initiatives related to the international development targets promote the Dakar EFA goals and basic education.

— They must hold national governments and the international community to their commitment to EFA through careful monitoring of the progress towards the EFA goals and targets. This will include monitoring of financing for (basic) education as well as identification of constraints and opportunities for planning, formulation and implementation of national EFA goals and targets.

REFERENCES

Arora, G.L., *Child Centred Education for Learning without Burden,* Gurgaon, Haryana, Krishana Publishing Company, 1995.

Dakar Framework for Action: Education for All*: Meeting Our Collective Commitments.* Text adopted by the World Education forum, Dakar, Senegal, 26-28 April 2000.

Haggis, S.M. (1991) *Education For All :Purpose and context.* Roundtable themes I. Paris: UNESCO.

Ministry of Human Resource Development, *National Policy on Education*, New Delhi, Government of India, 1986.

National Advisory Committee, Ministry of Human Resource Development, *Learning with Burden*, New Delhi, Government of India 1993.

Pradhan, B., Subramanian, A.,*Structural Adjustment, Education and Poor Households in India, Analysis of a Sample Survey.* Paper presented at World Bank Workshop on Poverty Reduction and Social Progress: New Trends and Emerging Lessons, April 1999, Dhaka.

UNICEF/EAPRO, *Education: Enrolment and Completion, Quality, Governance and Girls Education.* Fourth East Asia Pacific Ministerial Consultation—Goals and Strategies, Bangkok, United Nations Children's Fund East Asia and Pacific Regional Office, 1998.

5

Varied Educational Challenges

We are all well aware that keeping pace with knowledge change is a perennial challenge for higher education institutions. At research universities throughout the country; we engage in strategic planning, we invest in new faculty positions, we launch targeted fund-raising activities, alongside the daily work of tending academic landscapes. We add, merge, and delete courses, degree programs, and departments. While the prevailing image of knowledge change in higher education has tended to be either inertia or expansion, those who have made their professional lives within academic settings during the recent past also know otherwise. That is, they understand the threat, if not the reality, of selective consolidation and program elimination when priority-setting is mandated and when some academic areas are deemed dispensable as a result of insufficient centrality, quality, or cost-effectiveness.

In 1990s, public scrutiny and mandates to restructure are likely to continue in a new light: enrolments are expected to expand. For example in California, a state legislative committee has held hearings to consider how to serve the anticipated swell in enrolment, Tidal Wave II.

Several possibilities have been considered, including mandatory summer session, distance learning, and outsourcing of academic programs. Although growth is expected, the cost-savings mandate of the 1990s seems to persist where administrators and faculty do not have the option of widespread additive solutions that their predecessors enjoyed in the 1960s.

Thus, the basic challenge remains to consider which academic structures and resources are appropriate commitments to old and new knowledge areas, which are worthy of continued investment and how they should be organised. For the most part, deliberations over academic restructuring seem to occur in one of two ways. If there is some urgency, traditional mechanisms of academic governance are bypassed by an ad hoc committee, system-level or state-level agency.

In this case, faculty are unlikely to be asked to participate in deliberations over the alternatives or the likely consequences of proposed changes. If timing is not critical, academic processes can reign, including faculty committees engaged in re-evaluating their charge as well as the options. In this mode, given an awareness of external pressure and unprecedented public scrutiny, tensions may exist internal to the campus among proponents of different academic areas as well as between those who advocate compliance with external demands for demonstrated accountability versus those who argue for resistance often in the name of safeguarding faculty rights.

Although neither seems satisfactory as a wholesale approach, at least the involvement of faculty may lend some academic expertise to matters of teaching and learning that are entailed in proposed restructuring alternatives. Unfortunately though, as attention continues to be placed on managing the external pressures, we have yet to incorporate faculty expertise into such decisions or for that matter to improve tensions that fester within internal governance. Deliberations over whether or not and how to reorganise academic offerings are likely to be ongoing. At the same time though, little is known about the long term viability of many contemporary initiatives. These include recruiting star faculty, replacing tenure-line positions with term contracts and part-timers, establishing differential fees for professional schools, outsourcing academic activities (such as remediation or introductory languages), creating academic partnerships with industry and other nonacademic entities, and expanding distance learning arrangements. Little is known about the consequences of such structural and material resource shifts for the academic workplace, for our students, and for the broader society.

Moreover, we do not know whether there will remain any shared sense of institutional purpose or the perception of interdependence on any given campus and whether cross-subsidisation of resources across academic units will persist. We do not know whether core academic activities of knowledge creation, preservation, and transmission will remain viable, either as a complementary set or as separate functions. While the unknowns are daunting, this is an exciting time for those of us who make our professional lives in these settings. The major issues before us will be restructuring to what, by whom, according to what values and societal goals.

Among higher education observers, there seems to be consensus that the locus of academic reform, if not control, extends to a range of economic and political factors beyond local campus settings. In this era satisfying them all seems elusive as a result of either prohibitive cost or the irreconcilability of conflicting mandates. For public research universities in particular there are formidable expectations to improve access, enhance quality, and cut costs, alongside expectations to embrace new information and communications technologies that are in themselves costly and unproven. The assessment paradigm has an apparently unlimited reach to establish organisational and individual performance metrics in the name of demonstrating accountability.

The perspective of higher education as an industry, public colleges and universities are seen increasingly as a sector of the economy. As with firms or businesses, the root metaphor is production—to produce and sell goods and services in a competitive marketplace, to train some of the workforce, to advance economic development, and to perform research. A research university may be thought of as offering a very diverse product line, especially in the post-World War II era of Kerr's "multiversity". It offers courses and levels of degrees across hundreds of fields of study; professes to serve national, state, and local economic needs; and sells entertainment in sporting and cultural events to the local community.

According to microeconomic theory, organisation are managed based upon assumptions of economic rationality. The main services of teaching and research are variously supplied and priced to correspond to laws of supply and demand.

Students, parents, state legislatures, employers, and research funders are seen as customers. Particular customers have different tastes and preferences. Other people, such as faculty employed by the organisation, are presumed to participate out of calculative involvement. As such, they can be motivated to be more productive through the use of incentives and sanctions.

Major obstacles to maintaining the organisation's viability include fixed costs and inefficiencies, competition and oversupply, uncertainty and imperfect information. Guiding principles for the organisation's managers are to know it, liabilities and assets, to anticipate costs and benefits, to enhance efficiency and flexibility, and—as realised in the contemporary quality movement—to increase customer satisfaction.

This "industry" perspective focuses on the harsh realities of market forces and the urgency of staying competitive by planning strategically, scanning environments, attempting to contain or cut costs, re-engineering to correct inefficiencies, or doing whatever it takes to maximise flexibility adjustments include changing product lines, substituting technology for labour, and reducing fixed costs through such means as outsourcing and privatising as well as increasing the proportion of part-time and temporary personnel. Doing nothing is not an option.

Several types of markets are at work simultaneously—not only for obtaining students, but for placing graduates, hiring and retaining faculty, obtaining research funding, establishing collaboration with industry, maintaining endowments, and sustaining and extending alumni-giving to increase various revenue sources. The major barometer for managers is to read the market for constraints and opportunities relevant to the viability of their niche; if done well, a higher education organisation can capitalise on untapped demand, allowing it to supply the educational product at a higher price. The decision to add an academic program could be seen as a strategy to position the college or university to attract new customers and thereby increase revenue.

Similarly, an increase in tuition can be explained as appropriate because of increased demand or decreased supply of a particular educational product (for example, a professional degree in engineering, business, or law). Hence, programmatic changes can be seen as prudent market corrections.

All of this should sound quite familiar to observers of contemporary higher education management. The corporate metaphors of production in a competitive marketplace are omnipresent. Knowing one's resources comparative advantage, and strategy has become standard in the US and increasingly in Europe. Of course, one might argue that these principles are rendered irrelevant for public higher education, given that many of its markets are heavily regulated by state and federal government through several types of public subsidies, restrictions in pricing regulated degree offerings and admissions standards. Yet the industry perspective and its dominant production metaphor have nonetheless acquired a certain resilience, due in part to their parsimony to today's uncritical acceptance of business and economic rhetoric, and to the very real complexity of today's campus operations.

For example, it is not uncommon for university presidents to use an industry yardstick to convey the magnitude of the enterprise, as for example Duderstadt's characterisation of "the University of Michigan. Inc.," which, with an annual budget of over $2.5 billion, would rank roughly 200th on the list of

Fortune 500 companies. Given the size and complexity of university operations, adopting business rationales with strategic management principles has become de *rigueur* for repositioning higher education organisations to compete within new economic realities.

There are several consequences, of course, to such an industry conception of higher education coming to dominate as the legitimating idea that is used to make sense of and ultimately to redefine the parameters of, public higher education. It is worth noting that leaders of public universities today are expected to demonstrate some willingness, if not enthusiasm, to consider market forces and demands for relevance. There is increased concern expressed, for example, over new providers (some virtual, many private) that may draw students away from traditional university settings.

While such developments must be monitored along with pressing economic realities such as escalating costs and stock market fluctuations, these matters should not define the entire landscape, for they unduly narrow our sense of the present and the future. Within a strict conception of higher education as an industry, there is no attention to what is at stake in repeated adaptation to market forces; nor is there a provision for the public good that may exceed the market's reach.

After the World War II , not only an expansion of higher education, but also a dramatic diversification of the activities expected as the legitimate province of public higher education: to broaden access, to advance knowledge through research, to contribute to economic development by employing and producing workers, and to accelerate the development of industrial applications. Such expectations and definitions may be reconstituted over time thus signalling a major shift in the unwritten charter between higher education and the society it serves. Moreover, it could be argued that these legacies must be periodically reinterpreted in light of societal developments.

The language used to talk about higher education is important, for it not only reflects our thinking: it also contributes to a construction of reality. While this observation has been noted by philosophers, linguists and sociologists alike, Robert Bellah and colleagues state it powerfully: "Institutions are very much dependent upon language: what ire cannot imagine and express in language has little chance of becoming a ... reality". This observation carries with it even more weight when one considers the moral import.

According to Bellah et al., we often neglect "the power of institutions as well as their great possibilities for good and evil"; the process of creating and recreating institutions is never neutral, but always ethical . . .". If we heed that admonishment, conceptualising higher education as subject to a logic of "social institution" invokes normative considerations for campus planners and for faculty, students, and trustees, as they chart a course for the future.

Thus, in addition to the ways that contemporary public universities and colleges are being reshaped by their environments, the very discourse itself about those changes and challenges plays a significant role in the reshaping of higher education.

In this light we must ask whether public higher education has taken on principally economic functions to the neglect of a more comprehensive institutional mandate to perform not only educational but also socialisation and social justice functions. Evidence to support such an assessment would be that the logic of managerial production and competitive repositioning has rendered irrelevant or unvalued the notion of higher education as a place for creativity and the life of the mind, a place for caring and nurturing relationships, as well as a place for exploration, dissent, and even unpopular ideas.

All of these may be deemed inefficiencies or distractions, wasteful or unaffordable except perhaps for the elite. Even retaining the university "as a place" may be up for grabs.

Proponents of "higher education as an industry" are concerned that higher education's inability or unwillingness to adapt will result in a loss of centrality and perhaps ultimately a loss of viability as providers. In contrast, proponents of "higher education as a social institution" are concerned that adaptation to market forces gives primacy to short-term economic demands at the neglect of a wider range of societal responsibilities, thereby jeopardising democratising functions and the long-term public interest.

The three interrelated mechanisms that have converged to advance this process and the dominance of the industry perspective. First is the rise of academic management in colleges and universities, drawing upon discourse from management science and organisational theory for its professional ideology and position descriptions to monitor vulnerabilities and reduce existing dependencies by cultivating private revenue sources. The second mechanism is the rise of academic consumerism, moving beyond the post-World War II decades of massification and its attendant democratic gains, to elevating as paramount economic-consumer interests, particularly the student as buyer with preferences to be satisfied. Third is the re-stratification of academic subjects and academic personnel, based upon the increased use-value and exchange-value of particular areas of knowledge in the wider society.

For the third mechanism, we must understand that higher education is a knowledge-processing system as well as a people-processing system universities need to be seen as creators and distributors in the competitive knowledge industry. Thus, what has come to count as knowledge on our campuses has not simply unfolded or evolved out of existing areas, but has resulted in part from the differential valuing and resourcing of academic units, each competing for epistemological, organisational, and physical space. When additive solutions have not been possible, priorities are identified; particular units and employees are construed as failing to pull their weight and are targeted for down-sizing or elimination. For example, small humanities programs (such as foreign languages) have been losing resources and status. In contrast academic units related to computer software, microelectronics, biotechnology, and bioengineering have gained support, given their relevance to thriving industries.

•In the contemporary era, the rhetoric of selective reinvestment has gained ascendancy, while the viability of comprehensive field coverage has been questioned across many campuses as something that may not be affordable. Indeed, what it means to be comprehensive has been disputed as specialised knowledge itself advances. Thus, keeping pace with knowledge change is a central concern that should be at the heart of fiscal and academic planning; and accordingly faculty expertise from several fields is required to weigh alternative investments for the future.

The pressure to remain technologically cutting edge can be fuelled by the hope of expanding access and the hope of improving teaching and learning, but it is also accompanied by the pressure to contain costs. As we have become painfully aware, upgrading technology entails major overhauls of information systems in addition to providing students, faculty, and staff with the training to use it.

One challenge for higher education's leaders is to encourage collaboration and to share lessons learned—not only at the campus level, but in state and national arenas. At the same time the challenge for the rest of us is to participate actively and critically in determining the appropriate uses for new technologies and the appropriate arrangements for oversight and governance.

Even though technology could transform higher education, the nature and scope of such changes are still contested and not guaranteed. In a very short time, we have seen obsolescence: the tremendous initial investments which were made in computer systems that are now outdated, the cadres of students who learned computer languages which are now obsolete. Moreover, there is to date very little evidence of sustained improvements in student performance as a result of new information technology, either at the K-12 or post-secondary level. Although history has shown us that the impact of technology is impossible to predict and that the most outspoken advocates and naysayers have often been inaccurate in their prognostications, the rhythms of academic work have already been altered.

From a market perspective, there is concern about a changing landscape of providers, with private companies expanding their market share as they draw students from traditional higher education settings. However, other than market realities, the advent of virtual higher education prompts us to rethink many fundamental beliefs about universities as places, storehouses of knowledge, and communities of learning. It also prompts us to consider the respective roles of teachers and learners. As such, technological developments challenge academic leaders to preserve what is essential to the enterprise and perhaps even recast it in terms amenable to the new media. While new technology in itself obviously cannot solve higher education's problems of cost, quality, or accountability, we need to be mindful of the character of discussions about potential technological advances.

Many deliberations cast higher education narrowly as a service delivery industry. Thus, among the many educational and governance issues raised by new media for teaching, learning, and delivery of knowledge materials, a fundamental challenge for academic leaders is to define their universities in broader terms. While public research universities may clearly compete with other providers of distance learning, the key contribution that academic leaders can make is to remind participants and consumers alike that their enterprise is much more than service delivery. This may entail reinterpreting the land grant mission to have contemporary meaning. It may also involve selectively reasserting the value of knowledge as an end in itself; or the preparation of citizens as an essential institutional goal alongside serving the more utilitarian interests of employers. So, as campus leaders consider their market niches as service providers, they can also tout the many ways they function as a public good beyond immediate economic value.

The academic leaders have not received enough support to accomplish their broader institutional mandates. Of course it is essential to heed accountability demands and pressing market imperatives. Yet it is equally if not more essential to interpret today's mandates in the context of the historical charter to serve the long-term public interest and to preserve their educational character as places of inquiry, teaching, and learning, as well as places of personal development and socialisation for citizenship.

As academic leaders are asked to reshape the university enterprise, there is a responsibility, not only to pause and reflect, but also to act. Research universities are usually characterised as places of inertia, difficult to manoeuvre, like battleships. Yet, in this era, there is a clear opportunity—and at times a demand—to change course. Deliberations must involve all stakeholders, and they must proceed prudently with attention to the cumulative effects of incremental decisions.

Academic restructuring entails a potential reshaping of institutional purposes-in its people-processing activities as well as its knowledge-processing. That is in addition to confronting questions of how to serve the needs of the economy and especially the state, there are compelling social justice needs that must be brought to the foreground. Depending on how these questions are handled, it is possible that resource allocation decisions will result in further stratification of who and what matters, as well as qualitative shifts in what areas of knowledge are deemed worthy and who has access to and ownership of them. In decisions about appropriate revenue-generating activities, some discussion should attend to the ways in which research is integrated with teaching, especially in graduate-level programmes.

The academic programme establishment and review, procedural legitimacy is a critical factor. Who will judge the academic worth of specific subjects? Faculty? Students? State coordinating agency members? Legislators? Employers? Is there any room for renegotiating the process by which academic programme decisions are made, to include more faculty expertise? It is also up to the academic leaders to consider the extent to which a campus offers comprehensive field coverage as well as what that means for each academic area. Moreover, beyond considering the full range of academic offerings, it is essential to consider what will draw people—students, faculty, staff, alumni trustees—to a university, not merely as a cyber-link, but as a vital cultural and educational site.

In recent decades, immigration to the Unified States has increased to levels unprecedented since the turn of the 20th century. This high rate of immigration has lead to a dramatic transformation of the nativity composition of school-aged children. The term children of immigrants is here generally meant to include both the US born and foreign-born children of immigrants. Although some children of immigrants are foreign born, most are US born.

From 1970 to 1995, the number of children of immigrants aged 5-20 who were living in the United States more than doubled, from 3.5 to 8.6 million, and the share of all students in schools that they represented rose sharply from 6.4 per cent to 16.0 per cent, with children of immigrants outnumbering African American children in 1995.

In the past, schools have typically been viewed as critical to the successful linguistic, social, and economic integration of immigrants and their children. In recent years, with the enactment of the Bilingual Education Act and the Emergency Immigration Act and as immigration levels have reached nearly all time highs, expectations that schools will accommodate the increasing and diverse needs of the new immigrant population have grown.

Other researchers have investigated the implications of immigration for opportunities for native racial and ethnic minorities in a variety of contexts. This research has been motivated by the concern that the benefits and costs of the country's relatively generous immigration policies have not been evenly distributed, thus threatening to fragment US, society further along racial lines. Unfortunately, relatively little research attention has been paid to how the children of immigrants in schools affect native minority students' educational outcomes, despite the prevalence of the issue in the media. Much of the literature on immigrants and schools has focused instead on educational experiences and outcomes for children of immigrants or for students with limited English proficiency.

A negative relationship between the percentage of immigrants in a metropolitan area and the educational attainments of African Americans. As elaborated later, the changes brought about by immigration may have implications for the way instruction occurs in US schools and the educational resources available to US children.

In the context of the issue of racial differences in educational opportunity, these types of potential changes, should they be distributed disproportionately among "black" schools, could further widen African American white differences in educational opportunities and outcomes.

Examining the implications of immigration for US born students involves assessing the effects on educational outcomes, such as changes in test scores, of attending school with children of immigrants or language minority students, net of other relevant individual and school-level characteristics.

In addition to looking at educational outcomes, it is important to find out—and indeed possible with available data sources—whether children of immigrants even go to the same schools as do African American or other minority children. Thus, as a first step, the research presented here compared the percentage of LEP children in schools attended by African American versus white students to assess the degree to which immigration may be viewed as an additional factor that may affect racial differences in educational opportunity.

The literature on school composition effects to provide a basis for examining school attendance patterns. Research on school composition and segregation has been motivated by studies that have consistently shown a correlation between the racial-ethnic and socioeconomic composition of a child's schoolmates and the child's academic success. Children who attend low-status, high-minority schools learn less than do children who attend integrated schools. Much of the relationship between school composition and learning can be attributed to the selection of children from certain family backgrounds into particular schools. But even after controlling for family background and SES of the school, some effects of racial-ethnic composition on learning remain, particularly at high levels of minority concentration.

School composition has been hypothesised to affect learning outcomes through at least two pathways: normative processes that occur, among students and organisational or structural changes that may occur in school systems. Both mechanisms have garnered support from the research literature and could be operating simultaneously.

The idea is that students establish a peer society within which attitudes related to schooling and achievement become normative expectations, at the same time, social networks develop that facilitate academic success. "Good schools" are those attended by "good students" and are where academic achievement is valued and facilitated-even if not realised by most students. Research on young children in elementary schools has shown little to no direct evidence of the normative processes hypothesis. However, part of the reason may be that peer influences do not become strong until children reach adolescence. Another explanation is that pressure to conform to group norms may be offset by students using peer group norms as a basis for making judgments about their ability to succeed. That is, lower-class, minority students may give up more easily in the face of seemingly unreachable norms and expectations for high academic achievement.

Normative processes have been used to explain the observed effects of racial-ethnic composition. That is, minority-group children may bring to schools the negative attitudes and expectations that emerge from the social and economic disadvantages of growing up non-white in the United States.

On the other hand, Ogbu's research has suggested that, unlike youths in "castelike" minorities like African Americans, Native Americans, Puerto Ricans, and native-born Chicanos, minority youths from "voluntary" immigrant groups develop peer cultures that facilitate achievement and upward mobility. The extent to which immigrant concentration in a school is accompanied by a heightening of an "oppositional" versus "achievement-oriented" peer culture remains an empirical question and probably varies by immigrant group.

Researchers have found that teachers in white middle-class schools teach at a higher level and cover more content than do teachers in schools that serve minority students. One explanation is that teachers pace instruction to the class average. African Americans in middle-class white schools benefit because the calss average is likely to be higher.

The number and percentage of children of immigrants in a school may affect the way instruction occurs and place limits on the educational resources provided to nonimmigrant students because children of immigrants have distinct educational needs apart from other students. First, children of immigrants tend to have low english proficiency. Van Hook and Fix found that approximately 42 per cent of foreign-born students and an additional 20 per cent of US born children of immigrants do poorly in school, on average they receive lower grades, score below their classmates on standardised reading and math tests, and more likely to drop out of high school. Third, children of immigrants tend to come from disadvantaged backgrounds. Poverty rates among all children of immigrants are almost triple that of non-Hispanic whites. Foreign-born children, in particular, have poverty levels—at 43-8 per cent—that approximate those of African American Children.

The challenges that immigrant students bring to districts, schools, and classrooms may affect the way instruction occurs for all students. Districts and schools that serve large immigrant populations may make curricula and hiring decisions in ways that attempt to accommodate their increasingly diverse student body but nevertheless are less than optimal for any single group. Finally, teachers with classes that contain a large number of language minority children and children of immigrants may focus more attention and time on meeting the needs of these students (thereby attending to the needs of the largest group of students) and spend less time with other instructional groups.

Orfield and his colleagues examined patterns and trends in school segregation among Hispanics, African Americans, and non-Hispanic whites, they did not explicitly examine the level of school segregation among African Americans, LEP children, or children of immigrants. The reason for this omission is related to the availability of data.

The research on racial and ethnic segregation relies on a national-level database of all US schools, compiled by the National Centre for Education Statistics. These data contain information on the racial and ethnic distribution of students in-every public school in the country, but do not include information on the students' place of birth or language status. In addition, sample surveys did not routinely collect information about LEP students until recently.

Some expectations about the distribution of LEP students across schools may be formulated. In particular, these expectations are derived from ideas about residential patterns within a multiethnic, multiracial context, like areas with significant immigrant and LEP populations. On the one hand, theories on spatial, or place, stratification predict patterns of racial segregation, in which non-Hispanic whites position themselves spatially in ways that exclude racial and ethnic minorities from their neighbourhoods (and schools), thereby preserving "social distance from less advantaged groups".

When immigrants move into a neighbourhood or school district, majority whites may move out or send their children to private schools, but minority families may not have the economic or social resources to do so. The ethnic composition of a neighbourhood can shift as more incorporated immigrant groups become spatially assimilated and newer, less acculturated groups move in. However, the process of neighbourhood succession is thought to occur quickly, particularly in areas with significant African American populations. As a result, multiracial, multiethnic neighbourhoods containing African Americans are relatively rare and short-lived. Referred to here as the autonomy hypothesis, the expectation is that these kinds of neighbourhood patterns are replicated in schools. Thus, a pattern would arise in which new minority students (less acculturated children of immigrants and LEP students) attend schools apart from both African American and majority white students.

Since many children of immigrants are Hispanic, these results suggest there may be little contact between African Americans and children of immigrants in schools. The contribution of this research is to use national school-level survey data to assess the degree to which African Americans versus non-Hispanic whites attend schools with LEP students. It focuses on LEP students, rather than all children of immigrants, because LEP students are more likely to have distinct needs that require additional funds and attention from teachers. This is nevertheless a departure from examining the school-attendance patterns of all children of immigrants.

At the national-level, US minority students-particularly African Americans-may appear to encounter relatively few children of immigrants and LEP students in school because immigrants and African Americans tend to be concentrated in different regions of the country; the patterns specific to the South may overwhelm the national-level results. Even though the national-level results would be important for assessing the current impact of immigration on national-level educational outcomes for African Americans, they would not have much relevance for assessing whether patterns of autonomy.

Since secondary schools tend to draw students from a larger geographic area than do primary schools, the patterns observed for secondary schools are likely to be indicative of broad residential patterns that occur within school districts, while the patterns observed for primary schools are more likely to mirror finer residential patterns that occur within neighbourhoods. Thus, for example, if it appears that African Americans are less likely to have LEP schoolmates in primary school than in secondary school relative to majority whites, this finding would suggest that the patters observed derive from residential autonomy among all three groups at the neighbourhood level.

REFERENCES

Bean, Frank D., and Stephanie Bell-Rose, 1999, *Immigration and Opportunity: Race, Ethnicity, and Employment in the United States*. New York: Russell Sage Foundation.

Bella, R. N., Madsen, R., Sullivan, W.M., Swidler, A., & Tipton, S. M. 1991, *The good society*, New York: Random House Books.

Clark, B.R. (1993). The problem of complexity in modern higher education. In S. Rothblatt & B. Witttrock (Eds.), *The European and American university since* 1800. New York: Cambridge University Press.

Dreeben, Robert, and Adam Gamoran, 1986, "Race, Instruction and Learning." *American Sociological Review* 51:660-69.

Fulgini, Andrew, J., 1997, "The Academic Achievement of Adolescents from Immigrant Families: The Roles of Family Background, Attitudes, and Behaviour." *Child Development* 68:351-63

Rumberger, Russell W. and J. Douglas Wilms, 1992, "The Impact of Racial and Ethnic Segregation on the Achievement Gap in California High Schools." *Educational Evaluation and Policy Analysis*.

Wilson, Franklin, 1985, "The Impact of School Desegregation Programmes on While Public School Enrolment." *Sociology of Education*.

6

Citizenship Education: Learning at School and in Society

EDUCATION POLICIES OF JAPAN

Educational policies of Japan The foundation of the current Japanese education system was established after the Second World War. In 1947, as part of democratic reforms during the American occupation, the Fundamental Law of Education and the School Education Law were enacted. These laws established the so-called 6-3-3-4 system and the principle of equal educational opportunity for all.

The 6-3-3-4 system means 6 years of elementary school education, 3 years of lower secondary education, 3 years of upper secondary education and 4 years of higher education. Almost all students attend elementary and lower secondary education which are compulsory. The enrolment rate is 96 % for upper secondary schools and 48 %for higher education (in 1998). Some basic education also takes place in preschool - notably in kindergarten where 62 % of children participated in 1998.

The curriculum is tightly controlled by the government and the Ministry of Education. All text books used for teaching are screened and authorised by the Ministry of Education. In recent years the schools and curriculum has been under reform. Among other things classsize has been reduced from 45 to 40 students and the school week is being reduced from 6 to 5 days alongside with a modest reduction of total school hours. The reasoning behind this is to give children more time with their parents in order to strengthen moral learning in the home and also as a step towards international standardisation. More emphasis is being laid on improving the learning environment to make it *"enjoyable and free of worries"*.

The idea of learning to live together is in particular evident in the subject areas as "Social Studies" and "Moral Education" where "Dowa Education"—also known as "Human Rights Education"- plays an important role.

The history of Human Rights Education in Japan is also the story of the Buraku minority and that of Dowa Education. Three million people are known as the Bukaru minority, which has been discriminated for centuries. The discrimination is not based on a different ethnic origin but on a feudal caste system. The democratic reforms carried out after World War II were expected to make Buraku discrimination naturally disappear. However, the long-established custom of discriminatory practice was not overcome easily. Major companies prevented Buraku from working in the mainstream and their job-opportunities were therefore limited. Also Buraku children attended school to a lesser extent than other children because they had to work to help their families who were too poor to pay for text books or school-meals and thus ultimately because of the discrimination. Then in 1948 in a few so-called welfare teachers began trying to solve the problem of low enrolment ratios and longtime absentees among Buraku children. This was the emergence of Dowa Education. As a result almost all Buraku children attended school in the late 1950s and in 1963 textbooks became free of charge. In the 1980s the concept of Dowa education was broadened to cover other anti-discrimination and human rights issues.

As it is today Dowa education is not a special form of education. It refers to all kinds of educational activities that aim to eradicate all forms of discrimination. Consequently Dowa or Human Rights Education is a cornerstone in combating intolerance and thereby in learning to live together.

In Japanese schools the education on moral and social issues are according to the recently revised National Curriculum Standards primarily carried out in the subjects areas of "Moral Education", "Social Studies", "Life Environment Studies" and "Special Activities". Human Rights Education is not a specific topic in the curriculum standards but is taught in the subject areas of Social Studies.

Moral education is taught 35 school hours a year (one credit) in elementary and lower secondary school and is furthermore an important part of pre-school education. In pre-school and elementary school the students are "given the basic discipline and repeatedly taught what they should not do as a human being, what is right and what is wrong until they *understand thoroughly*". The need to cultivate a spirit of international cooperation, respect for life and the need of helping each other are also important issues.

— Social studies includes history and civics and equals 2 credits in 1st and 2nd grade, 3 credits in 3rd to 6th grade and rising to 4 credits in most of lover secondary school. Civics teaches the basic principles of the constitution including democracy, respect for human rights and peace.

— Life Environment Studies is taught with 3 credits in first and second grade. It promotes *"activities and experiences* in communities, in the environment and with people in their neighbourhood". Furthermore "interactions with infants, elderly people *and disabled childre*n" will been couraged.

— Special Activities (1 credit in 1st- 3rd grade and 2 credits from 4th-6th grade and lower secondary school) emphasizes that students have desirable human relations and acquire basic morals and social rules. In addition the issues taught in Moral Education and Life Environment Studies are repeated.

— In pre-school and elementary school the education in all subjects is based on a *"hands-on learning approach "with* plenty of group activities and project oriented problem solving, thus emphasizing the need of giving the learners experience in interacting and respecting each other.

The high degree of accentuation on group identity in Japanese schools and society sometimes creates the problem that individuals not fitting into a group could feel isolated or be out casted. This also makes the problem of bullying worse. At elementary and lower secondary schools, bullying most often involves verbal abuse, with physical abuse occurring more often at the upper secondary school level. Although the exact numbers are difficult to determine because some cases go unreported according to one study, one in three elementary and lover secondary school students has been bullied but more than one third did not report it to anyone. The problem is however taken seriously by both the government, schools and the press. The official policy is that *"it is never, ever tolerated for a person to bully another*" and measures such as "encouraging education that values individual personality", flexible school transfers and the establishment of the Office of Ombudsman for Children's Rights have been taken.

Two types of adult education on human-rights issues exists: Programs for Buraku adults who were deprived of education when they were young (for instance, adult literacy classes) and programs for adults to learn about the Buraku issue and human rights.

A survey on Human Rights Awareness was conducted in 1993 by the Japanese government. People were among other questions asked if they had ever enrolled in adult education programs on the Buraku issue or read relevant materials to learn about the issue. According to the survey a national average of 24 per cent had followed lectures on the issue and 13 per cent had participated in community-based activities. Between 50 and 65 per cent had read public information papers, newspaper articles or magazines dealing with the issue. A notable difference existed between western and north-eastern

Japan with a much higher awareness in western Japan. This reflects that Dowa Education is extensive in western Japan.

The methodology of teaching Human Rights Education (HRE) is a central point of debate. It is acknowledged that one-way transmission of knowledge from the teacher to the learner is not enough to cultivate empathy among learners. Knowledge-centred teaching does not encourage learners to solve the problems, but rather foster helplessness. Therefore many teachers are introducing participatory methodology in their human rights courses. Learning is activity-based and includes simulation, role playing, discussion and other group activities. The hope is that this new teaching methodology encourages learners to become actively involved and tackle human Rights issues in the real world.

In 1996 a project team of 20 teachers was formed with the aim of exploring ways to reduce the incidences of bullying and violence in schools and to develop students' awareness for peace, tolerance and international understanding. A basic assumption of this project that this goal could be achieved by teaching students communication skills such as assertiveness, listening, conflict resolution, mediation and out of school activities and exchanges of views and contacts with disabled people. Examples from the project include how a teacher enhances mutual understanding between a Chinese girl and her Tokyo classmates by letting the two parts introduce respectively Chinese and Japanese culture to each other. In another class a teacher plans an exchange between his students and physically disabled people by letting the students help push wheelchairs while communicating, achieving enjoyment and mutual understanding in the process.

Examples of HRE in practise can be found in textbooks containing human rights stories, historical accounts of human rights violations, stories of contemporary human rights violations in the classroom such as bullying, tales of discrimination in Japan and essays for peace education. A teachers' handbook on HRE was produced in line with the 1997

Plan of Action of the UN Decade for Human Rights Education. It aims to promote HRE by taking up issues such as Dowa education, education for understanding disability and disabled people, international understanding, bullying and education for the environment. The hand book promotes a practical approach by using case-studies and active learning.

THE EDUCATIONAL POLICIES OF NAMIBIA

At the time of the declaration of the independence of Namibia in 1990, SWAPO formed the government, and a constitutional right to 10 years of basic education was established. At the same time an extensive educational reform was initiated. In 1993 "Towards *education for all*" was published as the official policy of the Ministry of Education. The educational reform builds on four pillars: quality, access, equality and democracy. At the same time a decentralisation of the school system was initiated with the aim to refer all decisions to regional level. With this educational reform it was the intention to support lifelong learning and to move away from education of the elite alone towards education for all.

Citizenship education is not a subject as such in Namibia—the term is not even used. Still there is a lot of evidence that citizenship education is actually taking place all over the country. Especially the subject of Life science has played an important role in the development of educating engaged, participant and self dependent citizens.

Life science is a compulsory subject in the Namibian lower secondary school (8th to 10th grade). Life science combines the subjects of biology, agriculture, health and ecology. The approach to the subject is dual in the sense that practical work in for instance school gardens is supported by theoretical learning.

The immediate goal with this project is to prepare the pupils for working life and the life conditions of Namibia. Both at the pragmatic and the more ideological level: to be able to participate as equal citizens in a democratic society.

More over, the subject has had the function as spearhead in the Namibian educational reform. Before the independence of Namibia in 1990 the school system was dominated by learning by rote - very often knowledge relevant for a European context, with focus on certification and a tight authoritative hierarchy. Life science has a relevant scientifical content and is, in contradiction to the former teacher oriented education, based on learner centred education. The target group encompasses all pupils from 8th to 10th grade in the Namibian basic schools.

The subject Life Science was originally developed for the Loudima-school in the SWAPO refugee camp in Congo Brazzaville in the 1980'es. The practical agricultural part was here essential, among other things to secure food for the refugee camp.

The subject was developed by SWAPO incooperation with the Danish NGO, IBIS. It was introduced in Namibia in 1990 in connection with the educational reform. The implementation in Namibia was led by NIED (National Institute for Educational Development) in cooperation with IBIS. Along with the progress a shift in the emphasis of theory and practice has taken place so that the practical part to a higher degree works as a pedagogical tool in order to understand the theory or to take on a responsibility. The specific support for Life Science ceased in December 2000 and the subject is now part of the curricula like any other subject.

The Danish Ministry of Foreign Affairs supported the school in the refugee camp in Loudima through its anti-apartheid-grant through IBIS. Many governments, NGO's and UN-organisations supported the Namibian educational reform economically.

In 2000 the project was evaluated by an international group of researchers conducted by Ursula von Harmelen from the Rohdes University in South Africa. This evaluation will be published in the summer 2001.

The Namibian society is dominated by a gap between the skills of the traditional society and the demands of the new society. Based on a learner centred strategy Life science emphasizes the experiences and the knowledge already achieved by the pupils in school or in the local community. This way Life science is one of the attempts to build a bridge over this gap and also an attempt to involve the cultural backgrounds of the pupils in the education.

Life science education puts the learner in the centre saying that learning must begin at the learners level and encourage the learner to seek more knowledge and to combine it with practical experiences. This changes the role of the teacher radically. Many teachers build their authority upon their monopoly of knowledge and are afraid to loose the respect of the pupils if they no longer are the sole resource of knowledge. In Life science the teacher is more of an adviser and her job is more asking the right questions than providing the right answers. This makes a lot of teachers feel in secure, and pedagogical courses and work shops for the teachers were - and are essential. In order to create learner centred education the teacher must:

— establish learning environments that activate the pupils own ideas
— challenge the pupils in their perception of the world
— present new concepts to the pupils that relate to correlations they already know
— in as many ways as possible add new knowledge to practical use in the daily life.

This is a challenge for the teacher not just because of the new role. The implementation meets many obstacles. A teacher may find learner centred education feasible at a workshop, but meets the difficulties at home with overcrowded classrooms, shortage of textbooks and other materials etc.

It is difficult to move from a traditional authoritarian teaching towards pupil centred learning. Scepticism has been expressed and shows the fear that this new education method will create disciplinary problems and that the level of learning will drop due to fewer examinations. At the same time many teachers and parents—fear that the authority of the teacher will be undermined in the changes of the teachers role. Indeed, how is it possible for the teacher to open up for pupils participation and yet maintain an authority based on the teacher as a role model, the pupils respect for the teachers knowledge and ability of conducting the activities rather than respect based on obeying and fear of not knowing the right answers.

The old education system in Namibia was founded on control through a lot of examinations. Life science has introduced the concept of continuous assessment partly to take the place of examinations in order to find out what the pupils gain from the education. The goal is to decrease the necessity of examinations. Still, examinations are a vital part of the Namibian education system. The Life science project has dealt with this by asking different, more open questions at examinations than is usually being asked. The aim is to find out what the pupils actually know rather than what they don't know, and whether the pupils are able to use knowledge from their local area. The idea of continuous assessment is to assess the process-oriented achievements of the pupils: their capability of asking questions, analyse and collaborate. Within all subjects certain fields, skills and attitudes must be assessed along the school year both to get a fair impression of the pupils gains and problems, but also for the teacher to adjust her teaching. Thus continuous assessment implies the possibilities to involve assessment of the practical work e.g. in the school gardens. This provides a fair assessment for children who does not have the benefits of a reading tradition from the family, but who profits from the combination of the study and the practical work. This is possible for the teacher to assess on basis of the daily work, but still there are lots of experiences to obtain in order to develop methods to assess even better.

THE EDUCATIONAL POLICIES OF ROMANIA

Romania is a country in transition. After the change of system in Romania in 1990 an educational reform was initiated. But it was not until 1998 that the changes could be traced. The educational reform did not explicitly mention 'education for all', nevertheless it was a very important issue in the content of the reform. The concept was in the EFA country report associated with *"education for the quality of life"*. The report lists a number of parameters for life quality such as income, possibilities forwork, health and interest in (participating) in politics. All of them parameters on which a successful' education for all policy' would have had a stabilising influence. In the system of education for all there port emphasizes that education for all can only be carried through by including both the formal and the non-formal educational system.

In the Romanian educational landscape a number of so-called foundations and NGO's are operating. Many of them have specially exposed groups as their target groups, e.g. homeless children or gypsies. A number of the projects have a specific aim about learning to live together in a multicultural context. In many places around Romania several ethnic groups are found in the same area, all having smaller orbigger problems with images of enemies, marginalisation and victimisation the multicultural projects all have as a goal to help those different ethnic groups in a certain area to attain a daily life, based on a peaceful coexistence and mutual respect. To the projects there are often a European aspect in the coexistence: Understanding and respect for the cultural diversity on local level is the first step to an understanding at regional level.

Intercultural learning consists of a number of local projects in different counties, among others Bihor, Braila, Covasna, Sibiu, Caras-Severin—all with several ethnic groups.

A varied number of learning methods and activities are being used, for instance drama as an exercise to develop affective connections, intercultural celebrations and other specific social cultural projects. One kind of activity is the thematic workshop, such as: *Values of human solidarity; Customs; Socialroles; Intercultural communication; Why do we contest?; Do we know our neighbours?.*

A special theme is called *Scapegoat* which generally covers psychological aspects of interactive and equal participation of everyone in the local communities. It is meant to improve daily relations by provoking an open reflection in the individual in order to let off for instance a complex of inferiority or to help the participants to become aware of the real cause of victimisation.

Another interesting activity is the local memory documents. It can for instance be temporary or permanent exhibitions presenting all the citizens' daily life through items like the family albums of photos, the old significant cultural objects such as books, icons, pictures, genealogy trees, old agricultural or industrial tools etc.

In the perspective of lifelong education the project aims at learning and understanding the cultural codes of the different ethnic groups both in terms of their difference and similarity from one another. The project aims at using new techniques and strategies, and also to share an attitude of loyalty and respect for each other in a context of common responsive participation.

In the local community the projects are aimed at developing a personal and collective expression of local memory, and also at encouraging volunteer participation in the multi-ethnic communities in order to offer a positive perspective of a European, culturally integrated identity.

The target groups, coming from the school system and civic society at large, have been composed of students, teachers, decision-makers and volunteer social workers, as well as members of NGOs and GOs, media, teachers' trade unions and parents' committees. The participants are of Romanian, Slovak, Hungarian, Greek, Armenian Turkish, Jewish or Gypsyorigin.

The national Institute for Educational Sciences is the main organizer of the project. However networking is a fundamental part of the project, and the institute works together with both governmental (national, regional development agencies, departmental and local authorities,) and non-governmental (trade unions organisations, parents committees, public universities, art schools, libraries, museums) organisations as well as educational institutions and private or state schools and academic universities and media. To learn how to network has constituted an important part of the learning process.

The phases of the project has been:

I *Networking*: Investigating and extending the intercultural communication ideas and forming networks in the counties.

II *Preparation of intercultural dynamics to each local partner, autonomous for each participating group:* Every intercultural operator works together with each leader of an ethnic group in order to prepare their common meetings in the local community.

III Different intercultural practices.

IV *Ongoing activities, reiteration and transfer of the good practices:* E.g. Caras-Severin county economic and cultural activities involving all the local decision makers and social partners in order to enhance the associative and democratic local life.

Financing comes mainly from the EU, The Institute for Educational Sciences and Ministry of Education and Research. At the local level the operators use financial resources coming from local councils of communities, the contribution of community "in kind", the contribution of local NGOs and the sponsoring by economic institutions.

The project team has been periodically carrying out surveys on evaluation phases and levels focusing on: involvement in projects, results connected to objectives, effectiveness, transferability inside and outside own institution, satisfaction, environmental, political and institutional context development, management, funding and fund allocation, target groups, working and educational methodology. Any perceptions reflected in media or in local communities are also taken into account. The objects of informal and formal evaluation are cultural references, dissemination of information, artistic and cultural creation, openness to other cultures, sensitivity to the transversal cultural dimension, ability and complementarity in fulfilling the social role of cultural intermediary, and responsive participation.

A few 'outcomes' can be mentioned:

1. It is not possible to work with a fixed programme when you are dealing with intercultural learning. You must always consider the local conditions and adjust the activities accordingly.
2. The impact on the visitors at the local memory exhibitions was very remarkable. They recognized various significant cultural objects - books, icons, pictures etc.—they actually recognized themselves and felt proud of themselves and their local history, because they realized they did have a cultural image.
3. Several teachers—even at university level—realizes the importance of working with the multicultural aspect also inside the formal educational system. (this—and which is mentioned in point number four—is not a result of this specific project alone, but is rather a consequence of the multi-ethnical projects altogether).
4. At national educational policy level there is a responsive interest by the current government insolving the situation with for among other the Gypsy people: In each county of Romania centres for social and educational integration of the gypsies are to be established within a 10 years period.

Citizenship education: learning at school and in society is bringing the concepts of citizenship and learning to live together up for discussion with the aim to discuss the concepts in a global context.

Three cases from different places in the world have been introduced to represent three different ways of understanding and using concepts of living together, citizenship and learning. The cases illustrate different ways of learning to live together. Different traditions, assumptions and practices will together serve the purpose of crystallizing some points for debate that all will have a bearing for the global as well as local intentions of learning to live together.

The ICE 2001 contributes to the development of the global objective of Education for All and is placed centrally in the actual international discussions of learning strategies and objectives and of thc complex of problems and aims presented in the Jomtien-documents, evaluated in the EFA 2000 Assessment and then reformulated in the Dakar-documents. The international discussions of *citizenship* is placed centrally on the agenda in the UNESCO for a, and in the fora of developing the concept of sustainability, in the discussions of human Rights and in the debate of our multi-cultural societies. Thus, the paper presents an international angle to the understanding of learning about citizenship on basis of UNESCO's work up till now together with other international contributions to these discussions. Different levels of citizenship and living together

It must be pointed out that the concepts of citizenship and democracy are strongly connected to a Western European / Northern American philosophical and political tradition. Thus citizenship is one way—among many others—of living together in which the rights and obligations of the individual are emphasized and participation of the individual is stressed as an ideal. Everywhere around the world people are living together in communities described in other terms or without any term or concept for the way of living together as such.

For countries in transition it is quite new to the citizens that you have a right as well as an obligation to be an active participant in the development of society. In some of the old democracies the traditional participation in political and social life is decreasing. In both cases there is a need to develop the capability of citizenship within the individual.

Depending on where on the globe we live we as individuals, participate in far more and different communities than 50 years ago. The communities are shaped on both local, national, regional and on global level. This fact creates a potential field of conflict for the individual because of a clash between the expectations from and interests within the different communities.

To some nations it is a stated objective to become partners in a regional political and economical community. One of the ways to reach such a goal is to create a sense of regional citizenship in the nation's citizens. However, it is a question at which level and to which extent it as an individual is possible to engage yourself in daily life as citizen of a region. Furthermore, it is not at all clear how big a part of our identity and community spirit that is tied to the close environment.

At the individual level the increasing globalisation for some people means new possibilities to develop global networks of knowledge that among other can imply detachment from the local - and often binding -community. To others the new possibilities are completely overshadowed by the polarisation between rich and poor regions that is another result of globalisation.

Citizenship is not easy to define as it is a concept holding several layers and dimensions. One attempt to seize the many facets of citizenship mentions four different dimensions.

Citizenship is by many primarily understood as political *citizenship* encompassing political and juridical rights and obligations in a given society. But political citizenship does also bear an active dimension implying engagement and insight in the communities one is part of and where the citizen feels responsible towards society. A political citizenship like that pre supposes that the citizens have a common socio-cultural context. Here citizenship has a*social dimension* that refers to the mutual relations between members of a community and are essential to the relationship between the personal integrity and the community. Furthermore, there exists a*cultural dimension referring* to the awareness of a common cultural heritage that is essential for the community in relation to the surrounding society. Finally, citizenship has an *economical dimension* referring to the right of the individual to a job and to a certain standard of living. All four dimensions are closely inter-connected. When you act politically you do it on the background of your social consciousness. The cultural practice of an individual is e.g. dependent on the economical possibilities etc.

Each culture emphasizes different dimensions of citizenship. For some the religious aspect within the cultural dimension is of outstanding importance both in the under-standing of the individual and in the common understanding of rights and obligations. For some the ability of providing for one' self and one's family is a vital part of the rights and obligations of citizenship. As well the educational system and the economic life must be developed to ensure these needs.

Even if the political and the cultural citizenship can be separated theoretically they are in reality closely inter-connected. Some nation states have a historically based tradition for having several ethnic groups—each with their own cultural citizenship—living together in apolitical citizenship. Other nations have throughout history been dominated by an ethnical homogeneity or by a ruling group that has affected the national institutions with its own cultural distinctions. In both cases it implies a marginalisation of other ethnic groups whose culture is being claimed to be inferior by the ruling group.

An equal coexistence of different ethnic groups is a big challenge to the educational system, since an understanding of the values of other cultures simultaneously questions the superiority of the culture of the ruling group.

In some cases citizenship is intended due to a specific political goal. For instance in connection with the creation of a nation state or of a political region the need for a construction of some sort of citizenship may occur. Equally, global citizenship is a construction where the common problems of our earth - the environment, war, inequality -demand a responsibility for our common future as well as tolerance towards other cultural expressions and ways of living.

Furthermore, education for citizenship - civic education - and learning to live together are important in the major concept of sustainability: the ability of living together on a basis of sustainable social, economical and environmental developments now and in the future. These dimensions are equally important and mutual dependent in a sustainable development. Sustainability implies the production and consumption in the perspectives of renewal of energy and resources as well as the north-south aspect and cultural diversity and also includes the problems of poverty and distribution of wealth. Thus it shares common values with education for citizenship in aspects of learning to live together, moral responsibilities, demands for problem-oriented thinking and not least participation. In this way education for citizenship can be seen as a corner stone of Education for sustainable development.

Active citizenship depends upon the rising generation's education for and in democracy. This has e.g. been stated as one of the aims of the Danish Municipal Primary and Lower secondary Schools: "The school must prepare pupils for participation, shared responsibilities, rights and duties in a society with freedom and democracy. Thus, the school's education and entire daily life must be based on liberty of thought, equality and democracy".

How education may contribute to creating the conditions of active citizenship is not only a question of subjects being taught. The teaching methods employed, in addition to the atmosphere in the classroom are assumed to play a decisive part in the school's contribution. The dialogue among the learners, and between the learners and the educators is also an essential element. The learner's own critical investigations, familiarity with problems and dealing with controversial issues are other elements. However, the school is far from being the only source of influence in terms of guiding the learners in a more or less democratic direction.

Which skills and competences are required of us in order to learn to be a citizen? Which dimensions do you, as a citizen in different societies, have opportunities to develop and unfold? Which economical limitations exist for the school system? Which cultural and social barriers must be overcome for mastering to live together? From an ideal point of view you can point out four levels of skills:

To acquire knowledge: Basic skills such as literacy is a necessity for participating in the democratic processes at all levels. Eventually, computer literacy will also be crucial for the capability of participating in society. The ability to learn—*learning to learn* is essential for enabling the individual to learn new things throughout life to meet the rapid changing needs on the labour market and to be able to participate in the current changes in society.

To make use of knowledge and involvement: Regarding citizenship the basic skills cannot stand alone. The social dimension in which they are situated and the conduct and attitudes of the individual are essential. 'Life skills', 'coping skills' and 'participatory skills' involve the ability of participating at different levels in the activities of a democratic society as a responsible citizen. In this dimension also lies an emotional aspect. It is not sufficient to invest your knowledge according to a dissociated evaluation, you must as well invest part of yourself by expressing commitment and belief in the activities you participate in. Just as knowledge and information are crucial for the development of citizenship, moral and ethical responsibility are equally important.

To understand yourself: In order to be able to participate as an active citizen in the activities of a community you must as an individual be aware of your own stand points and affiliations. In earlier times the community was taken for granted, today we move in and out of communities and therefore we ourselves have to create coherence in our identity. This is the reason why some direct attention towards the narrative skills—the ability to place yourself in a continuous connection by means of your life history. Others point out the historical dimension: Once you see yourself as biography it all of a sudden makes a big difference whether you participate or not.

Learning to live together: Learning to live together is today a necessity at many levels. We must deal with bigger and more complicated cohesions than in earlier times. The ability to live together in the family, the local community, the nation or globally is closely connected to the skills of being a citizen - to be part of a community. In his/her actions, the citizen must focus on what is best for the community, not on narrow individual interests.

A very important dimension of (social) citizenship is the ability to live together. In aculturally homogeneous society where the political and the cultural group of citizens are identical this might represent a rather small problem, but many places it is extremely difficult to unite a national, political citizenship among several cultural citizenships. In Africa, for instance, it is not uncommon to see a gap between on the one hand the membership of the tribe that you are born into (which is often both a cultural, social and an economical citizenship) and on the other hand the general political citizenship that is taking place within the state and which often has been forced upon the tribe and therefore is regarded with scepticism. At the same time many of the countries that according to tradition have been characterized by a relative homogeneity are now under pressure both from abroad and from within the country. The rise in immigration means visible cultural differences in daily life. From abroad the globalisation implies a growing demand for relating to new and larger communities. But even in a relatively homogeneous society there will always be differences and inner contradictions. Therefore it is of great importance to emphasize that citizenship implies both rights and obligations. The citizen has civil, political and social rights. However, citizenship cannot be understood as a private life style but rather as a way of living together in which you share the responsibility for the society. You cannot, as a citizen, focus on what is better for yourself. You must estimate the interests of the community: the common good. Citizenship is via involvement, participation and the ability of dealing with disagreement the best tool to create understanding of the dilemmas encompassed in the ideal: the common good.

EDUCATIONAL AND LEARNING STRATEGIES

The development of citizenship must be seen as a mean to create active citizens who participate in the society at different levels and who feel a responsibility towards the communities in which they live and work. Thus, citizenship is both an individual and a collective concern. Individual because it pre supposes competences that enables the individual to act actively in relation to his surroundings. Collective both because it is a goal of the society to develop citizenship and because citizenship is based on shared responsibility and is implemented through collective actions. Thus, citizenship is based on a) lifelong learning and b) learning through experiences and interaction with the social practice in the community in question. Citizenship is the ability of living together, cooperating, having influence on your own life and reacting constructively on changes in the community. This demands competences that include a potential to solve unforeseen problems in different contexts.

The necessary learning that enables the citizens to function in various roles as individuals as well as part of the work force takes place both in the school and outside. To learn how to maintain a work function is in some societies a concern for the educational system, in other societies it is learned within the context of the family or the local community. The division of labour between the school and the society when it comes to qualifying the citizens is thus varying according to the type of society, economical structure or culture.

The acquisition of basic skills (reading, writing and arithmetic) is being considered a responsibility for the school, even in areas where there is little or no possibility to implement the ideals. The knowledge that forms the basis for values and attitudes has been learned more diffusely in a complex pattern encompassing the three forms of learning: formal, non-formal and informal, as for instance defined in the EU-Memorandum on Lifelong Learning.

Formal learning is structured learning taking place within the educational system and leading to recognized certificates and qualifications.

Non-formal learning takes place outside the formal school system - very often considered a supplement to the formal system. It does not lead to formal certification, however often to recognized skills. It can take place in the workplace, in structured leisure time activities and in various forms of volunteer work.

Informal learning takes place in everyday life. It is incidental, unstructured, not intended and very often not considered as learning by the learner. The informal learning also goes on informal as well as non-formal learning contexts. The three forms of learning supplement and reflect each other and the very fact that experiences and knowledge from all life spheres are being activated a learning takesplace that encompasses cognitive, emotional and social dimensions. Learning takes place when the established knowledge is being challenged and counteracted in one or all dimensions. Your knowledge, attitudes and values are being challenged if they are not in perfect harmony with the surrounding world experienced directly or via education, media or narrations. The individual's learning opportunities are directly dependent upon the knowledge that school and society make available.

The competences and qualifications that develop citizenship presupposes learning environments that support democratic processes: the actual goal for citizenship. Learning to live together and learning democratic processes is furthered in learning environments with a democratic practice, learning environments that give room for considerations for differences and respect for others and room for active participation and possibilities to make up one's mind about own learning and practice.

The formal educational systems have the possibility of playing a crucial role in the development of citizenship. The educational systems have a great responsibility for our development as citizens. Learning exclusively build upon transferring indiscussable knowledge, learning exclusively directed towards certification and where the teacher is considered to be the only source of knowledge, leads to inactivity in everyday life and working life and appeals to passivity and obedience rather than to independence. On the opposite side, learning that is based on human potentials and that builds upon responsibility, active participation, reflection and flexibility creates competences that develop active citizens and furthers democratic behaviour. The conditions for democratic participation can be created through:

a) relevance of curriculum
b) learning methods—i.e. possibilities to make critical investigations on your own, possibilities for problem-oriented and inter-disciplinary work and possibilities for team work
c) the atmosphere in the classroom—i. e. dialogue among the learners as well as among the learners and the teachers on a daily basis.

Relevance of the curriculum to the learner is not only essential for the motivation of learning. The content of curriculum is a matter of (re)consideration as the development constantly generates new demands. The curriculum of citizenship education is characterized by a complex set of values which are dependent on the cultural context. At the same time citizenship education concerns the political reality in society. The content of subjects like civics, history, geography, biology etc. must deal with issues of relevance and some times taboos to put the learners in a position to meet the challenges of the changing demands of society. We are entitled to know our own historical and cultural background even though it contains dark sides - in order to understand our selves as a part of it and at the same time to be able to act towards the future.

Learning to live together, mastering co-existence, presupposes a learning that is not build upon pre defined and "right" answers, but rather a situated learning based on problems and challenges that are relevant to the learners. A problem-oriented learning like that demands active participation from the learners in an atmosphere in which their conception of a problem is being respected. In the same way cooperation and team work are important skills to develop tolerance, consideration and respect for one another.

Education for citizenship should not be seen isolated within the formal education systems. When it comes to the ability of living together learning is deeply anchored in the social practice within the family, on the job, associations etc. where non-formal and informal learning environments are being found. They contain elements that furthers citizenship due to their connection to practice of everyday life—be it organised, intended learning or unconscious learning. The social practice unites the cultural, social and political aspects of citizenship.

The concept of 'lifewide learning' reflects a wideness in the learning uniting the experiences and recognitions of everyday life with the learning taking place in the more intended form. The concept of 'lifewide learning' stresses that learning can be of any form and take place any time throughout life and therefore also includes the concept of life long learning. By that formal, non-formal and informal learning are put into an organic connection with each other, thus complementing one another. Within the formal educational systems citizenship is there fore developed both through formal and informal curricula as well as through democratic participation in the learning environment.

Some attempts of assessment have been carried out stressing the difficulties of measuring educational aspects based on qualitative categories like values, attitudes, processes of learning etc. The recent IEA Civic Education Study is an extensive survey of pupils' knowledge about democracy and their concepts of, attitudes towards and actions related to citizenship. The tests and surveys were designed on the basis of reports and documents from the included countries. This material—along with other research material was investigated in order to find the key items of the survey. This way differences in views on democracy, citizenship etc. influenced the items in their making.

Assessment of educational activities are often rooted in the traditions of assessment and examinations of any education, e.g. testings of learners' knowledge and achievements at certain levels. Such tests are focused on the output and are seldom concentrated on the processes of learning or of the deeper understanding of the actual knowledge. The methods used for these tests are dominated by quantitative, rather than qualitative approaches, partly because of the overall interest in outputs and evidence of knowledge, and partly because it is very difficult to implement qualitative methods. Nevertheless it is vital to orientate towards new approaches in order to assess attitudes and practises in addition to knowledge and output.

Assessment of civic education must be based on a spectrum of key issues serving as standards. Those issues should be significant and central for the very concepts of citizenship and living together, thus we speak of issues of cultural and contextual sensitivity. Still, some common values will hereby be put to discussion as possible standards:

— global responsibility
— participation in practice
— moral values and responsibility
— sustainability
— marginalisation and exclusion
— cross-cultural aspects of learning

The question still left to be answered is how to assess such complex and extensive issues. Still, there is no doubt that it is crucial for the development of civic education and for learning to live together to develop methods and approaches for such studies and carry out attempts of measuring practises and attitudes of citizenship.

REFERENCES

Belanger, P., 1999, *Conference on Education for Democratic Citizenship: Methods, Practices and Strategies*, Warsaw, 4-8 December *1999 : Final repor*t, Council of Europe, UNESCO, European Commission.

Danish Ministry of Education, National Education Authority, 2001, *UNESCO Permanent* System of Reporting for Peace, Human rights, Democracy, International understanding and Tolerance : National report *from Denmark.* Copenhagen: Danish Ministry of Education.

Dohmen, G., 1998, *The future of continuing education* in Europe: Lifelong learning for all in *changed learning environment*s, Bonn: Federal Ministry of Education and Research.

Eichberg, H., 1997, Otherness in encounter thinking folk identity, democracy and civil society with the help of Martin Buber. In *Adult learning and the challenge of the 21st century. Ove* Korsgaard (ed.). Copenhagen: Association for World Education.

Hayashi, Shin-ichi (1999) *The History and Activities of Osaka Prefectural High School. Dowa* Education Research Associationhttp://www.erc.hrea.org/Library/curriculum_methodology/HRE_in_Asia2/chapter3.html#Dowa.

International Commission on Education for the Twenty-first Century (1996) *Learning : Thetreasure within : Report to UNESCO /* Jacques Delors (Chairman of the Commission). Paris:UNESCO.

Jarvis, P., 2001, Globalisation, citizenship and the education of adults in contemporary society. In *Journal of world Education, vol 31, no. 1, 2001,* 21-26.

Korsgaard, O., 2001, The battle regarding citizenship : From social citizenship to active citizenship, From adult education to life long learning. In *Journal of World Education, vol.31, no. 1, 2001,* 14-20.

Monbusho (1996) *Promotion of DowaEducationhttp://www.monbu.go.jp/hakusyo/eng/2_c03.html#2.03.7*

Monbusho (2000) *The Educational Reform Plan* for the 21st Century : The Rainbow Plan (The Seven Priority Strategies)http://www.mext.go.jp/english/topics/21plan/010301.htm

National Institute for Educational Research (1999) *Teacher Education for Peace and International Understanding*. - Tokyo: NIER.

Veldhuis, R., 1997, *Dimensions of citizenship, core* competences, variables and international activities. Speech given at the Council of Europe seminar, Strasbourg, 11-12 December 1997: Education to Democratic Citizenship: Basic concepts and core competences. http://culture.coe.fr/postsummit/citizenship/concepts/erap97_23.htm

7

Globalisation, Human Rights and Education

Education is a most powerful means to protect and promote the cultural identity of different societies and to maintain cultural diversity when globalisation tends to cultural uniformity. Education can contribute to the regulation of globalisation, in particular by establishing the conditions for respect of human rights—a prerequisite for a successful evolution of globalisation.

The phenomenon of globalisation is a result of worldwide integration of economic and financial sectors. It was made possible by:

- fast and significant technological progress, in particular in the area of information and communication technologies;
- geopolitical changes, in particular the collapse of the Eastern Bloc and the emergence of economic grouping of countries;
- a dominant ideology of regulation by the market, initially applied to economic and finance exchanges, and gradually proposed to all sectors of human activity, including the social sector (education, health, etc.).

The aims of increasing return to capital, added to the possibility of locating the units of production of goods and services almost everywhere, have thus contributed to uniting or globalising the world.

Among the main implications of the phenomenon of globalisation, one can mention:

— the emergence of learning societies, due to the multiplication of sources of information and communication;
— the transformation of the nature of work with, in particular, the need for more flexibility and mobility, the importance of communication skills, the necessity of teamwork, the increasing use of new technologies, etc.; and
— the progression of social exclusion, a large part of the world population being unemployed or misemployed and/or receiving inadequate remuneration, finds itself outside social integration.

Fifty years after the adoption of the Declaration of Human Rights, much progress has been made: more legal guaranties, including two conventions in 1966 (one on civil and political rights and the other on economic and cultural rights); more attention paid to the rights of women and the rights of the child; the end of apartheid in South Africa and of totalitarian regimes in Latin America and in Eastern Europe; and, more recently, following the adoption of the Rome Agreement to establish an International Criminal Court (ICC), the International Criminal Tribunal (ICT), with growing recognition and capacity for prosecution.

Although 142 countries have signed the 1966 Convention on Economic, Social and Cultural Rights, 144 countries the 1966 Convention on Civil and Political Rights and 191 countries the 1989 International Convention on the Rights of the Child, a number of countries have not yet adopted the three conventions (the USA has not ratified the first and China the second of these treaties). Outstanding and significant issues remain, based on:

i) *Ideological arguments*—some societies (governmental, religious and political bodies) challenge the universality of the rights, on the grounds that the Declaration is 'western oriented', putting the emphasis on the individual, when in other cultures social groups are most important. Another challenge addressed by some societies is based on the indivisibility of the rights. There is no human dignity with poverty, illiteracy, lack of adequate health services and other social protection.

ii) *Contradictions generated by scientific and technological progress*—new challenges for human rights—are to be addressed, resulting from conflictual concerns: environmental, genetic, communication. Here are a few examples that illustrate the arguments. How to reconcile the principle of freedom of expression in the era of the Internet when we want to protect privacy, avoid the exposure of children and youth to the pervasive effects of certain messages (drugtrafficking, pornography, violence), while at the same time respecting the right of children to access of information and knowledge? How to promote intellectual creativity by protecting copyright when, at the same time, 'downloading' books and messages is regarded a human right for a free flow of information and communication? Many other examples can be found from the consequences of the progress of science and technology. For example, research on genetics:

a) the use and abuse of analyses of DNAs to protect the rights of children from recognition of paternity against the wills of the adults concerned;
b) the risks of 'cloning' on the human species; and
c) the potential consequences of the general use in agriculture of species genetically modified, on the protection and equilibrium of the environment.

There is a rather broadly shared consensus on both the issues facing education today and the approaches and strategies that are offered. Indeed, there is a need to address the issues of access, efficiency, equality, gender, quality and relevance of education. At the same time, it is suggested that policy-makers, planners, decision-makers, educators and managers should adopt a change in their approaches to education, namely: less state involvement and more ownership, participation, collaboration and mobilization of educational protagonists.

Changes in focus are also recommended: from systems to institutions, from inputs to processes and resource allocations, from higher levels to lower levels of education, from initial to lifelong education and from teacher to learner-centred education.

Finally, a gradual process of integration of theories of learning is highlighted: from passive to active memorization, with inbuilt incentives (behaviourist), to constructivist or cognitive development of learning to, recently, a more 'learner-centred' approach to the capacity of each learner to build his/her own learning model, using the mediation of the teachers, a didactic environment, and both school and out-of-school educational resources.

There seem to be two grounds for combining the three areas of interest into one topic for discussion:

Convergence of focus of attention: i) Education, the issues, challenges and the process of learning are now focused on the 'individuals' and far less on the 'system'. In this respect, it is amazing to note that for very different reasons, the 'individuals' are the targets of economists, educators and political protagonists. The economists promote education vouchers and the freedom of choice of individuals on arguments of market efficiency. Educators believe that it is the learner who ultimately determines the construction of knowledge, on pedagogical grounds. As for the political protagonists, the values of alternative policies can only be assessed by their impact on the learners. (ii) The main utopian assumption of Globalisation is that there is a 'world market' where all 'individuals' can buy and sell, no matter where they live and how they live. We all know the highly questionable merit of this assumption, but the dominance of the ideology of the market is such that, while recognizing that there is no such thing as a 'perfect' market (free access, free information, etc.), the literature on Globalisation refers to individuals as the key actors of a 'world market'. Finally (iii) in the Declaration of 1948 and the other instruments of 1966 relating to the protection of Human rights, the 'individuals' (all individuals, children, youth and adults, male and female, of the whole world) are the subjects and the objects of concern; they have rights and their obligations are to respect human rights across country borders.

Emergence of new concerns: With the acceleration of Globalisation and the weakening of governments and intergovernmental authorities in their ability to regulate economies and societies, in most countries today the state has experienced erosion of its power, its credibility and even its legitimacy. The state is no longer in a position to unilaterally decide on public policy. A redistribution of powers is taking place between the state, companies, news and media agencies, etc. The respect for human rights, including the right to quality education for all citizens has so far been the responsibility of public authorities. Large numbers of treaties and different legal international instruments, concluded in written form between states and governed by international law, such as the Vienna Convention on the Law of Treaties of 1969, play (and have played) a crucial role in the progress achieved in the matter of respect of human rights.

More specifically, for education, the General Conference of UNESCO has adopted several recommendations during its different sessions. For example, in 1974 the General Conference agreed upon a recommendation concerning 'Education for International Understanding, Co-operation and Peace'—education relating to human rights and fundamental freedom. More recently, the Jomtien Declaration on Education for All, adopted in 1990, emphasises the need to ensure access to quality education to all.

The efficiency of such legal instruments depends upon the agreements of the states and on their capacity to respect them.

With the weakening of the state, the capacity becomes problematic. This has led to different scenarios for the future, in particular, to contradictions or support between the trends of Globalisation and the challenges facing education and the human rights agenda. Globalisation dynamic is determined by different factors from those that seem to affect the trends in the progress of human rights—they are primarily economic and financial, supported by the opportunities offered by communication technologies; when, in the case of human rights, the concerns are the moral and ethical convictions of individuals. The scenario assumes that if the present trends in Globalisation continue, they may generate political and social resistance and turmoil, but no concrete action is either possible or feasible. This is a *laissez-faire* scenario and a quite likely possibility when we analyse and compare some of the 'governing forces' of the three social processes: Globalisation, human rights and education.

Globalisation: Globalisation is based on market mechanisms which do not include the concerns of values: the driving forces of Globalisation are ideological (the market), economical (the capital) and political (the leadership). Individuals are 'economic actors' and, as such, their behaviour is based on narrow economic concerns. It assumes a market of individuals and not of 'social actors', when we know that behaviour of individuals is determined by their social characteristics and that not all individuals have 'equal' access to markets. Hence globalisation contributes to segmentation of societies and groups; the concentration of capital in Europe, Japan and North America, and the higher concentration of political leadership in the United States of America and strengthening of communitarian ideology and the weakening of universalistic values. The weakening of the states, whose capacity to monitor, regulate and manage national economies, taking into account social concerns, is severely restricted by the multinationals. Thus, the ability of the states to protect human rights and ensure access to quality education becomes more and more limited.

Humanrights: violation of human rights may be regarded as an obstacle for Globalisation and uniting of world markets. In practice, with some particular exceptions, 'are some societies being excluded from Globalisation because of violation of human rights?' The answer is no, when we compare the list of countries singled out by the Annual Report of Amnesty International and the degree of the integration of some of them into the world economy.

The Declaration assumes full equality of all rights to all when globalisation is clearly dividing the world and the people into three groups: 'those who globalise', 'those who are globalised' and 'those who are left out of globalisation', thus contributing to the violation of 'economic and social rights'.

In spite of significant progress in literacy and access to education, there is persistent denial of access to education and close to one billion illiterate people, meaning a violation of the rights to education and to the maintenance of a large proportion of the world population outside the main stream of development. The progress of respecting human rights rests on:

a) the capacity of individuals to keep monitoring closely the attitudes and behaviours favourable to human rights;
b) the political will of governments to ensure such respect; and
c) the capacity of supranational agencies, like the United Nations, to enforce the compliance of governments to international human rights treaties. Needless to say, these conditions are not always met.

Education: Education policies may be designed and adopted taking human rights principles into consideration, but more often than not, access to schooling and to good education is determined by market considerations and by prevailing social, economical, cultural and geographical inequalities (not consistent with the conventions on human rights).

Child-centred learning contributes to the promotion of autonomy and self-development—basic conditions for social and economic promotion in a global world. At the same time, child-centred learning may generate biases towards individualistic values (lack of interest in social concerns) and rejection of universalistic values (a basic feature of the culture of human rights).

Excessive emphasis put on evaluation and assessment (standards and excellence) may support the culture of globalisation and, at the same time, of selection and inequalities leading to denial of social and political human rights.

While the dominant suppliers of education are 'nationals', a growing number of producers of education services are multinationals: this may lead to less attention being paid to cultural diversity and even, potentially, to the domination by one culture. This would not necessarily be a bad thing if the dominating culture were to be really 'universal', when it embodies the creative work of world artists, architects, creators, musicians, painters, poets, etc.

Globalisation contributes to a wide diffusion of ideas and values (including human rights), mobilizing international attention to universalistic issues and challenges.

Pervasive effects of Globalisation—by generating social injustices and economic exploitation made visible by the mass media—can produce resistances and claims to protect human rights. The more educated and well informed a population, the more likely the mobilisation for an effective respect of human rights. The recent freezing of the Multilateral Agreement on Investment (MAI) by militant groups using internet facilities, later supported by some governments in Western Europe, is an example of this.

Multinationals are using universalistic values (protection of the environment, no child labour and human rights consideration) more and more in their marketing strategies. The Italian 'Benetton' is a spectacular case in point, but examples can be found in all sectors and in different countries: production and commercialisation of sportswear, films, theatre plays and music, saving water campaigns in international hotels, and promotion of the use of motor cars using lead-free petrol.

Negation of human rights is an obstacle to the participation of a large percentage of the population in education and Globalisation; it is in the interests of 'globalisers' to participate in the 'opening' of closed, authoritative societies and thus generate new markets. The ICT and the growing visibility of a human rights agenda borne by the multinational press and media agencies are, and will, gradually affect the mode of operation of some multinationals against child labour and the violation of social laws, as well as the market of armaments, in particular landmines, and contribute to more attention being paid by educators at all levels to universalistic values, such as respect for the environment, human rights, tolerance, and other cultures.

Respect for human rights can be a good condition for integration in a global world and involves universal access to quality education.

The concerns of human rights affect education on three grounds—contents, methods and values. There are countless education programmes on human rights, at all levels, and in a variety of countries, from a modest scale (NGO) to a more prestigious host (university).

Education is crucial for successful integration in a 'global world'; competencies needed: learning to be, learning to do, learning to learn and learning to live together. Even countries under endemic conflict with their neighbours, or having suffered from decades of discrimination, are revising their teaching of history and geography to 'learn to live together'.

This is the case in Israel, where new textbooks teach empathy with. Palestinians. More spectacular is the decision of the South African education authorities to rewrite their history/ geography textbooks to promote post-apartheid values.

Good education, efficient participation in the process of Globalisation, and the capacity to defend and promote human rights require 'fully autonomous' individuals. Putting it differently, *educating for autonomy* means building the capacity of individuals to participate in Globalisation and to protect their rights.

Education at all levels should devote particular attention to the potentials of the human diversity of our world: skills for globalisation include a better knowledge and understanding of the heterogeneity of our world, including information, in particular, on economic inequalities and social injustice. Moreover, educational curricula should include references to international concerns and experiences. In this respect, there are good arguments for facilitating mobility of learners and teachers, valuable means for contributing to widening experience beyond national boundaries.

Another priority for education is the promotion of the autonomy of the learner. A prerequisite for success in a global world is indeed autonomy of the individual; at the same time, respect for human rights is conditioned by autonomy. Autonomy means more knowledge of oneself and of the world around one. What are the implications for the adaptation of the curricula and methods of teaching?

There is also a large consensus on the priority to be attached to the development of negotiation skills by learning conflict resolution and peaceful human relations. The implications for policy-makers are: What to teach? In brief, 'learning to live together', economics, international law, social sciences—basically to train professionals in human rights; How to teach? Naturally an emphasis should be put on teamwork and participation, and learning to listen and become informed— learning to learn.

Education should be regarded as a social process of becoming a world citizen. Multidisciplinary approaches to teaching and learning should be adopted to promote the unity of the world and the interdependence of societies. The potentials of learning networks should not be minimized, as numerous recent experiences show.

Implementing education policies

Here is a tentative list for consideration:

i) revisiting educational aims to balance economic, social, cultural and ethical interests;

ii) allowing a large space for autonomy in design and implementation;

iii) ensuring participation of different protagonists: the world of work, the media, the different entities of governments at central and local levels, the civil society, the education profession, and the children and youth;

iv) organising channels of consultation on universalistic values;

v) updating the mission for teachers and teacher training;

vi) improving articulation between curricula, methods and teacher training; and;

vii) introducing in the curricula both human rights concerns and skills for Globalisation (autonomy, communication, and learning to learn).

International co-operation in education

The comments made under the preceding four sections suggest at least four priorities for consideration:

i) What is 'basic' in education (to be supported by donor agencies)? Communication (literacy), 'learning to learn' (focus on teaching/learning approach), autonomy (focus on self-learning).

ii) There is a case for supporting the promotion of 'universalistic values' in education at all levels: it is a basic condition for a 'humane globalisation'.

iii) In spite of traditional scepticism among co-operation agencies on the merit of new technologies, there is a strong case for investment in (Information Communication Technologies), ICTs in the education sector.

REFERENCES

Arjun Dev, et.al., 1996, *Human Rights: A Source Book,* National Council of Educational Research and Training (NCERT), New Delhi.

Arora, G.L., and Yadav S.K, 1995, 'Curriculum for Human Rights' *Progressive Educational Herald*, Vol, 10, No.1, Hyderabad, pp. 47-50.

NCTE, 1996, Human Rights and National Values, National Council for Teacher Education, New Delhi.

Dakar Framework for Action: Education for All: *Meeting Our Collective Commitments.* Text adopted by the World Education forum, Dakar, Senegal, 26-28 April 2000.

Education for All: Achieving the goal : The Amman Affirmation. Mid-Decade Meeting of the International Consultative Forum on Education for All, Amman, Jordan, 1996.

EFA 2000 Assessment (2000) *Draft Country Report*: Japan http://www2.unesco.org/wef/countryreports/japan/contents.html.

EFA 2000 Assessment (2000) *Country report* :Namibia.

Education for All Year 2000 Assessment:*Statistical Document* (2000). Paris: UNESCO, International Consultative Forumon Education for All.

Haggis, S.M. (1991) *Education For All :Purpose and context.* Roundtable themes I. Paris: UNESCO.

Ministry of Human Resource Development, *National Policy on Education*, New Delhi, Government of India, 1986.

UNO, *Children and Juveniles in Detention: Application of Human Rights and Standards.* Vienna, Crime Prevention in Latin America, Presentation for Managers, n.d.

UNO, 1994, *Children and Juveniles in Detention: Application of Human Rights and Standards.* Vienna, Crime Prevention and Criminal Justice Branch, United Nations Organisation.

WHO, 1998a, *Healthy Nutrition*, Geneva, World Health Organisation.

8

Challenges of Information and Communication Technologies (ICTs) for Education

In the last decades of the twentieth century, society has witnessed unprecedented technological advancements and economic, political and sociocultural changes that must be reflected in the school. Education is a process of human enlightenment and empowerment for the achievement of a better and a higher quality of life. A sound and effective system of education results in the continuous development of learners' potentialities, the strengthening of their skills and the fostering of positive interests, attitudes and values. All progressive societies have recognised the enormous potential of education and have committed themselves to the universalisation of elementary education with the explicit aim of providing 'quality education for all'. They have also recognised the need to expand secondary education to as near universal levels as possible, while simultaneously improving its quality for the increased empowerment and advancement of an ever increasing percentage of the population. While higher education also has great potential in this respect, it is often accessible to only a small section of society.

However, at present, primary education can be provided to practically all members of society and, therefore, its quality and efficiency attain a special significance within the personal, social and national context. Thus, effective teacher education acquires an even more crucial importance, becoming a key factor in ensuring quality school education. In other words, effective formal education implies effective teacher education. Teachers can act as trailblasers in the lives of learners and in the process of education for development. If they acquire the professional competence and attitudes that enable them to effectively perform their multiple tasks in the classroom, in the school and in the community, teachers become the single most important contributing factor in ensuring quality educational provision at primary and secondary levels.

There was a time, in most countries, when teacher education was just a single event that took place at the beginning of a career. But this once-in-a-lifetime model is utterly inadequate for the needs of contemporary societies. Indeed, these events have already had a very significant impact on schools around the world. In an effort to better meet the diverse needs of learners and ultimately of society, there have been numerous curricular reforms and the introduction of a range of new approaches and strategies in instruction and evaluation.

A COMPREHENSIVE PARADIGM

These changes have profound implications for the content and processes of teacher education. If teachers are to be able to provide quality education in the face of these challenges, there is an urgent need for ongoing reform of teacher education. Effective teacher education for both elementary and secondary stages of schooling has now to be conceived within a more comprehensive paradigm encompassing a number of inter-related components. These components include the following:

— *Preservice and initial teacher education*: To be provided in a systematic, professional way to all new teachers entering the teaching profession.

— *Recurrent in-service teacher orientation*: To be offered on a recurrent basis and in an organized manner to practising teachers through orientation seminars, workshops, tele-conferences and other such programmes in response to new professional needs and to ensure continued teacher motivation.

— *Continuing professional self-learning*: According to their individual needs, interests and specific professional responsibilities, teachers should pursue their own self-directed and lifelong learning through books, journals, audiovisual aids and other available information and communication technologies.

Professional orientation for school principals and department heads. When promoted or newly recruited as principals, supervisors, co-ordinators, etc., they should benefit from:

— Recurrent organized professional development opportunities.

— Continuous self-directed professional learning and enrichment.

— Opportunities for learning about international experiences and contacting colleagues in other countries.

Higher professional education: Planning and provision for increased access to higher education.

— Planning and provision for training of high-level specialists in different fields, such as curriculum development, textbook writing and preparation of other teaching/learning materials, evaluation and monitoring, planning and management, research and statistics, etc.

— Adequate planning and provision to prepare teacher educators and resource persons to provide effective preservice and in-service teacher education at the elementary and secondary levels.

— Provision of opportunities for international exchange.

Enrichment opportunities for teacher educators.

— Provision of opportunities for periodic enrichment of teacher educators through seminars, workshops, presentations and discussion of papers, etc.

— Facilities and opportunities for research and debate on different aspects of education including teacher education.

— Facilities for publication of different kinds of materials on diverse issues relating to school and teacher education.

— Encouraging international contacts.

The teacher education needs to include all of these componetns in a comprehensive and multi-dimensional manner. The first three components cited above are directly focussed on the education of all teachers. The other three components are essential for improving the quality of teacher education in various ways. An effective pre-service teacher education programme serves as a sound basis for implementing and developing each of these additional components.

COMPONENTS OF THE PARADIGM

The overall objectives are to ensure that elementary and secondary schoolteachers are professionally well-equipped so that they may become increasingly autonomous in their professional growth and, ultimately, maintain their motivation and effectiveness in their role and performance in the classroom, school and wider community. Pre-service teacher education should be the start of a process of transforming lay persons into competent and committed professional educators. The untrained entrants should possess the requisite educational background and stipulated qualifications. The aim of pre-service teacher education is to prepare the uninitiated to become sound professional practitioners. In the light of this definition the new curriculum for teacher education must be competency- based and commitment-oriented.

In-service teacher education refers to a recurrent, organised and needs-based continuing education for practising teachers so that they may update and enrich their professional competence, strengthen their commitment and enhance their role and performance in the classroom, school and wider community. As new developments take place in the curriculum, educational techniques, evaluation procedures, classroom management and other aspects of school education, new needs will constantly arise for in-service training, calling for recurrent provision.

In addition to these organised efforts, all teachers should be encouraged and given opportunities for continuous self-study related to their own professional needs, interests and responsibilities. A successful and dynamic teacher remains a self-motivated and self-directed learner throughout his/her career. It is this self-directed and lifelong learning that supplements and complements the organised sector of teacher education and becomes an important dimension in a comprehensive paradigm of professional education for teachers in contemporary society.

If these three components of teacher education are to be realised, a major review of existing teacher education provision needs to be undertaken. Any such effort must clearly establish and define the basic competencies required by teachers within prevailing social, economic, and cultural conditions, and also foresee the new educational needs and challenges likely to arise within the initial decades of the twenty-first century.

One of the important dimensions of renewing the curriculum, five performance areas were identified on the basis of job analysis and needs analysis. The purpose was to improve the quality and efficiency of school education. It may be noted that these performance areas will give rise to a series of practical activities which include the present programme of 'teaching practice', but in a more realistic and effective manner will cover evaluation procedures and classroom management in different situations, such as multigrade teaching.

However, they also include another important educational responsibilities in which the teacher should be given adequate practical training to develop pertinent skills. Thus, in the field of practical training, these performance areas mark a major shift from teaching practice to broader educational practice in which pedagogical skills remain an integral part, but where the development of other significant practical skills are also given their due place.

a) *Performance in the classroom:* includes teaching and learning processes, evaluation techniques and classroom management.
b). *Schoollevel performance:* for greater all round contribution to school organisation and management.
c) Performance in extracurricula and out-of-school activities.
d) *Performance related to parental contact and co-operation:* for improved enrolment, attendance and student achievement.
e) *Performance related to community contact and co-operation:* should focus on improving school-community relationship for mutual development and enrichment.

These are designed to provide adequate theoretical and conceptual understanding, empowering teachers to perform their responsibilities with professional insight and confidence. In essence, these are teacher competencies that should aim at the development of learner competencies and qualities at school. To achieve these multiple goals, teacher competencies include relevant conceptual elements, content elements, contextual aspects, transactional and evaluation aspects, etc. All the ten competency areas thus identified converge on one or more of the performance areas and interrelate theory and practice in a focused manner.

These competencies are first to be developed during preservice teacher education and further updated and strengthened during recurrent in-service teacher orientation, as well as through continuing and self-directed professional enhancement.

Information and communication technologies (ICTs) have a number of characteristics that permit significant innovation in pedagogical methods at all levels of education. These include the following:

— The digitalised form of information allows storage and dissemination of all types of data on computers (text, sound, still pictures, moving pictures), since all are encoded in the same format—a succession of digits.

— New possibilities for distance communication, whether simultaneous or deferred, permitting collaborative projects between classes, schools or the development of professional networks among teachers.

— The development of these distance communication techniques has led to a new structuring of information, bringing with it a new way of reading and discovering texts. 'Hypertext' permits the combination of linear reading with rapid connection to related texts, each linked to the other. Multimedia encyclopaedias are a good example of the very useful hyper-textual organization of information.

— Multimedia is becoming the principal way of presenting information, allowing information to be presented in different forms, with the result that it is more diverse and take up less space.

In the classroom, two main tasks may be identified in the use of these technologies:

a) *Mastering the technology:* the use of ICTs in education can permit both pupils and teachers to acquire skill in the use of these technologies, particularly in exploiting the computer, as these machines become essential everyday tools in contemporary societies. This objective is in accordance with the aims of vocational education, i.e. to teach skills that will equip learners to enter the job market.

b) *Tools for learning:* if used effectively, ICTs can enhance the possibilities for instruction and learning for all pupils at all levels of schooling. They should, however, be seen as supplementing rather than replacing the more traditional but proven educational tools and methods. They may be used in the instruction of all disciplines, as well as for interdisciplinary or cross-curricular projects. ICTs may also enhance learning in the following ways:

— *Searching for information:* The use of CD-ROMs or the Internet requires knowledge of research methods, such as those used in traditional library research, i.e. documentary research. To find the right answers to specific questions, it is necessary to identify keywords, find appropriate sources, and select relevant information from the identified resources. This process requires the development of critical abilities in order to assess the quality and validity of the information retrieved. The teacher's role is essential so as to develop documentary research and critical thinking skills in students. This responsibility cannot simply be delegated to the computer, which remains a tool to be suitably exploited.

— *Summarizing the information.* As with the above, the ability to summarize the information obtained is not a new objective of schooling. Again, it is the technology that allows a new *way* of formulating and presenting the information. Developing the ability to summarize and reformulate retrieved information should be one of the major objectives of learning. ICTs are ideal tools for developing this skill.

— *Distance communication.* Several sorts of communication are possible :

a) *Among teachers.* Using electronic mail, news-groups or websites, teachers can share their ideas, experience and innovations. This may be a very effective and rewarding means of professional development, as there are already numerous sites, news-groups and networks devoted to education covering wide geographical areas and subject ranges.

b) *Among classes or pupils.* This use is less developed because it is more difficult to realize. However, it has tremendous potential for developing the concept and practice of living together, of intercultural communication and international understanding. Classes in diverse geographical locations may collaborate together on a project, with the contribution of not only individual and collective student abilities, but also context-specific knowledge and data from the participating regions/localities. For this type of activity to be carried out successfully, teachers must be properly trained and the technical possibilities of networks and the available software (in particular the transmission speed) must be improved.

c) *Between teachers and groups of learners.* A new style of communication is being invented between teachers and learners in a distance-learning context. It no longer should be considered sufficient, for instance, to follow a lecture via a video-conferencing system. Nowadays, multimedia materials may be used to enhance instruction. Teaching styles have to evolve to keep pace with these technologies.

However, three principal challenges confront the effective exploitation of these technologies in schools:

— the price (of computers, of software and of communications);

— the capacity of telecommunications—which should exceed 2Mbit/sec;

— the development of software with greater capacities, especially for the sharing of documents.

It should be emphasised that the use of ICTs as a tool, like any other means of instruction, such as books, videos or mere observation:

— may be used for all disciplines: science, technology, languages, history, geography, art, as well as for trans-disciplinary projects.
— should supplement—not replace—other tools for teaching and learning. Pupils need to remain in close touch with the reality around them; they need to touch, manipulate, build and experiment with the natural world.

In the traditional teaching-learning relationship, the relation between the teacher and the pupil is frontal—the role of the teacher is to deliver knowledge to the pupil. There is some co-operation among pupils.The details are described in Fig. 1.

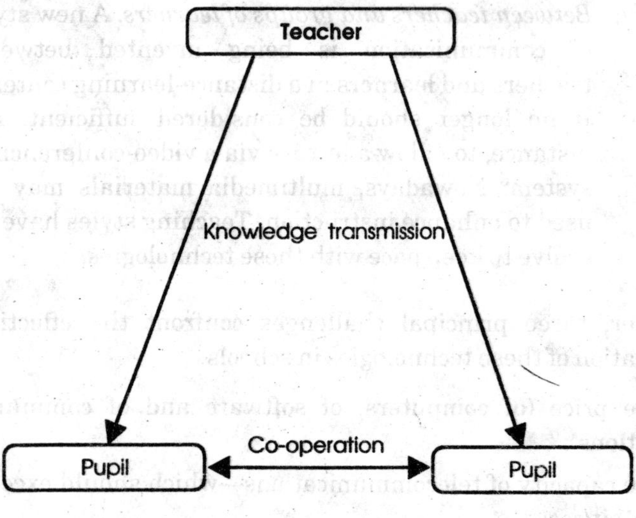

Figure 1: The traditional frontal pedagogical relationship

Often teachers do not possess adequate knowledge and skills for the effective exploitation of ICTs. In many cases, they are less expert than their pupils. Furthermore, there is likely to be confusion in the teacher's mind about his/her new role in relation to the use of these technologies, i.e. teachers find themselves in a situation where they are no longer the principal source and deliverer of information.

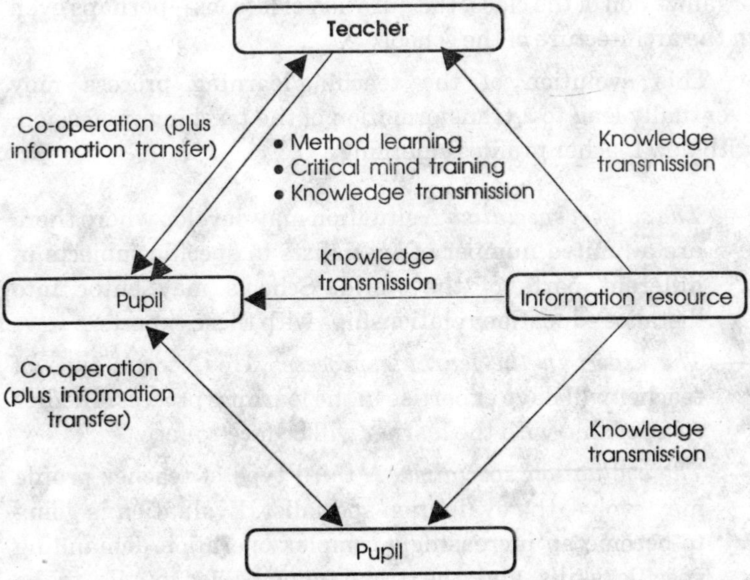

Figure 2: The new pedagogical relationship

If teachers are going to find themselves less capable of making effective use of ICTs in the classroom, they need first to be properly trained in pedagogical skills, so as to have adequate knowledge for developing pupils' learning abilities. The skills needed to use computers as tools for learning are similar to those needed to exploit other more traditional tools: how to transform information into knowledge; how to develop a critical mind; how to make links among different sources and types of information; how to find the right answers to the questions rapidly. The teacher's role remains vital in transmitting and developing these skills.

With these technologies, the traditional way of organizing teaching/learning activities may change, with many forms being used in different combinations: individual or whole class work; small group research; out-of-classroom activities, such as research in libraries. This would lead to changes in the organization of the class, the duration of lessons—perhaps even in the architecture of the school.

This evolution of the teaching/learning process may eventually lead to a transformation of the teaching profession, with new teacher profiles emerging.

— *The subject specialist.* A situation may develop where there are a limited number of specialists in specific subjects in different parts of the world. Schools may enter into distance education relationships with these experts.
— *The expert in the learning process.* This second type of teacher will have expertise in the learning process. His/her relationship with the learner will be face-to-face.
— *The evaluation specialist.* A third type of teacher profile may evolve: the evaluation specialist. Evaluation is going to become an increasingly complex operation demanding specific skills and the trend may be for pupils to be evaluated by persons other than their teachers.

Considering these possible important transformations, the adaptation of the teacher-training system becomes a fundamental issue. Two aims of training may be identified: *Preparing teachers for the introduction of ICTs in the classroom:*

— It is necessary for teachers to become skilled in operating the new technologies and in exploiting them effectively as educational tools.

— Teachers must master the use of information—skills of research, critical analysis, linking diverse types and sources of information, reformulating retrieved data—if they are to teach their pupils to develop these same skills.

— There needs to be more emphasis placed on training in pedagogy, as opposed to the current trend in many education systems where the major focus is on specialized knowledge in specific curricular subjects. Teachers must be adequately equipped with more didactic competencies so as to assume their new role as experts in the learning process.

Using ICTs as tools for the training of teachers. As sources of information and expertise, as well as tools for distance communication, ICTs offer many new possibilities for teacher education. Teachers may learn new forms of communication through the regular use of these technologies. Use of new media, new rules of communication—even a new language—have to be learned.

All new technologies initially provoke reactions ranging from apprehension, to caution, to curiosity, to excitement and expectation. There is considerable scepticism on the part of educators with regard to the potential impact of the new technologies on schooling, since the anticipated impact of earlier communication technologies—such as radio and television—has not been realised.

While communication between learners and mentors is the essence of education, in the traditional learner/ teacher paradigm, teachers largely dictate facts (that they themselves may not necessarily comprehend) to pupils who often just reproduce them on paper without interpreting or understanding them.

For education to be effective, it is essential that there be more opportunities for student participation in the learning process, more teamwork, more self-study and self-evaluation, as well as more peer-evaluation, and less examination-oriented teaching and learning. It is felt that the new technologies can assist in the promotion of more student-centred and interactive learning.

ICTs can be briefly summarized as the result of the convergence of technologies—telecommunications and television have merged with informatics. The computer, which can be described as an engine of the mind, has tremendous capacity to store and process data, to produce and disseminate information. With the emergence of diverse multimedia and networking possibilities, computers have increasing potential as tools for innovative teaching and learning.

The new technologies have enormous potential to revolutionize education as we know it, dramatically transforming schools. For the first time in the history of education students are proving more adept at mastering delivery systems than their teachers. It is obvious that the monopolies enjoyed by schools as formal education providers will diminish, with a lot of educational exposure and experience in future being provided outside these institutions. The scope of the new technologies for transforming existing educational provision is enormous and includes the globalisation of education, the adaptation of curricula, new teaching materials and the networking of schools.

The development of the Internet has already had a very significant impact on the structure of higher education provision. Traditional distance education institutions are fast changing to leading-edge 'virtual universities'. Today there are about 800 'cyber colleges' in the United States, with approximately 1 billion students plugged into 'virtual classrooms' compared to 13 million enrolled in traditional institutions. By the year 2000, this number is expected to triple. It is anticipated that fifty years from now, most of the professions will be taught through the Internet, causing many regional institutions and smaller universities to disappear. Bureaucratic structures are likely to diminish and there will be increasing use of information technologies and resultant networking and partnerships to convey resources for the running of institutions. Technological developments are leading to accelerating convergence between education and industry and between formal and non-formal education:

— Business organisations are becoming learning organisations;
— Distinctions between formal education and distance education are being reduced resulting in integrated classrooms;
— Lifelong education and training will become increasingly the norm;
— Through technology, education is becoming more closely linked to entertainment.

Some of these changes taking place at the level of higher education are likely to filter down to schools. Already in the United States, 'virtual high schools' are being established. Liberal entry and exit between the school system and the world of work may become increasingly possible. Courses of studies in traditional classrooms will no longer meet the public demand for tailored educational services, especially at upper secondary and higher education levels.

There is likely to be a move from rigid one-time, full-time, on-campus education to diverse programmes of lifelong learning. The content of courses will need to assume a more global dimension, with cross-cultural variations becoming more evident. The new educational enterprise will be developed around student outcomes and rigorous evaluation of achievement. The new technologies are also creating a demand for a range of basic competencies, including: improved numeracy skills, communication skills, technical skills and skills in creativity and design, the ability to work with and relate to others, to manage tasks and solve problems, and to foster one's self-development through lifelong learning. In the area of vocational education, there is scope for many new courses including Web design and Web publishing, repair and maintenance of personal computers, office records management and retrieval systems.

These changes are likely to lead to the development of outcomes-based education where each learning outcome will be defined, assessment criteria for each outcome will be clearly stated and guidelines for generating evidence of learning achievements will be laid down. Teaching methods and strategies, as well as accreditation and certification, will have to change significantly to meet these new demands. The professor/teacher will no longer dominate the teaching/learning process: Students will assume greater autonomy and responsibility for their learning. The teacher will become more of a coach, animator and co-explorer with his/her pupils. The process of learning will be emphasized more than specific detailed subject content, while learning will become more flexible and interactive. In some situations, the technologies make education more affordable.

With the use of a variety of new technologies in instruction, it is imperative to assess the extent to which true learning occurs. Sophisticated assessment methods need to be developed to measure and certify learning competencies. Incorporating the technologies successfully into schools requires careful advance planning and preparation. Significant financial and human resources are required, with training an essential component of the process.

REFERENCES

Chaurasia Gulab, *Teacher Education and Professional Organisations,* Authorspress, New Delhi, 2000.

Planning Commission, *Working Group on Early Childhood Education,* New Delhi, 1992.

Report of the Committee set up by the Ministry of Human Resources Development, Govt. of India, on *Minimum Levels of Learning at Primary Stage,* NCERT, New Delhi, 1991.

NCERT, *Concept of Evaluation in Education*, New Delhi, 1963.

Jangira, N.K., Singh, Ajit and Yadav, S.K., *Training Needs and Motivation of Primary Teachers,* New Delhi, NCERT, 1994.

9

Educational Change and Globalisation

After the Second World War, the Czech Republic entered a long period of communist rule (1948-89). The education system adopted Marxism-Leninism as an imported ideology. A rigid, centralised education system was introduced with a monolithic, federally controlled curriculum, leaving little room for individual pedagogical initiatives. Textbooks were provided by the state, and educational needs were guided by a centralised human power planning strategy. Conformity was promoted, and access to higher education was based on Communist Party membership. In 1968, Communist Party Secretary Alexander Dubcek sought to implement "socialism with a human face," reforming the country's economy and easing political oppression during the "Prague Spring." Unhappy with the new developments, Soviet authorities invaded Czechoslovakia and suppressed Dubcek's counter-revolution. What followed was an even more repressive system under the leadership of Gustav Husak, one that lasted for 21 years. After the fall of communism in Hungary and Poland and the fall of the Berlin Wall, the "Velvet Revolution" began to erupt in Czechoslovakia in fall 1989. Despite crackdowns, Czechs increasingly demonstrated and staged massive strikes in Prague and other major cities. By November of that year, the communist government had resigned and Vaclav Havel, the long-imprisoned playwright, became the Czech Republic's new president. The events immediately following the fall of communism prompted a series of changes in the political, economic, and education systems of the nation.

The constitution of Czechoslovakia was modified to eliminate the influence of the party and remove the ideology of Marxism-Leninism from its position of power in all sectors of society. A pluralistic parliamentary system was reinstated; a centrally planned, rigidly controlled economy as replaced with a free-market economy within a democratic framework; and privatisation of former state-run enterprises was permitted, as well as foreign capital investment and free market price competition. These events set in motion a major contradiction of values within the structure of the country's political and economic systems. The new principles as expressed in the legislation prompted the initiation of major structural changes in education as well.

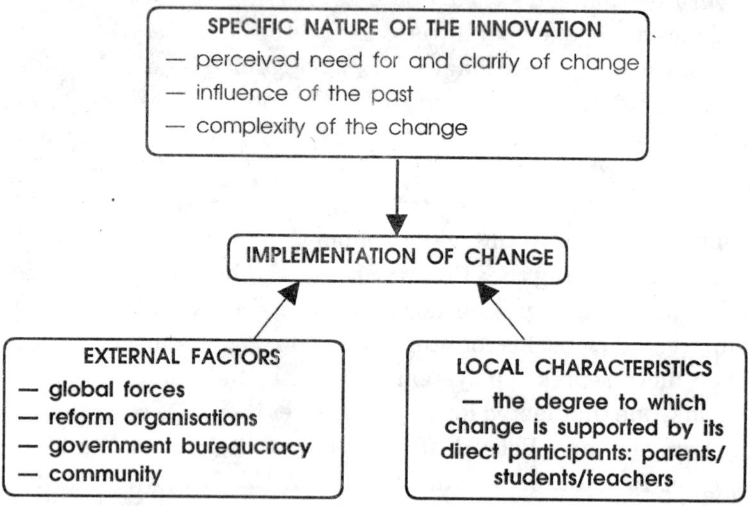

Figure 1: Factors affecting the implementation of change

According to Fullan a knowledge had three broad stages in the process of educational change: initiation, implementation, and institutionalisation. The first stage, initiation, consists of the process that leads up to and includes a decision to adopt or proceed with a change. The implementation stage, which is two-three years in length, involves the first experience of attempting to put an idea or reform into practice. Institutionalisation refers to whether the change becomes an ongoing part of the system or disappears by way of a decision to discard it or through attrition.

The initiation of change: Fullan says that there is a broad range of variables involved in determining whether a change programme gets initiated. He concentrates on the factors associated with planned or action-oriented change and identifies the following eight factors, taken from the literature, which affect initiation:

a) external change agents,
b) new policy/funds (federal/state/local) that support reform,
c) advocacy from a central administration that enables or inhibits change,
d) problem-solving and bureaucratic orientations characteristic of the government,
e) community pressure or apathy,
f) existence and quality of innovations,
g) access to information that facilitates change, and
h) teacher advocacy. Fullan suggests that change is initiated from a variety and combination of sources, which to us implies that there is no obvious order to these factors.

The implementation of change consists of "putting into practice an idea, program, or set of activities and structures new to the people attempting or expecting to change. The change may be externally imposed, or voluntarily sought; explicitly defined in detail in advance or developed and adapted incrementally through use; designed to be used uniformly or planned so that users can make modifications according to the needs of the situation." Fullan organises the factors that affect implementation into three main categories:

a) the specific nature of the innovation or change project;
b) external factors, which press for and facilitate change; and;
c) local characteristics, which affect the degree to which the innovation is supported by its direct participants or stakeholders.

In 1997, the authors conducted lengthy inter-views in Prague with over 30 key individuals, including members of the Ministry of Education, teacher educators, university researchers, members of advocacy and school reform organisations, teachers, school administrators, parents, and students. The authors also had an opportunity to informally observe selected classrooms at both the primary and secondary levels, in both state and private institutions for cognitively challenged children and youth. Interviewees were selected because of the central role they played in the transformation of the education system. The variety of participants interviewed was deliberate in accordance with Fullan's concept of "shared meaning of change." As a supplement to the interviews, important primary documents related to the change process of educational transformation there also provided by a number of interviewees. These documents described elected innovative programs, provided statistical data on various aspects of the education system, and described legislative changes that have been introduced an the Czech Republic since 1989.

In addition, the interpretations of events reflect the authors' own perspectives and, by necessity, are informed lay both the participants and the specific period in which the interviews took place. Nevertheless, a wealth of primary information was collected in the short time available. Data were: collected from key individuals, including members of the reform movement in Prague who played a critical role in the Czech Republic's initial transition period.

IMPLEMENTATION OF EDUCATIONAL CHANGE

Fullan's model of educational change speaks most directly to change and innovation at the level of classrooms, schools, or school districts, although it does not exclude change at the national level. In the case of the Czech Republic, educational change was not simply an innovation or project being introduced at some local level. The unit of analysis for educational transformation in the Czech Republic, at least for the original impetus for change, was the nation. The current analysis therefore, will focus on the implementation of change at this broader level.

In the first few years following the "Velvet Revolution," there was immediate national consensus in the Czech Republic that change, after 40 years of communist rule, was desirable. This period has been characterised as one of euphoria, of great expectations, and of an unwavering commitment to change. In the several months following November 1989, a rapid elimination of the most perceptible characteristics of the rigid communist system took place, as exemplified by the following:

a) the teaching of Marxist doctrine in primary, secondary, and university school curricula was abolished, inadvertently creating a vacuum of suitable instructional materials for teachers to use in history, social science, and civic studies;
b) new legislation permitted the creation of private and religious schools;
c) decentralisation of the school system was initiated giving more responsibility to teachers, principals, and local authorities;
d) institutions of higher education were accorded autonomy and political independence;
e) the teaching of Russian as a foreign language was no longer obligatory, resulting in english becoming the first foreign language of choice among students; and

f) a shift occurred from a needs-based approach for funding schools to a normative system of funding where money now followed the student; since students were free to select the school they attended, schools became very competitive, developing alternative curricula and unique programs to attract more students. While these initial legislative changes took place fairly quickly, the implementation of more systemic structural, curricular, and administrative changes in the Czech education system posed a greater challenge.

For change to be successful, there must be a perceived need for and clarity of change among the general populace (i.e., the goals and means of implementation must be clear). Fullan notes that many innovations are often attempted without a careful examination of a need for change. Recognition of a need is an important readiness factor associated with subsequent implementation of change. The people involved must perceive both that the needs being addressed are significant and that they are making at least some progress toward meeting them.

The administrative and ideological power vacuum in the Czech Republic that resulted in the months following the Velvet Revolution created an urgency for change. Although the public joined in the call fair legislative reform, there was no consensus regarding the direction the change should take or how to navigate through the difficult terrain ahead. One view was to allow the free market to decide the direction of educational change, while another suggested a slower, more cautious approach, allowing time for the development of a vision. Fullan cautions that, although vision is necessary for success, one needs reflective experience before one can form a plausible vision. "Vision emerges from, more than it precedes, action. Even then, it is always provisional .... Visions coming later, does not mean that they are not worked on .... They are pursued more authentically while avoiding premature formalisation."

Jaroslav Kalous, director of the Institute for the Development of Education at Charles University in Prague, addresses the concept of "inertia of acquired attitudes and behaviour patterns." He believes this legacy of the communist regime is an important, yet elusive, barrier to educational reform in the Czech Republic. By attitudes and behaviour patterns, Kalous means work habits that are deeply rooted in the past, such as acting only according to detailed instructions "from above" (i.e., following centrally prescribed curricula), or using outdated teaching methods and content (e.g., an authoritarian, teacher-entered method of instruction and encyclopedic curricular content). Cesar Birzea, director of the Institute of Education Sciences in Bucharest, explains that such a paradoxical coexistence of old and new structures is typical of states in transition.

The events in the Czech Republic immediately following the revolution led to a contradiction between the new principles of democracy, humanism, and liberalism and the old rigid, highly bureaucratic, educational structure. Evidence of this contradiction can be found within the centralisation tendencies of schools, in contrast to the proclaimed general principle of decentralisation. The newly created school offices in.districts are a case in point. Under the former system, education was governed through a number of district and regional national committees under the Ministry of the Interior and the Communist Party. Following the dissolution of these committees after 1989, new school offices were setup in each district to ensure links between the Ministry of Education and the individual municipalities. These offices were directly responsible to the Ministry of Education.

Although, in a number of cases, the school offices were instrumental in introducing innovative programs and methods at the local school level, the great majority remained mere delegates of the central ministry; thus, they recreated the very administrative structure they were designed to replace.

Fullan indicates that a reciprocal relationship exists between cultural change (norms, habits, skills, and beliefs) and structural change (physical environment, organisational arrangements, roles, finance, governance, curriculum, and training). He clarifies that "this relationship is much more powerful when teachers and administrators begin working in new ways only to discover that school structures are ill fitted to the new orientations and must be altered. This is a more productive sequence than the reverse when rapidly implemented new structures create confusion, ambiguity, and conflict ultimately leading to retrenchment."

The Czech Republic, it is evident that the relationship between cultural and structural change was not static or linear. This was not only reflected in the ministry's attempt to decentralise the education system but was exemplified in the new role of the school inspectorate. In the past, the school inspectorate was an important ideological, political tool of the totalitarian power for controlling schools and, over the years, its staff had steadily increased to a total of approximately 1,200 central, regional, and local inspectors in the Czech Republic. However, after 1989, the entire inspectorate body was dismissed, and experienced teachers were invited to compete for school inspector positions.

The old structure of the inspectorate was out of step with its new mandate and, as a result, it is currently undergoing fundamental changes in its function and goals as well as in its method of carrying out responsibilities. With the greater autonomy now enjoyed by schools, it is likely that the approach of the inspectorate will necessarily shift from being controlling and repressive to being more supportive and consultative.

According to Fullan, complexity refers to the difficulty and extent of change required of the individuals responsible for implementation. "While complexity creates problems for implementation, it may result in greater change because more is attempted. On the other hand, while complex changes promise to accomplish more, they also demand more effort, and failure takes a greater toll." In the Czech Republic, there is no doubt that change was massive, multilevel, and highly complex. It involved the governance and administration of the school system, the curriculum at all levels of education, the evaluation and assessment of programmes, the reallocation of financial resources, and the development of pre-service and in-service teacher training.

According to a recent Organisation for Economic Cooperation and Development (OECD) report, the change initiatives are entering unevenly into pedagogical practice and are encountering some resistance, including teachers who have a fragmented understanding of different elements of the curriculum (goals, content, process, and evaluation); a reliance on the central curricular model and an unwillingness to take risks or assume individual responsibility; concentration on the encyclopedic aspect of teaching without linking it to acquisition of skills, competence, and practice; and a preference for traditional authoritarian teacher-student relations.

The Czech Parliament is responsible for drafting education laws, but there is no nominated body of consultants at the Ministry of Education who can serve as advisors to Parliament. The OECD, in a recent review of the education system in the Czech Republic, proposed the creation of a National Curriculum Council to address this vacuum. The absence of a collaborative framework has been identified as a significant barrier to implementation of educational reform. Without such a framework, ownership and commitment to changes among those directly affected becomes more problematic. Following the break of the Czech Republic from Soviet rule, a culture of consultation is just beginning to emerge within the infrastructure of the current educational system.

According to Fullan, consultation is critical for any successful change, but it must be facilitated from both inside and outside a system. Instead of avoiding differences, one must incorporate them in problem solving, because this approach is more commonly associated with creative breakthroughs, particularly under complex, turbulent conditions. He continues, "Put another way, the two-way street of 'inside-outside' is a far more powerful metaphor than top-down bottom-up thinking . . . . It places internal collaboration (at the school, divisional levels), and external collaboration (at the state or national levels) as a high priority for success .... Effective organisations couple their internal problem-solving capacities with constant access to and consideration of external knowledge."

Educational reform in the Czech Republic was extensive, and while the need for change was nationally recognised, some reluctance and even inertia in the system was evident. A clear vision to guide the change process was absent; a culture of consultation had not yet had time to develop; and the educational heritage of the communist regime, both structurally and culturally, could not be discarded easily. The task of reshaping the education system remained a veritable challenge.

Fullan's discussion of change and reform is primarily from the perspective of classrooms, schools, and districts, rather than society, as a unit of analysis. While this perspective is suitable for an examination of change at the local level, one must broaden this view when analysing educational transformation in a post-Soviet nation. Global economic and political forces that resulted in the fall of communism and the removal of Soviet hegemony in Eastern and Central Europe provided the initial external impetus for change in the Czech Republic and the subsequent opportunity for influence by foreign agencies.

Foreign advisors and outside models of education after the Velvet. Revolution played an important role in the initiation and implementation of reforms in the Czech Republic. For example, after 1989, Western organisations, such as the European Union Program (PHARE): the Soros Foundation; the British Council; the American Information Agency; Man, Education, and New Technologies (MENT); Education for Democracy; and the Peace Corps provided substantial funding for various educational projects. There were also greater opportunities for teacher exchanges abroad, as well as conferences and professional development that held the potential for change or transformation at the classroom level.

Finally, there was increased access to scholarly literature from around the world by academics, policy makers, and educational researchers who, in turn, had the opportunity to work for change through the development of reform proposals. However, of all the external agencies, the OECD was the most instrumental in providing the first strategic approach for comprehensive educational change. Its 1992 "Report on Higher Education in the Czech and Slovak Federal Republic" has had a significant impact on policy development as it relates to Czech higher education. The 1995 visit to the Czech Republic by the OECD review team resulted in the document, "Reviews of National Policies for Education," considered to be a critical report that helped provide concrete directives for changing the national educational system as a whole.

After the revolution, reform groups in the Czech Republic argued for the introduction of autonomous schools, a child-entered curriculum, the humanisation of education, a focus on development of critical skills and problem solving, and diversification of curricular options. The three reform groups whose proposals were most influential were the Independent Interdisciplinary Group for the Reform of Education and School (NEMES), an independent, interdisciplinary group with several hundred members, including teachers, psychologists, sociologists, and economists; Independent and Diverse Educational Alternatives (IDEA), a group of mathematics educators; and Engaged/ Involved Teachers Association (PAU), a group of approximately 300 reform oriented teachers.

In some cases, proposals were shelved and ignored; in other cases, selected ideas were incorporated into concrete reform proposals. The Ministry of Education generally felt that experts from the academic community were often detached from political reality. Educational researchers, on the other hand, believed that policy makers did not have a sufficient understanding of the requirements of a scientifically based analysis. There is probably some truth to both views, but what cannot be disputed is that the role of the reform groups in recent years has perceptibly diminished. The Organisation for Economic window of opportunity for introducing change, initially wide open, has now significantly narrowed, and the influence of reform organisations has correspondingly declined.

Educational issues have occupied a relatively small place in the election platforms of both the Czech coalition and opposition parties, and they are addressed there only in very general terms. Political programs seldom include concrete proposals for reform. This does not mean that Czech political parties resisted reform, but simply that they were not the real initiators of reform.

Role of the Parliament in Educational Change

The role of Parliament is critical in that every major reform has to be approved, although not necessarily initiated, by the Parliament. Between 1990 and 1992, the Ministry of Education approved and financially supported numerous experimental programs in state, private, and church schools. Currently, however, the process of educational reform is slowing down considerably. Fullan refers to this phenomenon as the "implementation dip." The "fall" is both psychological (where the excitement about the innovation drops) and technical (where participants in the change process realise they need time to develop the requisite skills). Fullan explains that a "certain sense of failure accompanying success" is endemic to change.

A number of individuals interviewed also pointed to the absence of long-term planning in the new educational policy measures. In 1995, an amendment to the Education Act was introduced that required that all students complete nine years of education in basic school (years one-nine) before they were eligible to apply for entrance to secondary school (years 10-12). Formerly, students could apply after eight years of basic school and then move to an upper secondary school in their ninth year.

The unintended consequence of this new legislation was a dramatic decrease in student population in the first year of secondary school. This resulted in reduced classes, the need to transfer some secondary teachers to basic schools, and in some cases, even dismissal of teachers due to lack of student enrolment. In order to accommodate the students in grade nine, the curriculum content in the basic school had to be "spread out" by moving some of the lower-level subjects to the higher grades.

In 1989, the ministry summarily dismissed approximately 600 teacher trainers, only to discover that they were left with no mechanism for training current teachers. Schools now receive funds to "purchase" their own teacher-training services from ministry-accredited pedagogical centres and other organisations. This is not an a typical phenomenon with systems in transition; as Fullan explains, "the impatient search to address urgent problems makes the [education] system susceptible to . . . superficial solutions." Between 1992 and 1994, a conflict developed between the Parliament (through its Educational, Science, and Culture Committee), and the Ministry of Education. Noting the absence of a conceptually coherent programme, the Parliament repeatedly asked the minister to present a comprehensive educational policy for the country.

The community growing advocacy for children with special needs. The interviews in this study uncovered numerous accounts of personal experiences from administrators, educators, and parents whose children, for different reasons, had failed to thrive under the rigid structure of the communist system because they did not fit the "norm." These were the individuals who, for example, established private schools for children with special needs; worked in advocacy groups, such as the "Blue Key School" for the rights of multiply challenged youth; or founded parent organisations, such as "Rytmus," to lobby the government for the integration of mentally disabled students in state schools. These parents and educators knew, from personal experience, that the old system was particularly harmful to some children and that changes needed to be made.

Their drive and unswerving determination were powerful forces in making these changes come about. As one interviewee explained, the uniqueness of the change process as it relates to special education in the Czech Republic is that it is almost exclusively a spontaneous, grassroots-initiated phenomenon supported by charismatic individuals committed to making a difference in the lives of this neglected group.

Special education advocates in the Czech Republic are beginning to see some positive developments in the field. For example, educational opportunities were recently extended for students with cognitive challenges from eight years of mandatory schooling to 13 year; teachers have been given greater freedom to develop new, more flexible curricula that better meet the social needs of children with behavioural or emotional problems; increased parental involvement has been encouraged in the diagnosis of, and program planning for, children and youth; more at risk and troubled youth are being reintegrated into mainstream classrooms; and finally, educators are beginning to take a more humanistic, ecological perspective that provides more adaptive programming and talent development for students.

The fall of communism in Eastern and Central Europe, the influence of Western literature and scholars in the Czech Republic, efforts by national reform organisations, and the increasing voice of community members, particularly advocates for the rights of children with special needs. However, although islands of change have been evident, the Czech education system has been characterised by the conspicuous absence of a conceptually coherent reform policy. In 1993, new education legislation establishing school-based management sought to encourage parental involvement in education through participation on the newly created school boards. However, many of these boards were characterised by apathy arising from concerns on the part of parents that these boards, through proposed changes for a more liberal education, would negatively affect their child's ability to pass entrance exams to the next school level.

The role of students: The student involvement in the educational reform process is even less clear. The lack of empirical evidence addressing the role of students in die Czech Republic in educational change makes it difficult to assess whether they embrace or reject the basic principles engendered in the experimental programs introduced by the ministry. Furthermore, it is unclear whether student as support the innovations that have been adopted by their particular schools. Nevertheless, it is assumed that students accept the current changes more readily than do teachers, because the heritage of old habits influences the youth much less than it does the older generation.

Fullan notes that, it is the actions of the teachers, the frontline agents of change, that are critical to successful implementation of change. In the Czech Republic, individual teachers have often been the main initiators of educational change. The introduction of new course content or innovative teaching methods promoting a more liberalised, child entered philosophy of education has been successful to a great extent because of these creative-minded teachers.

The role of teachers: The majority of teachers in the Czech school system, however, remain cautious participants in the change process. While the position of teacher unions has not been entirely negative toward educational reform, these unions were against massive liberalisation of schools. Although it is conceivable that, in some instances, teachers were simply resisting "bad" change, it may be argued that, in other instances, teachers preferred the centralised prescriptive curriculum, because it not only provided homogeneity and comparability across schools but also protected them from the risks inherent in making choices and expressing views.

Educational legislation introduced since 1989 has ended the former mandatory curricula and textbook requirements of state schools and provided teachers with more choices. However, it is difficult to assess the extent to which curricular autonomy at the school level has, in turn, influenced the quality for teaching in Czech schools. Kalous estimates that only 10 percent of the schools have been able to produce significant curricular innovations and speculates that, in the majority of schools, the methods of, teaching have not significantly changed. Whether because of time constraints, lack of external resources, or little outside guidance, much of the teaching has remained teacher directed and fact based; pupils continue to be assigned a passive role; and learning outcomes are expected to mirror what has been taught in the classroom. As one OECD observer expressed during a visit to a number of schools in the Czech Republic in fall 1995, The school curricula may have changed, but the basic philosophy has remained the same.

Fullan indicates that "individual teachers and single schools can bring about change without the support of central administrators, but district-wide [and by implication, nationwide] change will not happen." In the Czech Republic, although some change has been observed within schools through lateral diffusion, active support by parents and students and innovative attempts by teachers, on the whole, tend to be rather isolated and uncoordinated. Since schools often compete for funds and students, there is little information sharing among innovative programs. Unfortunately, pockets of change and innovative approaches are not enough to profoundly transform Czech education.

REFERENCES

Paul Beresford-Hill, "Markets and Education in Eastern Europe and the Baltic Republics," *in Education and Privatisation in Eastern Europe and the Baltic Republics,* Oxford Studies in Comparative Education (Wallingford: Triangle, 1998).

Pitha, P. (1996) Building up a new citizen in a post-totalitarian society: an educational approach in the Czech Republic. In Prospects, vol *26, no. 4, 1996,* p. 749-755.

Jan Prucha and Eliska Walterova, *Education in a Changing Society*: Czechoslovakia (Prague: Charles University, 1992).

Kalous; OECD, *Reviews of National Policies for Education.*

10

The Principle of Learning to Live Together

During the last two or three generations, great changes have taken place in the living conditions of the young. In many countries, both parents spend more time away from the home at their place of work, while their children's links to the world of work and the learning that may be acquired there have waned. The impact of the mass media has grown continuously over the last decade, and schools have become increasingly multicultural. Social change is no longer an episodic set of events interspersed by periods of stability. Advanced societies are now open to a continuous process of change, difficult to predict scientifically and control socially. These societies are dynamic rather than static, and complex rather than simple entities. Advanced societies are 'risk societies'.

Social change has ambiguous consequences for the individual. It opens up new possibilities for human fulfilment, but multiplies the risks and hazards that confront the individual in achieving this fulfilment. In these circumstances, responsibility for shaping the conditions of existence in society should be devolved down to the grassroots—to the people themselves. Education can only meet the challenge of social change if it gives all pupils access to appropriate cultural resources in a form that enables them to take responsibility for actively shaping the economic and social conditions of their existence.

The organisation of the curriculum in terms of academic subjects for the purpose of systematic instruction is ill-suited to the aim of a general education. More consistent with such an aim is a curriculum that organises cultural resources in usable forms for the purpose of enabling pupils to deepen and extend their understanding of the problems and dilemmas of everyday life in society, and to make informed and intelligent judgements about how they might be resolved. Such a curriculum will be responsive to the pupils' own thinking and their emerging understandings and insights into human situations. Educational change implies a focus on both curriculum and pedagogy, and on the development of teachers as experimental innovators.

Learning has to be connected with the living experiences of students in a rapidly changing society. Different conceptions of education and of the curriculum presuppose different conceptions of society and the principles governing access to its 'benefits'. Recent trends in curriculum policy-making reflect the dilemmas with which all 'advanced' Western states are wrestling. States feel that they need to steer the curriculum in ways that are consistent with their economic goals, but find that the context of policy implementation is too complex to handle from the centre.

The dilemma is illustrated by, on the one hand, attempts at the State level to establish national educational standards through the concept of a core curriculum which will command a public consensus, and on the other, by pressure on schools to respond to the complex changes taking place in their locality. General education can be defined as 'that part of the student's whole education which looks first of all to his life as a responsible human being and citizen'.

The notion of citizenship should be central to defining the character of general education. Without it, general education tends to be defined as a common core of knowledge, skills, and values—a definition that fails to draw attention to basic curricular concerns, such as what knowledge is most worthwhile and what aims and objectives are best suited for schools in democratic societies. General education is more than a function of the curriculum; it is also an orientation to learning and to curriculum design. Generally speaking, all education justified under general education should emphasize a socio-civic content that promotes problem-centred inquiry and group co-operation. General education should also be marked by interdisciplinary subject-matter schemes.

The learner in this general education scenario is defined as an autonomously thinking, socially responsible citizen who is able to make decisions. In a broad sense, it is a perspective on learning that emphasizes citizenship priorities. Thus, the consequence of general education is a comprehensive concept of schooling. Conceptions of knowledge underlie curriculum development and can be defined in either of two ways: 'Curriculum as facts' and 'curriculum as practice'. 'Curriculum as facts' tends to have a life of its own and obscures the social contexts in which it is embedded. It often results in the curriculum being neither understandable nor changeable. 'Curriculum as practice' does not begin with the structure of knowledge, but with how knowledge is produced by people acting collectively.

According to Young, this connective model of curriculum integration does not start with subjects but with the broader notion of curriculum purposes and how subjects can achieve those purposes. It does not start from the requirements of the national curriculum, but with individual schools defining their curriculum purposes and asking how they can be made to correspond to the requirements of the national curriculum.

For schools to move towards a connective model, all staff need to endorse the curriculum criteria and agree to articulate how their subjects or areas of responsibility would be involved—both in supporting shared approaches to teaching and learning and in delivering the agreed outcomes. The model is 'connective' in the sense that subject specialists would be required to connect their subject teaching to:

a) the purposes of the overall school curriculum; and
b) the way other subjects are contributing to the overall school curriculum.

According to Young, the role of subjects would need to be made explicit in at least three ways; first, by identifying the specialist skills and knowledge they can offer; second, by showing how any of the specific skills and knowledge of particular subjects can contribute to the broader curriculum goals, such as personal and social education through collaboration with other subject specialists; and third, by identifying the contribution of subject specialists in enabling schools to develop their external links with employers, the community and other education providers.

Changes in society and the structural changes in education have made it necessary to re-examine the guidelines governing the purpose and content of education. An agreed minimum values framework has been developed in a number of countries, in the search for the common good. Thus, the process of promoting a consensus of values represents a negotiated view of the common good in a given society at a certain period of educational reform.

Globalisation in education should mean that there is one ultimate goal to be supported by general education in all countries—how to make citizens able to understand both the local and global societies well enough to learn to live together and act as responsible citizens in local and global terms.

When large-scale reforms were being introduced in primary, secondary and higher education in Norway, it seemed natural and fitting to provide a common formulation of the common core of the curriculum, with a view to emphasising how the stages of education are linked together, not forgetting adult education. Interdisciplinarity has to be considered not only across the curriculum at a certain stage or level of schooling, but in a vertical structure as well.

Consequently, curricular reforms are to be seen as a macro-educational planning process. How the reform concept is interpreted is dependent on the social, political, economic, cultural and educational conditions of a country. It is a policy issue to define the context of change, and to view and be willing to develop a holistic reform strategy, where elements of change are linked and provide for interventions enabling curriculum implementation to be realised.

Different levels of the education system in Norway is to be found in the following Acts of Parliament: the Primary and Lower Secondary Education Act; the Upper Secondary Education Act and the Vocational Training Act; the Adult Education Act and Folk High Schools Act. The main themes in the relevant sections of these acts fell into the following six groups:

— moral outlook;
— creative abilities;
— work;
— general education;
— co-operation;
— natural environment.

The introduction to the 'Core Curriculum for Primary, Secondary and Adult Education' in Norway states that the aim of education is to furnish children, young people and adults with the tools that they need to face the tasks of life and surmount its challenges. Education shall provide learners with the capacity to take charge of themselves and their lives, as well as equipping them with the will and determination to stand by others. Education must spur students to diligence and to close collaboration in the pursuit of common goals. It must promote democracy, national identity and international awareness.

The aim of education is to expand the individual's capacity to perceive and to participate, to experience, to empathise and to excel. It was recognised that if education is to achieve these aims, a number of concepts of the human being, illustrating our complex and diverse roles and identities, need to be defined for curriculum development. These include:

— The spiritual human being;
— The creative human being;
— The working human being;
— The liberally-educated human being;
— The social human being;
— The integrated human being.

Education should ultimately form integrated human beings possessing seemingly conflicting capabilities, attitudes, values and skills which permit him/her to lead a full and meaningful life, actively contributing to the common good, yet maintaining his/her own identity and dignity. From this perspective Norwegian education aims to:

— convey the culture's moral values, with its concern for others, while fostering the ability to plot one's own life course;

— provide familiarity with Norway's Christian and humanist heritage, while teaching knowledge of and respect for other religions and faiths;

— teach individuals to overcome self-centredness and belief in the right of the strongest, while inspiring strength to stand alone, to stand up for oneself, dissent and not to acquiesce or submit to the opinions of others unwillingly;

— develop an independent and autonomous personality and, at the same time, to be able to function and work as part of a team.

CORE VALUES IN PRIMARY AND LOWER SECONDARY CURRICULUM

In 1990, new curricula have been approved for Norwegian primary and upper secondary education. There are two main differences between the old and new curricula for compulsory education.

The former curriculum allowed local authorities, schools and individual classes a relatively large amount of freedom to decide and allocate the syllabus content at each level. To a great degree, the choices made corresponded to the content of the particular textbooks chosen. Therefore, there were considerable differences in the syllabuses taught from school to school, and district to district. The new national curriculum is based upon a national syllabus. Teaching objectives are set out for each stage, and instructions about what is going to be taught are formulated.

The old curriculum recommended pupil-oriented, challenging, working methods. However, more often than not, teaching and learning followed traditional methods. The new curriculum demands that schools, teachers and pupils implement pupil-oriented, challenging, working methods. This is evident in the curricula's general directives, the language used to describe objectives and main features, and the emphasis upon theme-based study and project work.

The compulsory school is a nationwide ten-year school characterised by community and adapted education, which means an all-inclusive school in a co-ordinated school system based on the same curriculum. Adapted education means that it is locally and individually adapted, and takes into account gender equality and linguistic minorities. The subject curricula are structured according to principles on centrally selected material, local material and adaptation, progression and more subject-specific teaching within a holistic and unified perspective. In the subject curricula, the selection of contents aims at promoting:

— fundamental values, cultural heritage and identity;
— creative abilities and creativity;
— all-round practical skills;
— basic knowledge and broad understanding;
— the ability to co-operate and independence;
— knowledge and awareness of nature, the environment and technology.

It is specified that fields of knowledge across subject boundaries are to be topics related to contemporary society and the individual and society. Teaching methods must include creative activities and modes of expression, play, practical work, independent work and in-depth study, and project work at all stages. The structure of the subject syllabi is as follows:

a) introduction;
b) subject-related aims;
c) subject-related objectives for each stage (primary, intermediate and lower secondary);
d) subject-related areas of study for each grade.

There are no individual objectives or targets related to the areas of study described. The objectives are an expression of the competence of the pupils to be achieved at each stage of schooling.

This provides important possibilities to schools and teachers to teach according to interdisciplinary themes and topics, in particular within the framework of project work. This focus on an interdisciplinary approach is expressed as follows in the curriculum document:

> Although the curriculum is arranged by subjects, it has been designed so those subjects support each other. Aims, objectives and areas of study must be viewed in relation to each other with a view to unity and connections, both within and between subjects. At the primary level, much

of the teaching is organised around themes. Structural and thematic connections between subjects and subject areas should be exploited throughout schooling. This helps pupils to develop overall understandings and to make the most of knowledge and skills across subject boundaries.

Certain fields of knowledge to be taught across subject boundaries have been identified, such as topical issues related to:

— *Contemporary society*—nature and environment, international understanding, human rights and peaceful coexistence, technology, information and communication technology, knowledge of the media, working life and vocational guidance, consumer knowledge, road safety.
— *The individual and society*—the family, sex education, homosexuality, preventive health work, drug abuse, crime prevention, bullying and violence.

The thematic structure of contents shall be based on the experience, interests and understanding of pupils, on connections with the local environment and on topicality. The methods to be used are creative activities and modes of expression in all subjects, practical and independent work, project work and in-depth study. Local work on subject curricula should mainly be decided by individual schools or co-operating schools. It shall establish the foundations for teachers' planning their lessons at all levels. Clear connections between the centrally and locally defined educational content of the teaching must be established, and the aims of the general part of the national curriculum should be borne in mind.

Co-operation between pupils, teachers and the school administration is essential to the development of the school in terms of creating a learning environment and a place for work. Such co-operation can strengthen the context and possibilities for interdisciplinary perspectives and approaches, helping pupils to see the interconnectedness of learning, and the links between school and the wider community. For the pupils to be included in a social, academic and cultural community, the staff of the school must co-operate, providing a model for the pupils. Co-operation will enable pupils to learn from each other, developing social skills and gaining insight into democratic methods.

It is stressed that the school should develop general social and civic awareness and active involvement in the life of the community. By encouraging pupils to approach new tasks and challenges actively, constructively and deliberately, the school lays the foundations for further learning and helps pupils to master their future work, and their participation in family and social life.

Important emphasis is given to practical and project work. Practical work is supposed to form an integral part of all classroom activities and should be designed so as to show pupils the connections between practice and theory and between action and knowledge. Teachers must provide adequate opportunities for independent work and in-depth study of subjects and subject areas, and in theme and project work. Emphasis should be on teaching research and analytical skills and on developing study methods and working habits which equip pupils for independent work and in-depth study, as well as group work. Teachers are expected to work closely with pupils in realising projects. It is stated that project work lends itself to both a single subject and an interdisciplinary approach, and can be linked to specific local themes. Teachers are expected to co-operate with each other to ensure that project work has an interdisciplinary character.

In short challenges for curriculum development in our time are to find ways of integrating general education and subject syllabuses—to organise knowledge for teaching and learning into meaningful units. The need for interdisciplinarity is obvious if knowledge is to be made really meaningful in a holistic way for the individual pupil.

The Norwegian model of the curriculum for primary, lower secondary and upper secondary education might be identified as a connective curriculum model. The outcome of the curriculum reform is presently being evaluated. Research-based evaluation will give some feedback on the success of operationalising the curricula for a better quality of learning.

VICTORIA'S SCHOOLS OF THE FUTURE

In 1996/97, there were 1,700 government schools providing education for 5- to 18-year-olds. The majority of these were primary schools. Another 673 schools were in the non-government sector. Total enrolments were 777,368 students, 517,882 of whom were in government schools. Twenty-five per cent of all Victoria's government schools cater to students from non-English speaking backgrounds, with a small proportion of students from an Aboriginal background.

The formal education system consists of primary schools from preparatory (P) grade to grade six (ages 5 to 12) and secondary schools from grades seven to twelve (ages 12 to 18). Most students (approximately three-quarters) complete thirteen years of schooling and attain the Victorian Certificate of Education (VCE). The total number of government schoolteachers in 1996/97 reached 18,159 in primary and 16,902 in secondary schools.

School education is supervised by the 'Office of Schools', which is divided into nine regions for administrative purposes. The Office of Schools is located within the Department of Education 1 and manages the government school system.

Several administrative units, including the Office of School Review, in charge of accountability framework, and the Board of Studies, in charge of the curriculum framework, support it. The Office of Schools reports to the Secretary of Education (the public service head) who reports to the Minister of Education. The latter has ultimate responsibility for the school education portfolio.

From the mid-1970s, Victoria became one of the leading states in the move towards a fully decentralised system of education. Between 1980 and 1992, a number of initiatives were taken by successive governments to devolve authority and responsibility progressively to schools. These moves culminated in a policy paper entitled 'Education: giving students a chance', published in late 1992 by the Liberal Government. It outlined that quality education can best be achieved by transferring educational decision-making and resource management to the school level.

A 'Schools of the Future' (SOF) Task Force was formed to develop a detailed report outlining the government's objectives and how quality education would be delivered. The task force released the SOF Preliminary Paper in 1993, which revealed that the key to schools' effectiveness would be a 'school charter'. The 'Schools of the Future' Programme and other legislation has increased the powers and responsibilities of school councils and principals dramatically. Victoria's principals have been placed on limited tenure contracts and local selection of staff was introduced.

In March 1993, the government asked for applications to place 100 of the state's schools into a pilot programme. The programme aimed at providing 'virtually full authority over the budget and personnel function to the school site'. Within a six-week period, over 700 schools applied, and in July 1993, more than 300 schools entered the first phase of the SOF programme.

By early 1994 another 500 schools had entered the programme and an equal number in July 1994. By mid-1995, all Victoria's schools were in the SOF programme. In an attempt to assist schools to understand their self-managing role, the Directorate of School Education published two information kits in 1994. To assist schools to formulate and implement procedures to achieve their respective visions, a Curriculum and Standards Framework was created.

This is a framework within which schools are able to create their own programmes, whilst taking into consideration the identity, aspiration and interests of their teachers. The Board of Studies provided curriculum frameworks for all schools, while the Office of Schools Review developed charter guidelines and an accountability framework. Victoria's model of school-based management (SBM) has two distinguishing dimensions:

a) the involvement of both internal and external constituencies, such as the principal and the representatives of the staff, parents, community and, in the case of secondary schools, students; and
b) the decentralisation and devolution to the school level as against the district or the local education authority level, as is the case with other countries, such as in the United States of America or the United Kingdom.

Victoria's experience of SBM, through the SOF Programme, is thought to represent one of the most comprehensive strategies at school decentralisation attempted anywhere in the world. It is the most sweeping move to decentralisation in the history of Australian public education, with nearly 90 per cent of recurrent expenditure distributed to schools within a global school budget.

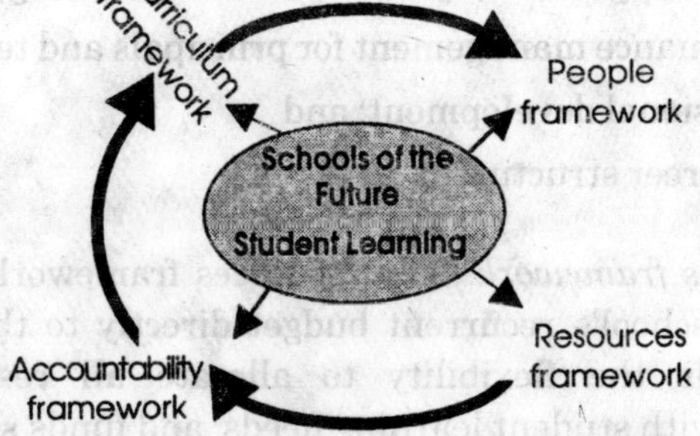

Figure 1: The dimensions of schools of the future

Victoria is the largest system of public education anywhere in the world to have decentralised such a large part of the state budget for school education. The stated objective of the reform was '[to improve] the quality of education for students by moving to schools the responsibility to make decisions, set priorities and control resources'.

Accordingly, SOF is intended to 'make more efficient use of resources for the benefit of students, provide a more professional workplace for teachers, and increase the level of community knowledge of, and satisfaction with, schools'. Basically, the reform has four elements, are described in figure 1.

The curriculum framework: The process of decentralising the curriculum made standards for student attainment explicit. The framework consists of two elements: the curriculum and standards framework (CSF) for years Prep to 10 (P–10) in eight key learning areas (KLA); and the Victorian Certificate of Education (VCE) for years 11 and 12.

The people framework: The career structures of principals and teachers were addressed in the people framework, consisting of five elements:

1) local selection of staff;
2) full staffing flexibility and workforce planning;
3) performance management for principals and teachers;
4) professional development; and
5) new career structures.

The resources framework: The resources framework allocates 90% of the school's recurrent budget directly to the schools; gives schools the flexibility to allocate all resources in accordance with student learning needs; and funds schools in a clear and equitable way through the school global budget.

The accountability framework: It has three elements: the school charter; the annual report; and the triennial review.

'Quality Assurance in Victoria's Schools' is the main mechanism through which the performance of schools is monitored. Each of these frameworks has several elements. Whilst most of the elements are in place, some are still to be fully implemented, such as full staffing flexibility in the people framework.

FEATURES OF SOF'S PROGRAMME

The School Charter is the official document produced by the school and the school council in collaboration with the school community. It is considered the major accountability agreement between a school and its community for the achievements of its students, on the one hand, and the school and the Department of Education (DOE), on the other. Each school develops its own charter which outlines how the school intends to deliver quality education to its students using the resources available in its global budget (the resources allocated to it by the DOE). Through the Charter, school communities have the opportunity to determine the future character, ethos and goals of the school. Figure 2 shows the process by which the School Charter is developed.

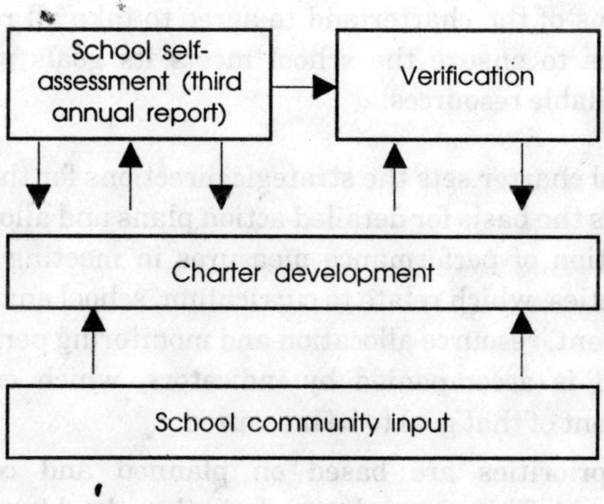

Figure 2: The process of charter development

The document of the charter includes: the curriculum profile, codes of practice, students' code of conduct, accountability, budget summary and an agreement to ensure that schools meet their objectives within the limits of available resources. In particular, the document gives:

— A description of the school's philosophy and future directions.
— The school's goals and priorities that are identified as requiring further development.
— How the school intends to deliver the eight mandated curriculum areas and any other special enrichment activities specific to that school.
— Codes of practice for school council members, principals and staff.
— A code of conduct and the discipline approach used for students of the school.
— Details of the processes used for monitoring and reporting on student performance.
— A prediction of student numbers and an indicative budget for the period of the charter.
— A statement that the school agrees to operate within the terms of the charter and to agree to take all reasonable steps to ensure the school meets its goals within the available resources.

The school charter sets the strategic directions for three years. It provides the basis for detailed action plans and allows for the identification of performance measures in meeting the goals and priorities, which relate to curriculum, school environment, management, resource allocation and monitoring performance. Each goal is accompanied by indicators, which enable the achievement of that goal to be measured.

The priorities are based on planned and continuous improvement. This places demands on the school to analyse its performance and, using the results of this analysis, to generate priorities for improved student performance. Schools report annually to the DOE and their local community on their performance in achieving their goals and priorities. Every three years a review is conducted at the school, in conjunction with the Office of School Review, to assist with the development of a new charter.

The school charter model adopted in Victoria has a number of features that place it in the category of the world's best practices.

— There is explicit detail concerning the areas identified for improvement and the goals that drive the school; it is not a document that focuses only on improvement, but includes details about the normal operation of the school.
— It is student centred with explicit acknowledgement of the central importance of curriculum and improved student learning. Measurement of both goal and priority outcomes are prominent features.
— The school charters are firmly located within a broad accountability framework that includes school review and school annual reports.
— There is detailed specification of the roles of the school community members and a profile of the school.

Most importantly, as an accountability instrument, the charter gives parents, via the school council, greater say in the conduct of the school, and increases the requirement to account for the enterprise to the government.

CURRICULUM AND STANDARD FRAMEWORK

A second important feature of the SOF programme is the Curriculum and Standard Framework (CSF). This is one of the elements of the curriculum framework noted above. The Board of Studies developed the CSF. There are eight key learning areas in the framework: arts; English; languages other than English; mathematics; sciences; technology, studies of society and the environment; and health and physical education. These guide the development of the curriculum from preparatory year through to year 10. The framework contains two components:

a) the curriculum content in several different levels to be attained over eleven years of study, across the various strands of activity within the key learning areas;
b) the learning outcomes for students for each of those levels.

The CSF incorporates both content and process standards. Student progress is assessed against the CSF in a programme of state-wide assessment, the Learning Assessment Project (LAP). The LAP assesses students in years three and five, in English and mathematics annually, and in one other key learning area on a five-year cycle. CSF is a teacher assessment of student performance based upon agreed performance levels contained within the CSF documents.

The LAP reports to the parents took the locus of information control on student progress out of the teachers' hands. It gave parents 'objective' feedback on their children, gave the school feedback on their performance vis-a-vis other schools, and gave the whole system information on overall attainment. In other words, in government schools, the LAP results became another instrument of accountability when added to school charters.

At the same time, the Victorian Certificate of Education (VCE), which is a two-year (years 11 and 12) school completion certificate, was revised and re-accredited. The VCE provides a wide variety of subjects for students to enable them to undertake studies for either university entrance and/or employment. It contains a series of Common Assessment Tasks (CATs) to be completed by all students undertaking a particular subject to ensure common achievement measures across the system.

Some CATs are assessed at the school and others through external examination, but a state-wide moderation system is used to ensure parity for all students' work. All students involved in the VCE are required to sit a General Achievement Test (GAT) to check on the distribution of student grades for school-based CATs within the certificate. Should the school's VCE performance fall within the tolerance range of that school's performance on the GAT, then the results for the VCE assessment will be confirmed. If not, the VCE results will be externally reviewed.

The third feature of the 'Schools of the Future' Programme (SOF), which is part of the accountability framework, is the systematic and local accountability processes. These are presented in Figure 3. According to this system, the Board of Studies provides curriculum leadership and assistance to schools on a state-wide basis, while the Office of School Review supports the attempts of individual schools to raise the quality of their teaching and learning.

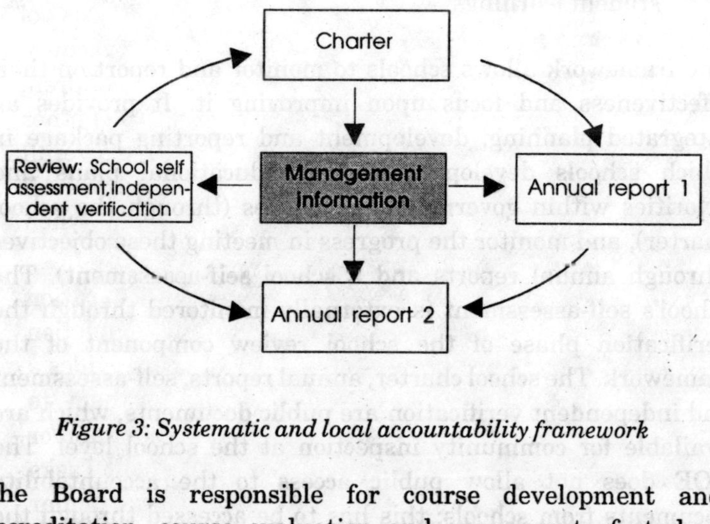

Figure 3: Systematic and local accountability framework

The Board is responsible for course development and accreditation, course evaluation and assessment of student performance (including school completion and certification). The Office of School Review is responsible for the co-ordination and management of the accountability processes, particularly as they relate to the development and review of school charters.

The school councils have the authority to determine the educational policies of the school within the framework of the School Charter. The councils are responsible for maintaining the school premises and grounds, employing non-teaching staff and contracting the services of teachers for particular projects. They are accountable to their local communities, to whom they report through the annual report, and to the Department of Education (DOE), through which independent auditors ensure that the financial Charter dealings of the school conform to the appropriate guidelines.

These elements of the accountability framework serve two main purposes:

i) they satisfy the 'legitimate expectations of government about accountability for the outcomes of schooling',
ii) assist 'schools and teachers to improve standards of student learning'.

The framework allows schools to monitor and report on their effectiveness and focus upon improving it. It provides an integrated planning, development and reporting package in which schools develop their own educational plans and priorities within government guidelines (through the school charter), and monitor the progress in meeting these objectives (through annual reports and a school self-assessment). The school's self-assessment is externally monitored through the verification phase of the school review component of the framework. The school charter, annual reports, self-assessment and independent verification are public documents, which are available for community inspection at the school level. The DOE does not allow public access to the accountability documents from schools; this has to be accessed through the schools directly.

The resource framework represents a significant feature of the SOF. Through this framework, the reform has implemented a new basis for funding government schools in Victoria through a well-developed School Global Budget (SGB). The SGB is primarily a formula-based funding model, which consists of a base element for all schools, together with an equity element based on the characteristics of the students enrolled. Hence, individual schools would have the flexibility to allocate all resources in accordance with local needs. Each school receives an SGB, most of which is made on a per student funding basis to reflect the different resource requirements across a range of variables related to learning needs. It provides funding for all school-based costs, including staff salaries, operating expenses and school maintenance.

Schools received support in the introduction of local budgets through increased funding for administrative support and with a software package called 'Computerised Administrative Systems Environment for Schools' (CASES). This assisted the schools to monitor their financial, personnel and administrative functions. Devolving financial management to the local level aimed to empower principals and schools councils to set and allocate resources for local priorities, to separate the purchase of education from its provision, and to decrease the need for a central bureaucracy.

The SGB has its counterpart in other places where there is a high level of school-based budgeting. In every instance, the task of determining the basis for allocation has proved difficult for a range of reasons, including the absence of information about allocations in the past and debate about the relative weightings to be given to the different factors to reflect learning needs.

In 1994 (and again in 1995), an Education Committee was called by the then Minister of Education to advise him on a mechanism by which the DOE could allocate 90% of its state's budget to schools. Most of the committee's recommendations in 1994 and 1995 were implemented. These included a per capita core funding supplemented by needs-based allocations for students at educational risk, students with disabilities and impairments, rurality and isolation, students from non-English speaking backgrounds, and priority programmes. The principles underlining these recommendations were detailed as follows:

Pre-eminence of educational considerations: This principle implies that determining what factors ought to be included in the construction of the School Global Budget and what ought to be their relative weighting are pre-eminently educational considerations.

Fairness :This principle implies that schools with the same mix of learning needs should receive the same total of resources in the School Global Budget. In accordance with this principle, SGB should redress the unfair historical allocation of resources, which involved some schools receiving more resources and others receiving fewer resources, when they were otherwise comparable.

Transparency: This principle implies that educational validity and the fairness of the SGB will be apparent only to the extent that the basis for allocations in the SGB is transparent—that is, it is clear and readily understandable by all those concerned. The basis for the allocation of resources to each and every school should be made public.

Subsidiarity. Subsidiarity is the principle that a decision should only be made centrally if it cannot be made locally. It describes the principle of maximising funds available for school-based decision-making. An implication for the construction of the SGB is that the starting point is to consider included all items of expenditure related to the operation of school. A case must then be made to exclude an item from the SGB. Exclusion of items from the SGB may take place if—and only if:

a) schools do not have control over the expenditure for that item;

b) there is excessive variation in expenditure for the item at the school level from one year to the next;
c) there is unpredictability in expenditure for the item at the school level;
d) expenditure is of a once-off nature; or
e) the item is one for which the school acts simply as a payment conduit.

Accountability: Accountability is a necessary counterpart of the educational focus in the SGB, given that the latter is concerned with matching resources to learning needs. A school which receives resources because it has students with a certain mix of learning needs has the responsibility of providing programmes to meet those needs, and should be accountable for the use of those resources, including outcomes in relation to learning needs.

Strategic implementation: When new funding arrangements are indicated, they should be implemented progressively over several years to eliminate dramatic changes in the funding levels of schools from one year to another.

INFORMATION SYSTEMS AND TECHNOLOGY

Another important dimension of the SOF is its extensive use of technology and computerised information systems. At the administrative level, and as noted above, CASES was introduced to assist schools to monitor their financial, personnel and administrative functions. This allowed the schools to interface with the central computer system. Schools were issued a standardised computer hardware and software system. CASES stores and processes a range of data including student records (often from teacher input), and financial, physical and human resource data. To enhance the value of information recorded and maintained in CASES, another type of software was designed.

This is the CASES Management Information System (CMIS), which is an 'add-on' software package to make better sense of CASES for management purposes. It provides a range of summary reports, often presented graphically, which have been developed in consultation with schools and central personnel. Both CASES and CMIS programmes have been developed in-house by the DOE.

To enhance the system by extending it to include student records, a third software application was introduced. This is a commercial product adapted to Victoria's requirements. The product known as Kidmap provides student assessment and recording, analysis and profiling of student progress/needs, preparation of reports for parents, and access to teaching resources. It allows schools and school systems to access student data, and to analyse and interpret this in a variety of ways.

At the central office and regions, the DOE introduced an Education Management Information System (EMIS), which has some linkages to the CASES/CMIS environment. The basic system in EMIS is the Corporate Information System (CIS) which contains basic school profiles, a diary of events, a phone directory and a range of documents.

EMIS also includes a decision support system (DSS) which contains the same databases as CIS, but with additional features. These features provide additional information to allow the construction of an individual school's profile. They also allow the provision of a range of statistical information for downloading to a spreadsheet/word-processing package.

The interface between these information management systems is shown diagrammatically in Figure 4. The figure illustrates the main channels of communications and the users of these channels in the SOF management information system. For both the annual report and school review elements, the processes are informed by an extensive array of school and system generated data on student and school achievement. This very much facilitates the collection and analysis of data used in the operation of the accountability framework, and the day-to-day operations of the school.

An Interactive Satellite Television (ISTV) programme was established in 1994. Both government and non-government schools installed satellite dishes to receive centrally produced programmes. Students could interact directly with the programmes' presenters using either a fax or a telephone. Professional development programmes for teachers and general access for other community groups were also made available through this new technology. Other technological initiatives in the curriculum included programmes which gave all schools access to the Internet and opportunities to develop methods of using the new technologies; and brought people from education and the entertainment arena to work together to develop computer software that both educates and entertains.

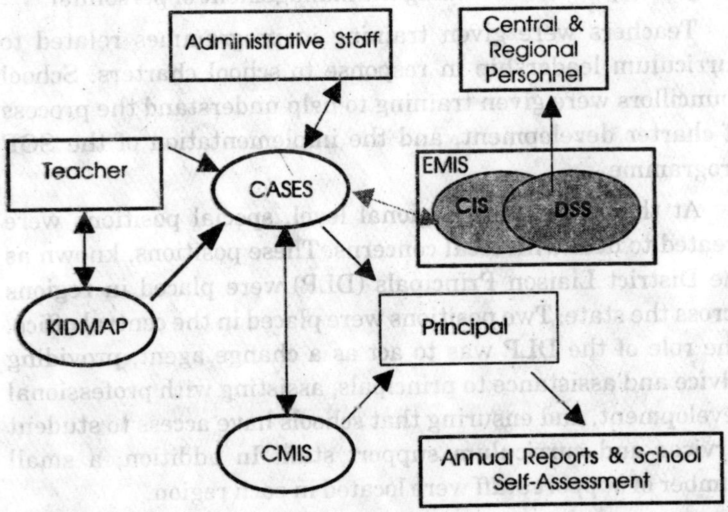

Figure: 4. Department of education management information systems

Staff selection was devolved to the local level and professional development was provided to build capacity in principals for their expanded roles, as well as to give teachers the skill to implement curriculum improvements. However, the school's personnel for the most part remain centrally employed. At the same time, schools were given an increasing capacity to select staff and determine the mix of professional, para-professional and support arrangements.

All of the restructuring noted above required considerable commitment from the central office to provide professional development for all school personnel: principals, teachers and school councillors. At the time of their entry into the SOF programme, schools had an induction period of six months to ensure that they were ready for their new responsibilities. Professional development for principals included issues related to the global budget, leadership and management. Administrative staff were given training to improve their understanding of the new computer system and the global budgeting process, including the management of personnel.

Teachers were given training in programmes related to curriculum leadership in response to school charters. School councillors were given training to help understand the process of charter development, and the implementation of the SOF programme.

At the central and regional level, special positions were created to deal with local concerns. These positions, known as the District Liaison Principals (DLP) were placed in regions across the state. Two positions were placed in the central office. The role of the DLP was to act as a change agent, providing advice and assistance to principals, assisting with professional development, and ensuring that schools have access to student services and curriculum support staff. In addition, a small number of support staff were located in each region.

Support for principals and teachers is an ongoing activity. Areas of support include leadership training, mentoring and coaching, with experienced principals supporting junior ones. These have helped to establish the longer-term future of leadership in schools. The Professional Recognition Programme

(PRP) offered teachers the capacity to opt into a system of enhanced pay and career structure, including annual appraisal. The main aims of the programme are:

— To provide a working environment that encourages and rewards skilled and dedicated teachers;
— To encourage the further development of an ethos that values excellence and high standards of achievement; and
— To provide formal feedback on a teacher's performance so that appropriate career development may occur through professional development and other means.

To achieve these goals, the DOE allocated in 1995, the total of A$240 per teacher in each school for professional development. This meant that appraisal could support improvement and provide the basis for promotions based on merit rather than seniority. Local staff selection, appraisal and professional development gave the school greater control over their human resources and greater flexibility in responding to local needs.

The SOF reform has devolved considerable authority and responsibility to the school level. Important features of its success include:

— The framework presents an integrated programme that works at two levels: for school planning and development and for system accountability. It is this dual utility that has been the key to success. Schools value the framework for providing them with a valuable developmental tool. Inspection programmes, such as those used in the United Kingdom, do not offer the same degree of support to schools as that offered by the accountability framework.
— The framework has been supported by the development of a range of performance measures. Some have been developed especially for the framework (staff and parent opinion surveys), whilst others have been developed as part of other elements of the reform (e.g. CSF).

Importantly, benchmarks of performance have been created which allow schools to assess their performance against those of both the state average and schools, which have a similar student population.

— The development of the performance measures has been supported by the development of software to facilitate the display and analysis of the data.

This process has provided schools with the tools to monitor performance, a quality assurance framework within which to operate, and a quality control process that meets systemic requirements. In essence, the accountability framework includes the benefits of a supervisor model of school supervision, with an explicit and extensive programme of support for school planning and development.

Extensive consultation and trialling occurred in the development of the school charter, the annual report and the triennial review. The Office of School Review also consulted widely with experts throughout the world, and its personnel have been active in gaining experience of best practice.

The independence of the Office of School Review from the schools section has enabled it to develop the accountability framework without the constraints that it might have been subject to had it been part of the bureaucratic structure of the Office of Schools.

At the early stages of SOF inception, the DSE published 'The schools of the future information kit' and 'Schools of the future guidelines for developing a schools charter' to assist all schools in their transition to SBM.

The documents reinforced the trend for principals to be recognised as true leaders of their schools and to be expected to build and lead their teaching teams by clarifying important responsibilities which are determined at the school level.

The unique character of each school and community is reflected in distinctive curricula selected from a broad range of studies established by Victoria's Board of Studies.

So as to achieve the overall aim of providing quality education for every student, enabling each to realise his/her full potential, different approaches to learning and teaching are encouraged to optimise the advantages gained from technological progress.The school charter, developed within the guidelines of the DSE/DOE, encapsulates the school's vision and establishes a framework for the allocation of resources.

The crucial element for the success of the school would seem to be its ability to respond to the needs of the community and to provide a service which sustains an ongoing demand for places within the school, as well as a boost to the employment potential of its graduates.

However, there remain considerable constraints on schools. For example, the leadership role of a principal of a SOF is a demanding one. The tasks carry onerous responsibilities, both 'upwards' to the DOE and the Minister of Education, as well as 'outwards' through the members of the School Council to staff, students, parents and the community.

Moreover, there is evidence of increased teacher workload and time demands, concern over the level of resources, increased reliance on local fund-raising, including the collection of fees, teacher disempowerment and a decrease in school diversity.

There is also frustration at the inability of parts of the reform to be fully implemented, especially the promise of school control over staffing and the implementation of the principal performance management plan.

On the other hand, the new arrangements of decision-making and the increased community involvement give a clear impression that education is a partnership between the staff and the parents. However, much of this seems to have been undermined in favour of more power being given to the principal.

REFERENCES

Education and Development, 1968, National Commission on Education 1966, Government of India, New Delhi.

Government of India, 1966, Report on the Education Commission 1964-66, Education and National Development, GOI, New Delhi.

_______________, 1992, Programme of Action, National Policy on Education, 1986, GOI, Reprinted by UGC, New Delhi.

_______________, 1985, Ministry of Human Resource Development, Challenge of Education—A Policy Perspective, New Delhi.

Pike, Grham, Selby, David, 1998, in the Global Classroom, Books 1 and 2, Toronto, Pippin Publishing.

UNESCO/ICE-EFA, 1999, Assessing Learning Achievement, Paris, United Nations Educational, Scientific and Cultural Organisation.

Wright, S., Morley, D., 1989, Learning Works: Searching for Organisational Futures. York University, Toronto, ABL Group, Faculty of Educational Studies.

Zandstra, H., et al, Caqueza, 1979, Living Rural Development, Ottawa, International Development Research Centre.

11

Formal Structure of Academic Organisation

Over the past two decades, higher education scholars have turned their attention to the study of knowledge legitimation, specifically the role of organisational contexts in the social construction of knowledge. Few recent studies address the formal structure of academic organisations. That studies have addressed this domain tend to focus on the nature of the imperatives for priority setting and selective reinvestment that accompany academic restructuring and retrenchment. In addition, that studies offer several anchoring assumptions that support a line of inquiry for higher education research.

— Post-secondary organisations are a primary societal arena in which knowledge is developed. That is, universities and colleges both reflect and reconstitute classifications of knowledge and in so doing establish categories of expertise and knowledge worth knowing.

— Organisational context plays a role in what comes to count as knowledge. Influential factors range from the shared understanding of mission and institutional legacies to the allocation of material resources (money, space, etc.) across fields of study.

— Academic organisations tend to respond to knowledge change with additive solutions, while the complete elimination of structural units is rare. This is due in part to the proponents of academic fields who actively work to promote their ideas and protect their turf. At the same time, existing departments have a self-sustaining momentum as they achieve both local recognition as an established field and material resource flows for tenured faculty lines.

These three premises suggest that the study of higher education can benefit from further analysis of the interdependence between organisational context and what counts as knowledge. In this chapter, we bring to the foreground the formal organisational structure and examine its significance for knowledge legitimation. Our primary objectives are to provide a rationale for the study of academic structure and to illustrate how our conceptual interests translate into empirical inquiry. We argue that changes in what counts as knowledge are reflected in the bureaucratic and programmatic structures of universities.

THE CONCEPT OF ACADEMIC STRUCTURE

Academic structure, which anchors our theoretical and empirical approach. Next, we review the literature that provides the intellectual ancestry of our work. We then identify and develop two research questions as a basis for exploratory analysis:

1) how does the formal organisation of knowledge change or remain the same over time? and
2) are there differences across knowledge areas?

The concept of academic structure as the main conceptual anchor in this line of research. Two propositions about the functions of academic structure are central to our argument.

— Several structural dimensions of academic organisations shape what counts as knowledge.

— Modifying the academic structure enables universities to reconcile competing imperatives for stability and change.

Some elaboration about each proposition is warranted. The formal organisational structure has been neglected in higher education research, even though it is well known to those who work and live in academic organisations. Many different structural units exist within academic organisations: departments and programmes, faculty lines and budgets, course requirements and sequences. Together they make explicit the division of responsibilities, rules and roles, flows of information, and resources. Although such structural elements contribute to rationality within an organisation, they do not assure it.

Dynamism at several levels is noteworthy. Over time, there may be normative changes across the academic workplace, such as an increased emphasis on the commercialisation of knowledge and other revenue-generating activities. There may also be varying degrees of social harmony and conflict within units; some of these may even prompt structural change. Within a department, for example, there are changes in course offerings, course content and pedagogy. Across departments there are emerging faculty research interests and interdisciplinary collaborations. Such dynamics within the informal structure potentially reconstitute what knowledge becomes recognised and valued.

Acknowledging the co-evolution of knowledge and structure, we highlight the role of structure in shaping the Intellectual terrain and supporting those ideas that become established as recognisable fields and specialisations. We examine two dimensions of the formal organisational structure-the array of academic departments and the array of degree programs offered. These two dimensions are distinct yet interrelated. Both are highly visible components of academic organisations, and they are comparable not only over time but across a diverse range of higher education settings. Moreover, academic departments an degree programs signal continuity or change over time in intellectual jurisdictions (albeit with contested borders), and as such they serve as organising principles to those inside and outside higher education.

Our second proposition is that modifications of academic structure accomplish a critical organisational function for universities and colleges, providing a powerful symbolic mechanism that signals the intention, if not the actual ability, to reconcile competing expectations from the external environment. When it comes to knowledge functions, academic organisations have a well-established social charter to embody both stability and change for society. While they are expected to preserve existing knowledge for transmission to future generations, universities and colleges are also expected to incorporate and advance new knowledge and to engage in priority setting and retrenchment when mandated.

Historically, the ideal structural response to these institutional expectations has been additive. Yet over the past three decades changing economic conditions and enrolment fluctuations have prompted academic leaders to question the long-term feasibility of addition ad infinitum. The realities of constraining organisational factors, such as money and space, have pressured universities to select among existing commitments those most worthy of continued investment. Times of priority setting often entail pruning academic units that are perceived to have proliferated excessively and weeding out those that have been deemed obsolete.

In the contemporary era, such targeting and consolidation of academic units have been justified due to fiscal constraint and rationalised by criteria that may characterise units as of poor quality, less central to mission, or too costly. In fact, mandates for such priority setting have become so widespread in the 1990s that some experts have declared that the principle of additive solutions has been replaced by a new principle: "change by substitution;" that is, if something new is added, something old must be eliminated. In this way, the pressure to adapt runs directly counter to the organisational inertia embedded in established structures, thereby posing an apparently irreconcilable challenge for the organisation.

Two sets of literature inform our conceptual and empirical approachs are:

i) the new sociology of knowledge,

ii) academic change in higher education organisations,

The new sociology of knowledge: The new socialogy of knowldege, which illuminates the relationship between post-secondary organisations and knowledge legitimation. Unlike the traditional sociology of knowledge, which examines the link between the development of ideas and the particular social locations or interests of individuals or groups, the new sociology of knowledge examines how kinds of social organisation make whole orderings of knowledge possible. As a scholarly domain, this conceptualisation asks how institutional structures and practices support and reconstitute categories of knowledge. This line of inquiry addresses the role of institutional settings in shaping the content and form of ideas, not only those structures of knowledge developed by specialists but also the structures of knowledge or consciousness that shape the thinking of laypersons. Sociologists refer to this focus as a "middle" level of analysis, in between analyses of large-scale macro forces such as the economy and individual-level interests. This middle level, what Smelser calls "meso-sociology," warrants examination in its own right for its function as a powerful shaper of cognitive categories and social boundaries with consequences for both micro and macro levels.

Some theorists claim that these functions are most apparent in educational organisations, especially at the post-secondary level, given that colleges and universities define categories of expertise and certify individuals for participation in the labour market. Yet the creation and evolution of knowledge classifications are evident in other societal domains. For example, in his studies of high culture, DiMaggio has argued that artistic classification systems are mediated by the organisational settings in which art is produced and genres are enacted. These processes have organisational as well as cognitive significance.

Extending DiMaggio's insights to academic organisations, the ritualisation of knowledge categories occurs through the creation and maintenance of departments and degree programs. In these settings, the knowledge categories and their labels contribute to what counts as knowledge. They not only provide a location where participants generate local knowledge of departmental procedures and programme completion expectations, but they also designate the knowledge most worth knowing within the field. The latter is achieved by requiring proficiency of students in certain subjects and by hiring faculty with particular research and teaching interests. So, while these institutional settings structure the educational milieu for learning, they also shape the landscape of "what is thinkable."

The formal organisation of academic knowledge in the United States occurs at several educational levels (elementary, secondary, and post-secondary) although these levels are not structurally aligned. For example, social studies in high school has no corresponding category in college. Knowledge categories become more prominent in the uppermost levels of education. At the lower levels of education (K8), the organisation of knowledge is less apparent, as grade levels dominate in structuring educational activity (e.g., fifth graders are educated separately from first graders).

Moreover, some knowledge categories are considered co-curricular activities that tend to occur outside the regular classroom setting (e.g., physical education, art, music). Although academic subject matter and departmentalisation do become visible at the secondary school level, it is in postsecondary settings where academic categories move to the foreground in structuring educational activity, and grade levels move to the background. Academic departments (chemistry, history, economics, for example) and degree programs (degree subjects of the bachelor's, master's and doctorate) are the basic building blocks. Thus, the knowledge categories in higher education are organising principles for students' learning, faculty work, and credentialing.

Knowledge categories also have symbolic value for the organisation with respect to the environment even if there is little or no productive activity in some of those areas. Consistent with institutional theory, the academic structure itself can have important consequences for the organisation's legitimacy. For example, the maintenance of a full range of knowledge categories in the academic structure can enhance the legitimacy of a campus that strives to be seen as a comprehensive university. Similarly, the establishment of new programmes may further the aspirations of those campuses seeking to emulate the academic offerings of higher status campuses.

According to Clark, the conventional approach that dominates higher education research is to focus on people processing functions: students undergo personality development, learn skills, develop human capital, or obtain degrees for status attainment and upward mobility. In contrast, Clark proposes that knowledge-processing functions should be seen as the defining core of academic organisations. He argues that knowledge is "the prime material around which activity is organised .... Knowledge materials, and advanced ones at that, are at the core of any higher education system's purposes and essence. This holds true throughout history and across societies".

These knowledge-based activities have a wide array of intellectual, professional, economic, and social consequences. Following Meyer, Clark suggests: "As educational institutions in general evolve, they develop categories of knowledge and thereby determine that certain types of knowledge exist and are authoritative. They also define categories of persons privileged to possess the bodies of knowledge and to exercise the authority that comes from knowledge. Educational structures, in effect, are a theory of knowledge, in that they help define what currently counts as knowledge". Certain historical periods have been characterised as times of dramatic knowledge expansion, where external political and economic demands for knowledge have penetrated the academy. The decades following the end of World War II are often characterised as a period of knowledge explosion in the United States. In addition to expanded research activities and a concomitant diversification of academic specialties, there was a proliferation of enrolments and career-oriented degree offerings.

At the same time, widespread interdisciplinary efforts, such as cultural studies, feminist studies, and science studies, have had far-reaching impact for what counts as knowledge in several domains and have even sought to unravel, if not dismantle, established borders that heretofore defined academic jurisdictions. By the latter part of the twentieth century, scholars have proclaimed a new knowledge-based economy in which the production and consumption of knowledge have become the primary mechanism for economic development, technological innovation, occupational advancement, political action, and societal change. This implies that the categories and content of the existing academic landscape are increasingly salient to those in the wider society.

Academic change in Higher Education Organisations, which provides the rationale for a line of inquiry that is both longitudinal and multidimensional. This study is research on organisational change, specifically in university and college settings. Two lines of inquiry are foundational to our approach. One encompasses competing organisational theories of inertia and adaptation. The other provides empirical analyses of academic change. Together this literature suggests the need for research on academic change that is longitudinal, multidimensional and considers variation across academic fields. Theorists offer opposing understandings of change dynamics within universities and colleges.

On the one hand, there are those theorists who emphasise organisational inertia. They suggest a tendency for large, complex organisations with contested goals and ambiguous technologies to resist fundamental change in their technical core and an inclination to retain the organisational arrangements established at their founding. These theorists find ready examples in higher education, because colleges and universities show a tendency to retain the essential structural characteristics of their origins.

The structure of academic organisations has been much maligned for its inertia, failing to respond effectively to changes in student demographics, labour market requirements, and technological advancements. Academic organisations have been criticised for bloated bureaucracy, professional stagnation and ineffective management. Not all characterisations of inflexibility in academic structures carry negative connotations, however. Enduring organisational features, such as classical curricula, faculty tenure, and the importance of symbols, rituals, and traditions, may be seen as embodying cherished academic ideals. Thus, while observers may lament the inherent inertia of enduring structures, others may view organisational inertia as an essential source of cultural stability, continuity in professional identities and knowledge classifications.

The adaptation theorists suggest that organisations manipulate their structures and processes in the face of strategic imperatives, such as those generated by shifts in the availability of key resources. In times of changing environmental conditions, adaptation theorists are among those who advocate restructuring and applaud the flexibility of academic organisations. Structural changes, such as re-engineering, networking, and outsourcing, have been offered as adaptive responses to environmental demands. Amidst the vocal calls that higher education must change in order to survive, several scholars have argued that the structural complexity of academic organisations and systems has enabled them to adapt responsively through the addition and subtraction of subjects that reflect shifting intellectual pursuits. Although the opposing assessments of inertia and adaptation offer alternative frameworks, a common denominator between the two is the need for evidence on the extent to which there is continuity and change in the structure of academic organisations.

These theories affirm the centrality of structure and the potential to modify structure to enact the many institutional functions expected of academic organisations. With this in mind, we can examine how higher education organisations structurally respond to the paradoxical imperatives faced by the U.S. higher education system to adapt to the changing needs of society while remaining a stable social institution. In light of these theoretical arguments, there is much to learn from the empirical study of structural change in higher education organisations. Below we review three studies that are significant to our approach in that they supply models for identifying and measuring change in major dimensions of academic structure. More generally, they also have value in their assertion that academic structure should be studied empirically in its local organisational manifestations.

Hefferlin's study of change identifies the curriculum as a primary structure around which legitimate knowledge is formally organised. Hefferlin was interested in the process of knowledge change in the form of expansion, differentiation, and specialisation. He focuses on course offerings and examines those fields that are eliminated from the knowledge structure, either through mergers with other subjects or wholesale removal from the academic program. Among Hefferlin's key findings is that curricular reform is most likely to occur under conditions of organisational instability and vulnerability. Hefferlin's argument presents change in the context of academic reform. This explanation of change in the organisation of knowledge suggest the need for a multidimensional conceptualisation of academic structure. That is, we think changes in the formal structure of departments must be examined separately from changes in academic program offerings, for those elements may likely be subject to different organisational and societal forces.

Metzger analyses the proliferation of academic units due to knowledge growth accompanying the expansion and specialisation of the professoriate, and he emphasises the differentiation and specialisation of academic knowledge as it is formally organised in the disciplinary affiliations of university faculty. His historical approach illustrates the value of studying knowledge change over an extended period of time. He also offers a more refined explanation of how knowledge specialisation occurs. For example, he distinguishes between (i) subject parturition, in which subspecialties are spawned from more inclusive subjects; (ii) programme affiliation, in which new academic pro-grams are created to accommodate training in the "learned" professions (law, medicine, divinity), and (iii) subject dignification, in which previously marginalised subjects or new subjects gain currency in traditional academic settings.

Although Metzger does not consistently distinguish between the basic structural forms of knowledge and seems to imply that the same forces drive changes in degree programs and departments, his distinction among types of specialisation suggests that it is worthwhile to examine the life course of accepted knowledge categories within the academic landscape. These pioneering works is the foundational notion that the formal organisational structures of departments and degree programs are defining features of academic organisations. Although they identify a number of potential links of empirical study, none of these researchers problematises whether the dimensions are linked to one another, whether modifications in structure are critical to the legitimacy of the academic organisation.

TWO DIMENSIONS OF ACADEMIC STRUCTURE

Bureaucratic elements: The delivery and production of knowledge through teaching and research are core educational functions of colleges and universities, then we can identify two related but distinct elements that structure these core functions: (1) bureaucratic (e.g., schools, divisions, and departments), and (2) programmatic (e.g., degree programmes offered). A great majority of organisational inputs and outputs are mediated through these two structural elements. Both elements reflect the differentiation and stratification of knowledge, embody political contests over organisational resources and power, and help form the identity of participants as well as the organisation as a whole.

In post-secondary organisations, the bureaucratic structure takes its shape in academic departments and other formal units that consume resources, manage personnel, and occupy physical space. This conceptualisation is consistent with a Weberian approach, highlighting the circumscribed domains of administrative responsibility, personnel, and procedures that structure organisational authority and work. Bureaucratic units also include other hierarchical levels, such as divisions, schools, and colleges. Departmental units are typically organised around an established field of study and are responsible for the administration of academic degree programmes, the hiring and support of faculty, and the flow of resources—a large proportion of which are fixed in tenured positions.

Thus, the bureaucratic structure is characterised by both vertical and horisontal differentiation. This results in nested levels of bureaucracy the higher levels of which represent schemes for organising related groups of knowledge activity and their administration. Almost all academic activity in a college or university is tied in some way to a formal bureaucratic unit. All regular faculty appointments have departmental ties, and the administration of each student's degree programme flows through the departmental bureaucracy. Thus, the addition or elimination of a formal unit is a significant event. For the most part, however, departments do not merely appear and disappear; rather, the organisation of units evolves over time as departments change names, merge with other departments, or split into multiple units. Such changes are related to the legitimation and de-legitimation of knowledge categories as well as to significant economic and political factors that are both internal and external to the organisation.

Programmatic element: The second element of academic structure is programmatic. As an empirical dimension for study, we focus on the array of degree programme offerings. Like the bureaucratic structure, academic programmes are horisontally differentiated by subject. However, vertical differentiation in this structural dimension takes a different form.

In the most common hierarchy, degrees are vertically differentiated by certification level the associate's degree representing the fewest requirements for certification, followed by the bachelor's, master's and doctoral degrees. Differential status of knowledge can be inferred from degree level, because the adoption of graduate degree programmes in a particular field is often interpreted as a stronger commitment to that field by the organisation. Like departments, the array of degree programmes offered changes over time. Programmes are added and eliminated, albeit with fewer consequences for the allocation of resources or personnel than the addition or elimination of an entire department, division, or school.

Nonetheless, degree programme offerings are important for several reasons. They signify areas of faculty interest and expertise, locate students within the academic organisation, and contribute to the external identity of the organisation. In fact, the highest degree level offered is a primary determinant in the Carnegie Classification of Institutions as well as a substantive factor in the choices of students and parents as they consider alternative educational programmes.

Additionally, students carry their degrees with them into their work and social lives, which serves as an important mechanism for the diffusion and legitimation of knowledge classifications into other societal domains. Thus, changes in both the bureaucratic structure and the programmatic structure: represent important organisational dynamics as well as broader shifts in what counts as knowledge.

These two dimensions of academic structure are closely related. In practical terms, departments administer degrees. Resources and personnel (faculty and administrative staff) are committed tee the establishment and management of departments in order to offer a curriculum and degrees in a given knowledge area. However, the experience of academic administrators and professionals tells us that the internal factors involved in adding new departments are much different than those involved in changing academic program offerings. University-wide committees that are charged with planning priority setting, budgeting, and promotion and tenure decisions tend to affect the establishment (or elimination) of departments more so than degree programs, which tend to re-quire approval (and renewal) from curriculum committees often working through academic senates. Thus, when considering the structural location of changes in the organisation of knowledge, the programmatic structure and the bureaucratic structure must be examined separately.

Many other organisational elements, such as individual course offerings, independent research units, continuing education, and professional development programs are essential to the academic mission of institutions and represent additional structural arrangements through which knowledge change processes occur. Despite the obvious importance of these elements, we think that departments and programs are two primary dimensions that are the most highly visible in structuring educational activity, identities of students and faculty, and the [illegible]l identity of the campus. Together, bureaucratic structure and programmatic structure enable academic organisations to fulfil their multiple functions: as settings for educational practices of teaching and learning, for organisational practices to coordinate and manage academic work, for elaborating careers and professional identities, and, in turn, for supporting and reconstituting knowledge categories.

College course catalogues provide a comprehensive historical record of many aspects of academic organisation. They list all available course and degree offerings as well as detailed information on the organisation of schools, departments, and programmes. These data allowed us to track changes in the formal bureaucratic organisation, including what departments existed each year, and during each five-year interval whether or not departments were added, eliminated, merged, split, or renamed. Catalogues also allowed us to track similar changes in degree programmes offered. The data for both the bureaucratic structure and programmatic structure were coded separately to produce a longitudinal history of academic change. For the bureaucratic structure data, we recorded the exact name of each academic operational unit that appeared in the ten catalogues.

An academic operational unit is defined as any formal administrative unit that administers courses or degrees, has dedicated faculty lines, and occupies a physical office located on campus. For the programmatic data, we recorded the names and degree levels of every programme offered during each academic year studied.

Objective of the analysis was to track change in the bureaucratic and programmatic dimensions of academic structure with respect to the evolution and legitimation of broader knowledge categories. To that end we classified the names of departments and degree programmes using a taxonomy of seven knowledge areas: Humanities, Social sciences, Engineering/Computer science, Life science, Physical science, Health science, Professional and applied fields.

The appearance or disappearance of departmental units occurred as the result of the addition of a new field, a name change, the merger of two or more departments, the dissolution of a department into two or more new departments, or the elimination of a department. A detailed history of each unit was recorded and analysed over the 45-year period, noting changes in name, faculty, office location, and curricular offerings. This qualitative analysis not only helped us gain conceptual clarity on the interdependence between academic structure and knowledge change, but also allowed us to gain a more refined sensibility of the nature and range of academic structural changes.

Degree data from the Integrated Postsecondary Education Data System (IPEDS) were used to track changes in degree production from 1966 to 1997. Unfortunately, data on degree production and faculty were unavailable for the earliest years of our study, and departmental level financial data were unavailable for the entire period under study.

Knowledge differentiation is reflected in the process by which departments and degree programs are split into multiple, new entities representing more specialised fields of study. Between 1982 and 1992 the degree programmes in Physical education were differentiated into five programmes (Athletic training, Movement science, Pedagogy, Adult Adapted/Corrective Therapy, Society Studies and Sports Management). These examples point to a proliferation of units that reflect an increasing specialisation of knowledge and mirror emerging career specialties. Another type of change is knowledge promotion, which also occurs in both the bureaucratic and programmatic structures.

When a bureaucratic subunit labelled a "department" is changed to a "division," "school" or "college," or when a degree programme formerly offered at only the undergraduate level is offered in subsequent years at the graduate level, the knowledge area is promoted. For example, between 1992 and 1997 the Department of Nursing became the School of Nursing.

In degree programme offerings, promotion is the most common type of expansion in the overall academic programme structure.

A third type of knowledge change is knowledge evolution, which is reflected primarily in name changes. This often signals a substantial change in the knowledge associated with a category or a change in professional or occupational legitimacy. The transformation of the Librarianship Department to the Department of Library Sciences between 1982 and 1987, and then to Library Information Sciences by 1992 provides an example of this point. Similarly, between 1977 and 1982, the Home Economics Department was changed to the Department of Nutrition and Food Science.

Fourth, knowledge consolidation is evident primarily in departmental mergers, and is often accompanied by name changes. Between 1977 and 1982, for example, six separate departments in the School of Business were consolidated into three: Accounting, Management, Marketing, Office Administration, Manpower Administration, and Finance, Insurance and Real Estate became Accounting and Finance, Organisation and Management, and Marketing and Quantitative Studies. By 1997 these three units underwent further name changes when the latter department was renamed Marketing, Management Information Systems, and Decision Sciences.

The example of consolidation is Environmental Studies, which merged into a single department with Geography in 1972. Between 1977 and 1982 it split from Geography, merged again, then split again by 1992. Stability of knowledge categories is reflected in the persistence of departments or degree programs that do not evidence any of the above four types of change. The departments of Music, English, Chemistry, Occupational Therapy, and Social Science are examples of departments that have persisted at SJSU without changes in name, departmental merger, dissolution, or promotion during the 45 years studied. Of course both pedagogy and the content of the courses offered in these departments and programs have surely changed over time, but the stability of each category itself is noteworthy. These qualitative examples illustrate a range of possible organisational trajectories for different academic fields. While some may reflect organisational dynamics that are idiosyncratic to San Jose State, other examples reflect larger national trends in knowledge evolution and societal expectations. It is also important to note that changes in labels and structures serve to advance knowledge evolution as much as they reflect them.

Specific to comprehensive state universities, Harcleroad and Ostar stress that the broad mission of these campuses reinforces the public's expectation that they will adapt to meeting changing economic and societal reeds. Although this mandate is clear, it is less clear how to manage academic structures for such flexibility. On the one hand, it could entail name changes that correspond to a changing knowledge base, as in library and information sciences. On the other hand, it could involve restructuring a group of established units to correspond to changing domains, as in business and physical education. The latter involves not only resource reallocation (money and space) but also redefining faculty's organisational location, which is difficult given the fixed nature of tenured appointments. In this sense, there are more obstacles to modifying the bureaucratic structure than there are for modifying the programmatic structure.

The data on bureaucratic structure suggest an overall pattern of early growth followed by relative stability. In the period between 1952 and 1997, the total number of departments rose from 25 to 61. This follows expected patterns of bureaucratic expansion and differentiation explained by Blau. A closer look at the 45-year time period shows that expansion in bureaucratic structure slows and then subsides in the period after 1967, with a net growth of only 7 departments between 1967 and 1997 (54 to 61).

Over the entire 45-year period there is very little net change in the number of departments in the life sciences, physical sciences, and health sciences. It is important to note, however, that these three areas represent a very. small proportion of the total number of departments. Departments in engineering and computer science, the social sciences and the humanities more closely reflect the overall pattern of early growth and then stabilisation in the period after 1967. Between 1972 and 1997 there was a net growth of two departments in engineering and computer science (8 to 10), and a net decline of one department in the humanities (13 to 12) and social sciences (12 to 11). Departments in professional and applied fields. primarily business and education, represent the largest subset of the bureaucratic structure.

Conversely, the changes in departments within the applied and professional fields may reflect their predisposition to adapt more readily to changes in the external environment, such as advancements in information technology and changes in career opportunities. Moving from the data on bureaucratic structure to programmatic structure, the longitudinal data on degree programs offered illustrates a trend of steady expansion, consistent with the predictions of Metzger regarding disciplinary specialisation. Unlike the stabilising trend in the departmental data in the latter period, growth in degree programs offered continued after 1972.

In the period after 1982, a general trend of stability is evident in the life sciences, physical sciences, and health sciences. Alternatively, degree programs offered in the humanities, professional and applied fields, and to a lesser extent social sciences and engineering, demonstrate patterns of steady expansion throughout the period under study. One noteworthy pattern in the degree program data is the proliferation of humanities degree program offerings. We have speculated that growth in professional and applied fields dominates expansion trends in the bureaucratic and programmatic data because they are more responsive to external influences, either directly from labour market changes or indirectly as mediated by preferences of career-oriented students. There are several possible interpretations of this pattern.

— From a market perspective, anticipated student demand plays an important role in decisions about the establishment and disestablishment of academic programs. For example, increases in humanities degree programs may be the result of increased student demand for particular humanities degrees. Although not a direct proxy for demand, degree production data does serve as a measure of productive activity within those units. Between 1972 and 1987 the number of humanities degrees awarded declined by over 50 per cent, from 993 to 415. Thus, in spite of such declines in degree production, the number of humanities degree programmes continued to increase. An alternative market explanation might hold that adding new programs may be a strategic initiative by the university to cultivate new student demand. Computing the ratio of degrees awarded to degree programmes offered more explicitly illustrates that if there was strategic intent, it did not succeed. Between 1972 and 1987 the number of degrees awarded per degree program offered in the humanities decreased by almost 70 per cent, falling from 35.5 to 10.9. This evidence suggests that a simple market explanation is not sufficient for understanding the complex dynamics of academic program change.

— The expansion of degree program offerings in the humanities may reflect an increase in more specialised graduate education. When we disaggregate the data on degree programs offered by level, we see that an increase in the number of graduate programs far outpaced growth in undergraduate degree program offerings. It does not appear, however, that the growth rate of graduate degree program offerings in the humanities is any greater than that in the professional or applied fields.

— The increase in degree programme offerings in the humanities may be the result of changing faculty interests and activities. This interpretation could have

> several dimensions, all tied to recent national trends in knowledge. For example, faculty participation in interdisciplinary programs within the humanities, such as various ethnic and regional studies programs, has become increasingly legitimate. Concurrently, as a result of protracted debate over the canon. the humanities have become increasingly fragmented. Both trends reflect a decline in consensus over what counts as knowledge. As such. these trends could yield a corresponding proliferation of degree programs generated by faculty who wanted to move out of established programs.

We have already noted that in both the humanities and professional fields, degree programmes were added steadily and that expansion occurred primarily at the graduate degree level. However, while professional degree production at the graduate level increased, graduate degree production in the humanities declined. Thus graduate degree programs in the humanities were added while graduate degree production in those areas decreased.

The relationship between bureaucractic and programmatic structures more precisely by computing the ratio of degree programmes offered to the number of departments across the seven knowledge areas. In a given year, this ratio shows tie average number of degree programs offered in a particular knowledge area relative to the number of departments in that same area. The change over time in this ratio illustrates whether or not the evolution of knowledge categories, as reflected in the programmatic and bureaucratic structures, follow similar patterns. Especially in the period after 1972, the separate data for degree programs and departments show steady growth in degree program offerings in contrast to relative stability in the number of departments. The ratio of degrees to departments captures this set of trends.

In the period prior to 1972, the proportion of degree programs to departments shows a decline for most knowledge areas. The declines are accounted for by a pronounced increase in the number of new departments created in this era. The resultant expansion in enrollments was accompanied by an increase in resources and organisational capacity that entailed a dramatic proliferation of the bureaucratic structure. In this era, degree program offerings also grew steadily, and our data show a notable change in the academic program. However, the major trend in this period is dominated by expansion of the bureaucratic structure.

The discontinuity between the nature and rates of change in bureaucratic and programmatic structure may indicate a structural capacity of academic organisations to mediate competing imperatives for stability and change. That is, while the bureaucratic structure is relatively fixed in the resource flows, tenured faculty positions, and vested interests for turf protection, the programmatic structure is more open to adaptation. Thus, the multi-dimensionality of academic structure enables universities to reconcile the divergent forces of inertia and adaptation.

There are several implications for empirical inquiry on the formal organisation of knowledge. We derive these out of the limitations we encountered in gathering and analysing data for this case study. Although the use of a single case obviously limits generalisability and does not produce definitive empirical claims, the case study data illustrate one approach to operationalising structural features of the academic landscape. Clearly, if one wants to make generalisable claims or to study causes, the sample of campuses must be expanded. Yet limitations in the availability and comparability of data remain a significant obstacle to constructing a large data set. National data collected at the institution level are not disaggregated to the department level.

Additionally, any study of knowledge change must, by its very nature, consider a long period of time. Unfortunately, data collection practices of institutional research offices tend to change over time, and many institutions keep surprisingly poor historical records. For this study we manually collected data on changes in the departmental structure and academic programs for a 45-year period by analysing campus archives and college catalogs for each of the years in the study. Certainly, the construction of a large longitudinal data set of bureaucratic and programmatic change across many types of campuses would open limitless possibilities for studying the co-evolution of knowledge and academic structure.

The quantitative data analysis, we calculated changes in the number of departments or degrees representing each knowledge category as net increases or declines, which obscures many intricacies of change that occurred within a knowledge area for each period. In a given year, the net change in departments representing the humanities could have been plus one, even if three new departments were added, two removed, and several renamed. Thus a net change does not reflect the volatility that may be occurring.

Future research could use more advanced quantitative methods to analyse longitudinal change within academic organisations. For example, by coding each departmental or programmatic name change, merger, or split as a discrete entry or exit event, event history analysis can be employed to compare the rate of change in departments and degree programs across different knowledge areas, and models can be developed to predict differential causes-both internal and external to the organisation-of structural volatility or stability within knowledge areas.

In universities structural modifications tend to be made incrementally, within shared governance practices as well as through phases of academic planning initiatives. However, the results for the organisation and its participants are cumulative. From the perspective of campus leaders, a number of concerns may arise: Is there a widening gulf between enduring departmental structures and vital educational processes (teaching and learning)? Is programme expansion excessive? In our opinion administrators and faculty need not malign either the enduring nature of bureaucratic structures or the proliferation of degree programs, for they each serve a vital function. The former enables the organisation to sustain legitimacy for its enduring commitments, while the latter simultaneously permits much-needed flexibility to launch experimental or short term programs that can be responsive to shifting faculty interests, student demand, or labour market needs.

Since institutional settings shape knowledge classifications, it is worthwhile to develop a more refined conceptualisation of the, interplay between context and knowledge categories. Educational settings are ideal sites for examining the co-evolution of knowledge with academic structure. The work of new sociologists of knowledge suggests that the analysis of the institutional settings may yield new insights about the interdependence between context and ideas, specifically how structure and content reinforce social hierarchies as well as the authoritativeness of knowledge.

REFERENCES

Astin, A., 1977, *Four critical years.* San Francisco: Jossey-Bass.

Bergmann, B.R., 1991, Bloated administration, blighted campuses. Academe 77 (6). 12-16.

Blau, P.M., 1973, The organisation of academic work. New York: Wiley.

Clark, B.R., & Neave, G., Eds. 1992, The encyclopedia of higher education, Volume 4: Academic disciplines and indexes. Oxford: Pergamon.

Frank, D.J., Wong, S., Meyer, J. W. & Ramirez, F.O., 2000, What Counts as history: A cross-national and longitudinal study of university curricula. *Comparative Education Review*, 44, 29-53.

Gumport, P.J., 2000, Academic restructuring: Organisational change and institutional imperatives. Higher Education: The International Journal of Higher Education and Educational Planning, 39, 67-91.

Meyer. J., & Rowan, B., 1978, The structure of educational organisations, In Meyer (Ed,), Environments and organisations. San Francisco: Jossey-Bass.

12

Women in Schooling: A Worldwide View

At the beginning of the twenty-first century, a majority of children in most regious of the world attends school, and although the formal education of girls and women long lagged behind that of boys and men, it has by now caught up in many countries, International declarations, focusing attention on those countries in which school enrolments, and those of females in particular, remain behind, put women's schooling high on the policy agenda for immediate action. The expansion of mass schooling started during the nineteenth and twentieth centuries. Questions of what part schooling has played in the social transformation of that period, and whether its effects were positive or negative, have been extensively considered and debated in the social sciences.

During the last twenty years, however, an international consensus has emerged, based on large-scale survey research conducted in the developing or low-income countries that embraced mass schooling after 1950: Schooling, particularly that of females, has beneficial effects, and more schooling brings more benefits to individuals, families, and society at large.

Observational research on childhood environments tends to support the idea that maternal schooling is beneficial to children's development. In other words, empirical studies seem to have confirmed the Enlightenment conception of formal education as a major pathway for human improvement, and the schooling of women as the most potent ingredient in the pervasive influence of mass education. In some respects, however, the international evidence concerning school effects is very thin. It lacks the perspectives of history, social anthropology, and—most remarkably educational research. It also offers no view of education beyond years of school (or highest level) attended and rarely includes direct data on what skills, attitudes, or other tendencies boys and girls acquire in school.

The "black box" of imputed links between school attendance and its socially beneficial "outcomes" remains large and murky' as do the institutional and cultural contexts that selectively facilitate or block the processes of individual development. Thus, the taint of speculation clings to the voluminous findings of school effects, raising the suspicion that researchers and policymakers have jumped to conclusions they were predisposed to accept as ideological heirs to the Enlightenment legacy.

In this chapter we re-examine the problem of school effects from a multi-disciplinary perspective, providing an overview of the evidence, building a theoretical model of the institutional and psychosocial processes that might be involved, and presenting relevant findings from our own research on maternal literacy in culturally diverse settings.

INTERPRETATION OF EMPIRICAL EVIDENCE

In the middle of the twentieth century Demographic theory suggested that women's schooling has an influence on the widespread trends toward lower birth and child mortality rates. It was only in the late 1970s, however, that syntheses of large-scale studies across the developing world showed women's schooling to be positively related to child survival and inversely related to fertility, even when other socioeconomic factors were controlled for.

In the 1970s, many developing countries were facing two major population problems, namely infant mortality and population growth. Infant mortality rate dropped sharply between 1950 and 1970, but had stabilised levels far shove those of the developed industrial countries. Furthermore, the earlier declines in mortality, combined with rising fertility, had created very high rates of population growth that threatened long-term survival. Many countries, including China, India, and Mexico, instituted family-planning programmes to curtail fertility, and many others put in place primary health-care programmes as well, with a special focus on maternal and child health in order to reduce the morality of infants, children and mothers. In this context, the findings concerning female schooling as a factor in reducing child mortality and fertility were of direct policy relevance.

Twenty years later, birth and death rates have come down almost everywhere, though they are still relatively high in sub-Saharan Africa, South Asia, and some Middle Eastern countries. Analyses of massive datasets from the World Fertility Survey and the more recent Demographic and Health Surveys have confirmed the importance of women's schooling as an influence in demographic transition, at least before 1990. The policy question driving recent demographic research on the effects of female schooling has been whether and to what extent low-income countries should invest in the further expansion of women's school attendance as a means of improving the survival, health, and welfare of children and families. Despite an international consensus on the value of gender equality in access to education and on the assumption that mass schooling for girls is generally beneficial to society, nagging issues of causal inference, as described below, continue to divide those who interpret the evidence for policy purposes.

In the last quarter of the twentieth century, however—and particularly after publication of the World Development Report 1980 that summarised evidence that schooling had a positive impact on agricultural production, child survival, and fertility decline—the consideration of school expansion as a policy for developing countries was renamed for national policymakers in those countries as a means of achieving these (and other) demonstrable outcomes. This view has been attractive to public decision makers, as it offers them the option of expanding schools, and especially female school enrolments, as an accessible policy lever for attacking social problems Differences of opinion concerning how tightly schooling is tied to demographic change, economic productivity, and social inequality now generate much of the interest in this topic for policy researchers.

There is more to schooling than its effects on health and population. Research on the effects of schooling is not needed to justify gender equality in access to education, which can be treated as a matter of fundamental values rather than simply a means to other ends. The question of how education and learning might be implicated in these processes is important in itself and significant for both theory and practice.

Demographic surveys that indicate a relationship between female school attendance and falling birth and death rates in the countries of Latin America, Asia (outside of Japan), and Africa during the second half of the twentieth century. In these countries, fewer than half of the children aged six to eleven were enrolled in primary school in 1960, and girls' schooling was rare; by the mid-1990s, 81 per cent of girls aged six to eleven were attending primary school.

Major socioeconomic and demographic changes occurred in the same countries during the same period: growth in economic infrastructure, output, income, and consumption, urbanisation, expansion of transportation networks and health and family-planning services; and reduction in mortality and fertility rates. As data concerning these trends became available, social scientists examined the interrelations among them and attempted to explain change and variation.

Women's schooling emerged from these analyses as an important factor in and perhaps a determinant of demographic transition and other social changes. The sheer magnitude of the demographic transition was enormous for the developing countries as a whole, mortality among children under age five was 216 per thousand live births in 1960 and 96 in 1997; total fertility declined from 6.0 in 1960 to 3.1 in 1997 (UNICEF, 1998). In Mexico, for example, the under-five mortality rate dropped from 134 in 1960 to 35 in 1997, and the total fertility rate declined from 6.9 in 1960 to 2.8 in 1997.

The facts concerning the relationships between women's schooling and demographic change are not in serious dispute and can be summarised briefly. Demographers have found that women's school attendance (from none at all through the tertiary level) is negatively associated with child mortality and fertility and positively associated with use of health and contraceptive services, even when statistically controlling for other socioeconomic factors (urban or rural residence, household income, and husband's schooling and occupation).

The major accomplishment of these statistical analyses has been to demonstrate that, although women's schooling is associated with indicators of socioeconomic advantage, it is not simply a proxy for these indicators but has independent relationships with health behaviours and reproductive change. These relationships are usually stronger than those of men's schooling and are frequently the strongest associations at the household level. These relationships are not identical for all demographic and health out-comes. Maternal schooling is more consistently related to child mortality than to fertility, and it is more robustly related to post-infancy child mortality (13-48 months) than to infant mortality (first 12 months).

Furthermore, while a mother's preventive health behaviour (immunisation, prenatal care) is almost always robustly associated with her schooling, the child's survival during infancy and early childhood may still be jeopardised by inadequate diet or exposure to infections such as HIV, hepatitis B, and drug-resistant malaria, for which no vaccines or cures exist. Maternal schooling alone does not guarantee child survival. Consistently and robustly, however, it is associated with some of the key components of child survival.

In the poorest countries, particularly those of sub-Saharan Africa, a curvilinear rather than linear relationship exists between fertility and maternal schooling; in other words, women with primary schooling bear more children than unschooled women, and only those who attended to the secondary level or higher shoe; the effects of contraception or delayed onset of child-bearing. When economic conditions improve, this U-shaped pattern changes to a linear one, as a did in some African countries between the World Fertility Survey of the 1970s and the Demographic and Health Surveys a decade later. Furthermore, the mass sterilisation of unschooled rural women in parts of South Asia indicates that school attendance is not a necessary condition for effective contraception there.

These variations raise questions concerning attitudes toward "contraception," which in one context refers primarily to sterilisation and in others to reversible methods such as the pill. There are, in other words, enough exceptions and qualifications to the inverse relationship between women's schooling and fertility to make the point that it is a contingent, context-dependent relationship rather than a uniform and universal one. At the level of crossnational variations, the average female schooling of a national population is inversely related to its total fertility rate, but regional variations exist in the strength of the relationship, suggesting that cultural influences are at work.

The relationships between maternal schooling and child mortality and fertility, examined through cross-sectional surveys, are clearly dependent on support from variable economic, social, and cultural conditions and they may also be relatively weak in magnitude (though consistent and robust) in the short run. Historical time-series analyses suggest, however, that women's schooling has been an important condition of long-term reductions in child mortality and fertility among developing countries during the period from 1960 to 1995. Furthermore, contraceptive prevalence, a strong predictor of lower fertility at the cross-national level, is also positively related to the average level of women's schooling across developing countries.

There is little doubt that women's schooling is implicated in the social processes of demographic transition, but the evidence can be read in different ways—like the glass that is half full or half empty. Those claiming the necessity and potency of women's schooling in demographic transition find an overwhelming pattern of recurrent, supportive findings, though with some exceptions. Those casting doubt on the importance of women's schooling point to the exceptions as disproving claims of universality, to the increasing number of exceptions concerning fertility, and to problems with the evidence, particularly as a basis for causal inference.

Two primary factors arouse skepticism concerning the causal inference: selection bias and ignorance of the causal links that may be connecting school experience to reproductive change. The problem of selection bias arises because the available evidence comes from cross-sectional sample surveys and population censuses that were not designed to answer causal questions about the effects of school experience. Schooling arms an independent variable is not randomly assigned, as it would be in an experiment, so the possibility of selection bias exists from the start.

A survey designed to mitigate this problem would involve a longitudinal study of girls beginning before school entry and continuing until the end of their child-bearing years (about 40 years), so that a direct assessment of their differential starting points (parental advantages, preschool ability), reasons for leaving school at different levels, learning influences, marriages, and other life events could be made. Several successive birth cohorts would have to be studied to disentangle cohort-specific historical factors from those at the level of individual differences. No study that was designed in advance to identify the causal impact of schooling has been conducted.

Another problem with the causal hypothesis is that the links between school experience and its hypothesised reproductive and health outcomes are unknown. More precisely, such links have been the focus of abundant speculation and a modest amount of research. Without a model of the intervening processes that is both plausible and supported by empirical findings, the credibility of women's schooling as a causal influence on social change is always in jeopardy. Approach has been to begin with the most common patterns of demographic findings from across the world and attempt to fit explanatory models to those patterns. Even highly sophisticated syntheses, however, remain speculations until direct assessment of the pathways sheds light into the "black box" of intervening processes.

The relationship of women's schooling to reduced fertility, for example, although partly reflecting the later marriage of those who have spent more time in school, is largely accounted for by the use of contraception of one sort or another, with or without organised family-planing programmes. This finding narrows the range of possible explanatory models: the primary problem is to explain why women who have attended school longer are more likely to use contraception with the intention of limiting births.

Similarly, many studies have shown that women with mole schooling ate more likely to use maternal and child health services (immunisation and prenatal care) more frequently and effectively, to adhere to domestic dietary and sanitary practices recommended by healthy authorities, and to attend to the mass media in countries ranging from Bangladesh and the Philippines to Egypt and Brazil. All of these findings suggest that maternal participation in bureaucratic health services is a path through which schooling influences reproduction and health—in the clinic, through the public health information media, or through social contacts with those who have been directly influenced by clinic or media exposure.

School attendance introduces girls to the communicative activities characteristic of bureaucratic institutions, thus facilitating their later responsiveness as mothers to authoritative guidance from clinics and public health messages in the media. Recent studies also point to the role of literacy practices in this process. In national surveys of mothers in Morocco and South Africa, directly assessed maternal literacy skills predicted better child health and lower fertility, with socioeconomic factors controlled for. The skills assessed through a brief test of health-related literacy (reading a medicine label) in the Morocco study, and one of reading comprehension in the South African study, point to a literacy pathway from school to the kinds of bureaucratic participation that affect, health and reproduction.

The spread of schooling throughout the world during the nineteenth and twentieth centuries was due largely to nation-building efforts by political leaders seeking, to establish their peoples and geographical territories as modern nation-states. While it is true that Christian missionaries had first introduced schools in many of the countries under European colonial rule, when these countries became independent in the mid-twentieth century, their leaders—like the Japanese of the 1870s tended to see universal schooling as an advantage held by the more powerful nations that they wanted for their own people. A nation, as it was increasingly conceptualised, had to have a school system as much as it did a government, an army, a civil service, a postal system, and hospitals.

Competitive nationalism fostered hasty imitation of other countries, and since no other way existed of determining which school systems were best, those systems associated with the most powerful and prestigious were also most imitated. Few national or culture-specific experiments in formal education were conducted, as national policymakers sought conformity with emerging "international standards" based on Western models. The spread of the Western school were facilitated by its attractiveness to leaders and people alike. Schools were seen by political leaders and presented to their constituents as the universal equipment of a modern bureaucratic state, as well as an import from the West. Bureaucratic schooling could be adopted as the means of realising differing ideological visions: liberal democracy, Marxist and social-democratic socialism, militant nationalism, laissez-faire capitalism.

The rhetoric linking mass schooling to these ideologies could be used to build popular support for a regime; thus the school became the major symbol of hope in much of the world. Furthermore, leaders saw bureaucratic schooling as a way to create loyal citizens, effective soldiers, productive workers—all essential to the growth of a powerful nation-state.

School expansion has formed part of each plan for establishing a nation-state as the primary institution for collective action, citizen responsiveness, and national growth and development, however conceptualised. The diffusion of organisational models of nation-building and schooling from the west to other countries is a historical fact. It is not an essential or intrinsic feature of cultural evolution or human progress, but rather the outcome of a particular history that might have taken a different turn. Among nineteenth-century nation builders as an extremely convenient way of harnessing people on large scale to the nation-state in order to fulfil a national agenda. As with the proliferation of nation-states themselves in the world during the twentieth century, the expansion of formal education has continued at a rapid pace.

Bureaucracies are designed for expansion by replicating standard units and coordinating their operations under hierarchical control. Standardisation of explicit rules for all activities, including communication, is central to the values of efficiency and equal treatment built into bureaucracies, which generate formal codes of conduct and discourse that deliberately transcend local customs and vernaculars of their participants. Schools are units in bureaucracies, and hypothesis is that schools prepare children, deliberately or not, to participate in other bureaucratic organisations by providing them with the skills, aspirations, and models of interaction appropriate for such participation.

PROPERTIES OF SCHOOL

School properties include group membership, age-grading, status hierarchy, intensified social comparison, adult-child interaction, verbal communication, and formal participation structure.

Group membership: Schools constitute membership in communities outside the family. At school entry, children learn that they belong to a community beyond the boundaries of the village and kin network, of which the nation-state is most important and has the right to claim loyalty and obedience and to confer the identity and privileges of a citizen. For children in rural villages of developing countries, this can be an important discovery.

Age-grading: Schools typically organize children into age-segregated groupings, creating peer reference groups. In the homes and communities of many agrarian societies without schools, a child grows up as part of a multi-age, often hierarchical, group of siblings and other children. By putting children of the same age in a class segregated from those older and younger, schools make children more dependent on the teacher for their learning, since they are isolated from other examples of more mature practice. But this segregation also establishes the conditions for childhood social relations to develop through peer groups, which can affect a child's attitudes.

Status Hierarchy: Schooling introduces the child to the ladder-like series of age-graded statuses in school that maps onto the ranked status system of adults in a socially stratified urban society, that is, the academic-occupational hierarchy in which level of school attainment is associated with occupational status, as opposed to the age-gender hierarchies of local communities without schools. Children learn through years in school that those with more schooling are entitled to jobs with higher income and social Power than those with lower levels of educational attainment. This message embodied in schooling provides awareness of the incentives embodied in socioeconomic standing and acts to motivate status-seeking behaviour during and after the school years.

Social Comparison: School attendance involves public evaluation of individual performance, legitimising and intensifying social comparisons, invidious distinctions, and competitive pressures, This practice often contrasts with the indigenous values of agrarian communities in which personal advantages are kept from public view in the interests of reducing interpersonal competition and promoting harmony and cooperation. Schools force a child to work for herself rather than helping others and to endure being publicly compared to others, in the classroom and outside.

Adult-child Interaction: The school classroom can be a unique setting in many agrarian communities by its dedication of the full-time attention and activities of an adult to interacting with children for purposes of instruction. Classroom interaction in schools everywhere consists of an adult expert dedicating his attention to child novices. Such an interaction pattern is taken for granted in societies with schools, but in many agrarian communities children grow up in interactive settings where they are peripheral to the activities of adults -in other words, where they are never the centres of adult attention or interaction for more than a few moments at a time. The adult-expert/child-novice structure is an institutionalised instructional format that can become prototypical for other teaching and learning interactions in a population.

Verbal communication: Verbal communication is an aspect of the institutional format of adult child instruction, but it deserves to be emphasised. In the rural communities of many largely agrarian countries, the school classroom may be the only place in a child's experience where words—in speech, reading, and writing - are treated as primary objects of attention themselves rather than as means to other ends. The school classroom, in its literacy instruction and in other ways, also promotes a unique self-consciousness about language, or metalinguistic awareness, that is a highly salient aspect of the school environment forts pupils.

Participation Structure: Classroom participation structure is undoubtedly influenced by local conversational norms and local conceptions of hierarchical and other social relationships; it is thus culturally diversified, rather than a uniform feature of schooling. Classrooms outside the United States and Canada may not follow the IRE sequence but are equally scripted and standardised according to other cultural formulas.

Since all pupils participate in these interactional structures not once but innumerable times in the course of their schooling, it is plausible that these structures have an impact, that the pupil learns not just the script as a sequence of actions but also the code that lies behind it. It may be that the formality of the participation structure in other words, its standardisation and control of attention in a learning situation - has a similar impact everywhere regardless of the particular script for participation.

As properties of schools and classrooms that could be universal, these structural features can be plausibly hypothesised to have cumulative effects on a woman's reproductive and health behaviour with additional years of school attendance, through secondary school and beyond, rather than effects specific to the curricular content of a particular level.

Every theory of education clearly requires a theory of society as a whole and of how social processes shape education. A theory of formal education also requires a theory of how learning and thinking skills develop in an individual member of society, and how educational processes contribute to the shaping of these skills. The demographic evidence leads us to focus on four path-ways through which schooling might affect a women's reproductive and health behaviour:

1) aspirations influenced by the occupational structure;
2) identity formation and empowerment;
3) communications skills influenced by bureaucratic language; and
4) models of learning and teaching as adaptive strategies, influenced by the instructional relationship with an expert.

Schooling influences the motivations of girls in low income countries, leading them to desire improvement in their own and their children's lives according to the standards of an urban industrial occupational order. Where women are barred from higher occupational positions, prolonged schooling may nonetheless qualify them (according to local standards) for marriage to men of higher, status who can provide them and their children with access to more advantages.

Where women select their own mates, their school-heightened desires for personal and filial improvement may lead them to marry men of higher status. Surveys of poor and developing countries typically find that the schooling of husbands and wives are positively correlated, reflecting the impact of this mate-selection preference in current cohorts of child-bearing women. Women with more schooling often want smaller families and more schooling for their children than they themselves had, similarly reflecting their elevated aspirations for improvement according to contemporary standards.

The impact of schooling on aspirations is a socialisation effect in which school experience motivates women to seek higher status. Such a conceptualisation is a standard sociological view of schooling. One problem with this view, particularly in many agrarian communities, is the assumption that women gain access to higher status and the advantages that go with it through their own motivation and efforts, rather than through those of their parents and husbands. In societies where marriages are arranged by kin, the woman's marriage to a man with more schooling is likely to reflect her parents' status-seeking rather than her own, and once she has an advantageous marriage, her access to better health and contraceptive services and information may simply reflect her husband's social location.

Insofar as this situation holds, one need not posit that school has a socialisation effect on the female pupil's aspiration level, only that she is willing to follow her parents' desires and use advantages that accrue to her from marriage. This reasoning represents another common sociological view of schooling, in which behaviour is explained in terms of social conditions, both constraints and opportunities, in the adult environment rather than in terms of the influence of earlier learning and socialisation.

WOMEN EMPOWERMENT

Empowerment is the term most widely used at present, often with an emphasis on the social rather than on the psychological in other words, on the freeing of the woman from the constraints of "traditional" women's roles. This proposed pathway between schooling and health behaviour brings into focus the sharp differences in views about women's education that characterise policy-relevant social science at present. Empowerment models of roomer's education die versions of an Enlightenment narrative that has been an established Western ideology for two centuries. In the Enlightenment narrative, schooling liberates children from the shackles of superstition and archaic customs so that they can think rationally and act autonomously.

This powerful moral story has inspired social reform and school expansion from the eighteenth century to the present day, and it is enshrined in recent declarations of the United Nations. As an ideology, it predisposes those influenced by it to believe that schooling is a universally positive process associated with rationality and freedom. Like other ideologies it tends to foreclose or bias empirical inquiry, establishing truth by presumption rather than by open-ended investigation. It is important to treat its application to women's schooling in developing countries with skepticism—and to ask, what evidence exists to support or falsify its premises?

Empowerment models have been criticised on the basis of anthropological perspectives and evidence. A cultural relativist framework prevalent among anthropologists makes them suspicious of claims of universality such as Kant's universal human reason unfolding in the course of child development or the assumption that personal autonomy is a universal human value.

These anthropologists are particularly suspicious of claims that worldwide institutions of Western origin, like the school, are necessary for individuals to reach higher stages of intelligence, rationality, and freedom. Their field experience tells them that the unschooled people with whom they have worked have alternative standards of personal maturity and interpersonal effectiveness that are unknown to those who assume modern Western standards to be superior.

Contemporary formulations concerning the psychological and social benefits of women's schooling in developing societies, then, insofar as they imply that unschooled women are lacking in rationality and social competence, arouse criticism from anthro-pologists, who see Western cultural superiority emerging once again in the guise of science and well-intent-ioned policy. Anthropological research has also uncovered instances of communities in which the schooling of women does not empower them.

The actualities of women's lives in a situation of educational transition do not resemble the enlightenment narrative with its liberationist model of schooling. Such cases, in which the more privileged segments of the population, whose daughters go further in Western-style education, are also those that have embraced religious orthodoxy including its greater restrictions on women at and during marriage demonstrate, at the very least, that female empowerment as conceptualised in Western thought is not a universal consequence of schooling worldwide.

In the classroom, where she is expected to apply herself for her-own benefit, a girl who at home is being raised within a male-dominated structure to be compliant and to work for the good of the family, undergoes a process of resocialisation. School is a new universe that operates according to different rules .... A girl can and frequently does beat out the boys for first place. The longer she stays in school, the more likely she is to be convinced of her own efficacy—*vis a vis* males in particular—a conviction that stays with her into adulthood, marriage and motherhood. She is likely to discuss family problems and make decisions jointly with her husband, rather than her husband keeping his own counsel and making decisions on his own.

A small-scale survey of mothers in the same working-class neighbourhood from 1983 to 1985 also found associations between maternal schooling and (reported) egalitarianism in the husband-wife relationship, (reported) less harsh discipline of children and knowledge of news events in the mass media—as proposed by theories of "psychological modernity" and other liberationist models of change. These findings came from an urban population with employment opportunities for women, in which schooling was expected to launch adolescent girls into jobs for a few years before marriage and to help them support their children after marriage should their husbands fail to do so.

Women's schooling can be a liberating force and be experienced as such by girls in school and thereafter; it can also have other, even opposed, meanings and consequences. It would be premature to conclude from the evidence that empowerment and identity formation simply explain the widespread effects of schooling on demographic outcomes. Yet the role of empowerment and identity formation as a pathway of influence between schooling and demographic change cannot be ignored.

Some social scientists have presumed that schools automatically and universally confer the literacy and numeracy skills they are officially intended to transmit. This presumption is embedded in the conventions of censuses and statistical yearbooks that report female literacy figures based entirely on years of school attendance. According to a standard international convention, any woman fifteen years or older who attended school for five years is presumed literate; in the censuses of India and Nepal, any female six years old or older who is currently attending school is classified as literate, just as are adult women who attended school. This equivalence of schooling and literacy is incompatible with contemporary conceptions of literacy in educational research, but the demographic analysts who adopt the equivalence notion apparently believe they are following a respectable precedent. Thus the equivalence position, though obsolete from the perspective of educational research, has not died out in demographic and economic analyses of women's schooling.

The acquisition of skills such as literacy and numeracy—or knowledge gained through health and population curricula—could not account for the impact of school on reproduction and health, for three reasons.

i) the global relationships of maternal schooling to child survival and fertility do not exhibit the kinds of discontinuities across countries, communities, and levels of schooling that would be expected if they reflected the impact of school quality or particular curriculum contents.

ii) school expansion has reduced school quality in many countries so much that it would be foolhardy to assume that "years of school attendance" accurately measures skill acquisition. Given the fact that there are functionally illiterate high school graduates in the United States, it is easy to imagine that women who have attended primary school in rural Kenya or Bangladesh might have acquired little skill in reading, writing, or calculation.

iii) In many low-income countries, few post-schooling supports exist for the literacy of married women, who are rarely exposed to printed materials after leaving school: Thus, it has seemed likely to these analysts that even if rudimentary literacy skills had been acquired in school, they would have been lost afterwards for lack of practice. Yet it is a fact that in such populations even a few years of primary schooling is associated with improved child survival. On these grounds, it seems impossibly naive to assume a literacy pathway from school attendance to demographic change in poor countries. The socialisation of women in school increasing their sense of self-worth, autonomy, and empowerment rather than their learning is more promising as an explanation.

Brown and French stated, commenting on the Yucatan research by Cole and his research group:

> Schooling, like tailoring or carpentry, promotes certain task-specific skills. The particular skills engendered by school experience involve the ability to apply a specific set of strategies to the task of solving decontextualised academic problems commonly encountered in school curricula. In these studies, gars of school experience is associated with the tendencies to use deliberate memory strategies, name superordinate categories in free associating to nouns (e.g., animal in response to the noun dog), use formal reasoning in verbal problem-solving, and other verbal skills that the investigators related to tasks learned and rehearsed in school.

Sharp, Cole, and Lave also found in their Yucatan research that more highly educated subjects more readily engage in intellectual activities which are not rigidly predetermined by the structure of the task and which promote efficient performance. It is not differences in the information about the stimuli per se but differences in what people do with commonly available information that is critical.

They argue further that what differentiates the subjects by schooling is not their familiarity with the content of the tests but familiarity with the task structure of the assessment procedures, which simulate tasks learned in school. Sharp, Cole, and Lave analysed in detail the selective bias in school attendance in the Yucatan and concluded that it did not account for the performance differences by level of formal education. Pointing out that only a longitudinal study could demonstrate the causal influence of schooling, they nevertheless conclude that schools augment performance on those cognitive tests that most resemble school tasks.

They question the relevance of learning such tasks to the real-world tasks faced by adults in the Yucatan or elsewhere, yet reluctantly concede that:

> the information-processing skills which school attendance seems to foster could be useful in a variety of the tasks demanded by modern states, including clerical and management skills in bureaucratic enterprises, or the lower-level skills of record keeping in an agricultural cooperative or a well-baby clinic. These activities may well be facilitated skills currently transmitted in schools.

Wagner's longitudinal study of Moroccan school dropouts lends additional support to the retention hypothesis: When children who left school after fifty grade were followed up three years later, they were found to have lost skill on math tests, remained stable on nonverbal cognitive tasks, and gained in their scores on both Arabic and French literacy tasks, This suggests that literacy may be an area particularly susceptible to retention.

The cross-cultural research on the cognitive consequences of schooling has shown that school experience affects proficiency in a variety of specific verbal skills, that these skills tend to be retained into adulthood, and that literacy practices in the broad sense are involved.

The skeptical demographers who saw literacy as an unlikely pathway through which schooling could influence reproductive and health behaviour. Any simple dichotomy that could support a distinction between literates and illiterates — but includes comprehension, discourse processes, meta-linguistic awareness.

These last three abilities are often referred to as "cognitive" by psychologists, but they are also communication skills that grow and develop with years of schooling. No general agreement exists as to how many skills should be included under the rubric of "literacy," but experts do agree that its definition has varied with its social functions across historical periods, cultures, and communities with different levels of formal education.

The direct assessments of literacy and language skills among mothers who varied in amount of schooling in Mexico, Nepal, and Zambia the findings from correlational and multiple regression analyses stowed that the mothers of young children retained such skills and that the skills were related to their health behaviour, even with other socioeconomic factors controlled for. These surprising results led us to formulate a new theory of how women in poor countries might acquire in school and retain into adulthood literacy and associated language skills that could influence their reproductive and wealth behaviour as mothers.

The discourse skills taught in school classrooms, in usher words, skills in using the language characteristic of written texts for purposes of comprehending and producing oral communications. This type of oral language skill has been conceptualised by Snow as "decontexualised language ability," and it has syntactic, pragmatic, and lexical features that distinguish its use from ordinary vernacular conversation in most speech communities.

In contrast with conversation, this mode of speaking assumes less shared context, involves the frequent use of abstract nouns, and explicates particulars that are taken-for granted among familiar conversational partners. Cummins refers to this kind of academic communication as "context-reduced," and Wells calls it "the synoptic mode of speaking and construing experience." Valdes and Geoffrion-Vinci have argued that it constitutes an academic "register," or an institutionalised situation specific use of language with distinctive linguistic features. Children are exposed to academic language in school, often for the first time if they have been raised by parents with little schooling, and their mastery of it influences their performance on school tasks involving verbal communication.

Since academic language is used throughout the years of schooling, proficiency in it could plausibly increase with years of attendance and help explain the linear relationship between school attendance and health behaviour. That the academic register, with ins features of formality, impersonality, explicitness, and abstractness, is the official language of all bureaucracies, including health and family-planning clinks as well as schools.

Children of university-educated parents begin learning this language during their preschool years; other children who attend school begin learning it at school entry; and those who do not attend school may never learn it at all. The longer the child attends school, the more practice she gets in using the academic register and the more proficient in it she can be expected to be. Proficiency in using the academic register is advantageous in oral communication with the health bureaucracy for example, in understanding public health messages in the media and medical instructions in the clinic, and in giving a coherent account of symptoms and their emergence to a doctor or nurse.

Thus, women who have spent more time in -school know in advance much of the language used in public health and clinical settings not the technical vocabulary but the use of general terms, forms of interrogation, and forms of explanation. This knowledge enables the mothers to learn from professional verbal communications about health, making it more likely that they will take preventive measures, recognise emergencies, and act promptly in health crises. Furthermore, women who lack the language skills expected are more likely to suffer frustration in seeking treatment and suffer humiliation at the hands of officious medical staff, leading these women to avoid going to the hospital or clinic until disaster's imminent. In their world, academic language proficiency and other communication skills acquired in school are the passports to maternal and child health.

MODELS OF LEARNING AND TEACHING

The regardless of curricular content and the idiosyncrasies of the teacher, children learn something about how to learn and how to teach -in a context structured by unequal authority and knowledge, and that the longer they attend school, the more they internalise the instructional schema of the classroom and spontaneously use it in other expert-novice settings involving unequal authority. When women who have attended school longer are in the subordinate position, they are more likely to assume the role of the pupil seeking to learn; when they have greater authority than the other, they are more likely to assume the role of the teacher seeking to instruct. Since classroom instruction is primarily verbal interaction, those with more schooling are: more inclined to prefer verbal communication in their adult learning and teaching behaviour. This process of internalisation can be understood in terms of Vygotsky's concept of movement from the interpsychological (or- interactional and interpersonal) arena to the intrapsychological (or intrapsychic) realm.

The child acquires an instructional schema from scripted social experience that provides a model for future authority relations in terms of the teacher-pupil relationship. The practical consequences for a woman's relations with health experts and own children are enormous. In a changing society, one needs information but never has- enough of it, and those who have new and valuable information become authoritative experts. Nation-building, often based on a metaphor of development, almost always entails rapid social and technological change that renders most of the population novices in the face of new conditions. Health care offers an extreme case of this phenomenon, with a small corps of professionally trained experts using a mysterious technology of potential benefit to all.

In this situation, mothers who have gone further in school tend to act mare like pupas than those with less; schooling—paying closer attention to public health messages in the maps media, following medical advice more obediently, attempting to gain access to health information they believe will help their children, and, above all, using health services more frequently so as to bring themselves into closer contact with the experts. Much evidence supports the idea that mothers with more schooling do behave this way, and even opt for measures that carry the authority and prestige of modern medicine but that actually elevate health risks. School experience has taught these mothers how to be novices who learn from experts, and the mothers then apply their knowledge and skills in the novel health situations they face as child-bearing women.

School also teaches women how to act like experts when they are responsible for and in a position of authority over novices, as in child care. Women who attended school longer are more likely to structure the care of infants and young children as pedagogical interaction, taking the role of the teacher in talking frequently to the preverbal child, responding contingently to the child's initiatives with speech, tutoring the child, scaffolding the child's learning (e.g., by recasting and extending the child's speech, or breaking down a task into smaller units the child can understand), and interrogating the child about lessons previously taught.

The idea that women acquire an instructional schema in school that leads them to act like pupils in relation to health expects and like teachers in caring for their children helps make sense of the survey data on utilisation of health and contraceptive services and the child development data on verbal responsiveness to preschool children. It suggests a process of learning through which a girl's social experience in the classroom influences her subsequent maternal behaviour.

In this chapter explain how school learning by rural and urban women in developing countries might have contributed to the major changes in child survival and fertility rates that have been documented by demographic research. The variations in women's schooling at the individual and cross-national levels arc related to birth and death rates and to the use of health and contraceptive services in much of the world during the last half of the twentieth century. The theoretical model that might explain how the expansion of mass schooling has contributed to this alteration in basic population parameters through an educational pathway that includes learning and is not restricted to status enhancement or personal empowerment.

The organisational entailments of nation-building policies have created a social tautology for individual development in which only those who have learned the norms of bureaucratic communication in school can be effective in the new, bureaucratised world of the nation-state. Those who do not attend school find that the standards of competence have been changed so that their skills and intellectual capacities shaped by indigenous education and once valued socially and rewarded economically cannot lead to success unless reshaped through bureaucratic schooling. To most poor and unschooled adults, the tide of school expansion cannot be opposed; their only hope is to make sure their children go as far in school as they can.

REFERENCES

Aries, P., 1962, *Centuries of childhood*, New York: Vintage.

Bicego, C.T., & Boerma, J.T., 1993, Maternal education and child survival: A comparative study of survey data from 17 countries. *Social Science and Medicine,* 36, 207-228.

LeVine, R.A., 1980, Influence of women schooling on maternal behaviour in the Third World. *Comparative Education Review*, 24 (Suppl.), 78-105.

Jain, A., & Nag, M., 1986, Importance of female primary education for fertility reduction in India. *Economic and Political Weekly*, 21, 1602-1608.

World Bank, n.d., *The Wolrd Bank and Girl's Education*, Wahington, D.C., World Bank Human Development Network, Education Advisory Service.

WHO, 1999, Child-Friendly Schools: A Mental Helath Promotion Initiative, Geneva, World Health Organisation.

13

Role of Transnational Advocacy Networks in Education

The end of the Cold War; rising evidence of global economic, social, and cultural integration; and the increasingly visible activities of networks of transnational social movements focused on such issues as the environment, women's rights, human rights, Third-World debt, and globalisation have given impetus to a renewed interest in the influence of non-state actors in the world system over the past decade. From a purely empirical stance, studying the growing complexity and volume of international relations among non-state actors and characterising the way these interact to structure a single, world-level political system has become a major challenge to the entire field of international relations. At the same time, an ethical or normative question lies at the core of a growing interest in the capacity of non-governmental networks to influence world order.

International links between non-governmental organisations, citizens groups, expert communities, and trade unions began to thicken in the middle of the nineteenth century, often stimulated by the desire to share information and offer mutual support and solidarity for national reform movements. Once an international link was made, many of these organisations played a key role in the establishment of formal inter-governmental agreements and institutions key examples include. The antislavery movement of the nineteenth century, the child survival movement of the early twentieth century, and the work of the international labour movement in the formation of the International Labour Organisation and its conventions.

Yet because international non-governmental organisations were largely dependent on resource, provided by nation-states and because they were often marginalised in the decision-making processes of international organisations during the Cold War era, there was a widely shared sense that these organisations were not significant or sufficiently autonomous players in international politics. Until quite recently, political scientists have viewed transnational non-governmental actors as marginal to state-based power politics. Today that sense of insignificance has evaporated, for two broad reasons.

The first set of factors influencing the new salience of international non-governmental actors is largely contextual. This century has seen the steady institutionalisation of new global structures of governance and political power that have "transformed world politics into a global politics of agenda setting, coalition building and multilateral regulation." Moreover, recent intensification of processes of economic, political, and cultural globalisation raises questions for each about the appropriate locus of political decision making in an increasingly complex, interdependent world. The problem is of a world order in which decisions made by centres of power have repercussions beyond national boundaries, while forms of democratic participation and societal compromise remain territorially grounded in increasingly hollowed-out welfare states.

The second set of factors such as the number, size, professionalism, and the speed, density and complexity of international linkages, has grown dramatically in the last three decades. This growth is especially marked around the issues of women's rights, the environment, peace, development, and human rights, where a variety of non-state actors have come together as advocates of major social and political change in what scholars have described variously as transnational advocacy networks, principled issue networks, and transnational social movements. The expansion and visibility of such transnational non-governmental advocacy networks have raised many questions for international relations scholars.

There is broad consensus: working without significant financial or electoral resources, these new collective actors use telecommunications and transportation technologies to build networks and generate international public interest in an issue. They develop highly publicised campaigns that target international organisations or intergovernmental regimes, and they link domestic and international groups in collective protests against both governments and international organisational policies in what Margaret Keck and Kathryn Sikkink describe as a common "boomerang" strategy designed to provide domestic movements' greater leverage against their home governments.

These networks have had a cumulative impact: they increasingly interact, use similar strategies and repertoires for action, and mobilise around overlapping collective action frames. Most scholars agree that their greatest impact to date has been at the level of agenda setting, the spreading norms and changes in intergovernmental and governmental discourse. But very different assessments have been offered of their success in holding nations and international organisations accountable to new agendas, or in achieving the deeper democratisation of international organisations and intergovernmental forums, which is so often a key part of their agenda. Thus, while many scholars have gone so far as to describe these new non-governmental networks as the harbingers of 'global civil society', others raise serious questions about the long-term capacities and representativeness of the new advocacy movements. They prefer to think of them as uneven transnational networks whose development into an effective global civil society needs to be empirically studied rather than naively assumed.

NON-GOVERNMENTAL NETWORKS AND EDUCATION

According to Marie-Claude Smout international non-governmental organisations (INGOs) derive their legitimacy from their ability to make demands in terms of collective needs and from their innovative capacity to suggest ways to meet these needs by focusing on the mobilising frames or ways in which global educational problems and their solutions are talked about and used to legitimate and motivate collective action among non-governmental actors.

Non-governmental actors have long played a significant role in the field of education, beginning with the role played by religious organisations in spreading western forms of schooling. The late nineteenth century and early twentieth century, a period that saw the rapid global spread of western models of compulsory mass schooling, also saw the growth of secular international organisations and networks with educational interests and programs taking up such causes as child survival, children's rights, child-centered pedagogy, peace education, the need for internationalism among youth and students of higher education, and teachers' rights.

The evolution of formal intergovernmental organisation in education during the twentieth century owed much to periods of intense non-governmental activism, especially at key historical conjunctures when new institutions for international cooperation were being formed. After World War I it was primarily non-governmental actors, including international women's organisations, international teachers' unions, and transnational groups of progressive educators, who pushed the League of Nations toward the formation of an International Institute for Intellectual Cooperation, despite the hesitation of member governments.

Some of the same non-governmental actors helped to create the International Bureau of Education, which later became the first intergovernmental body focused on the problems of public education. Non-governmental organisations were again instrumental in the inclusion of education in the mandates of international organisations formed after World War II. In 1945, a group of predominantly American non-governmental organisations lobbied and drafted the wording that eventually led to the inclusion of educational cooperation within the charter of the United Nations organisations. The same group of NGOs also convinced the American delegation to insist that the Economic and Social Council of the United Nations take on responsibility for the promotion of international educational cooperation, despite considerable governmental resistance.

Later, a wide range of women's and child-welfare organisations helped to further secure the legitimacy of education as a field for intergovernmental cooperation by introducing the right to free elementary education in the 1948 Declaration of Human Rights and by urging the adoption of a separate Declaration on the Rights of the Child in 1959. In each of these instances, international non-governmental actors overcame the hesitation of national governments, insisting that education was a legitimate, indeed morally necessary, field for international organisation.

Although the number of non-governmental organisations with an interest in education rapidly expanded in the post-World War II era, these organisations also remained highly fragmented and marginalised within what emerged as a fairly expansive arena for intergovernmental relations in education. The era saw the development of an expanding group of membership organisations, each narrowly focused on different levels of education, or specific educational issues. Some of these organisations, most notably international teachers' unions, were divided into American-led or more social democratic- and Soviet-oriented organisations.

At the same time, there was an explosion of church-based and secular charitable organisations who carried out smaller-scale educational projects in local communities, but whose work generally remained limited to supplementing national educational systems and thus concentrated in such fields as non-formal, adult, and literacy education. Actors across these two groups rarely came together to discuss global educational problems. Their work developed in relative isolation from each other, with only marginal linkages to the expanding work of intergovernmental organisations, which had been charged in the period after 1945 with constructing education as afield for international action.

During the period 1945-80, the relationship of international non-governmental actors woththeir relationships inter-governmental organisations become more constrained. This occurred in part because intergovernmental organisations came to view international educational problems as linked, first and foremost, to the achievement of national economic and political modernisation and, thus, as primarily in need of technical expertise delivered to governments and governmental actors.

Non-governmental actors were quite absent in this conceptualisation of educational development. Furthermore, the escalation of Cold War politics pushed intergovernmental bodies like UNESCO to rigidify its relationships with non-governmental organisations and focus more fully on governments as their chief partners. It is thus not surprising that non-governmental actors ended up having highly formalised and superficial relationships with organisations like UNESCO, nor is it surprising they were absent at such formative international organisation (IO) sponsored meetings on education as the 1961 DECD meeting on education and economic growth, the major regional conferences on education hosted by UNESCO in the 1950s and 1960s, the influential Bellagio conferences on education of the 1970s, and even the UNESCO-sponsored literacy conferences in Tehran and Persepolis.

The absence of a standardised model of national responsibility left a vacuum that was quickly filled by a host of non-governmental actors whose interest in literacy and adult education extended back to the nineteenth century. These NGO interests gave birth to the International Council of Adult Education and ushered in a vibrant period of transnational advocacy during the 1970s, when networks of literacy and adult education organisations were formed and engaged in highly popularised debates about the appropriate purposes and organisation of education. Yet although this new movement into educational advocacy achieved some degree of formal recognition within UNESCO, the idea of alternative educational structures or of a right to adult and literacy education made little substantial headway in the programs of the new giant in the field of international cooperation in education, the World Bank, and still less in the practices of national governments.

In the late 1980s, as sources of finance to support literacy became increasingly scarce, the cohesion of the literacy and adult education network began to erode. In the second half of the 1990s has seen a remarkable explosion of international non-governmental activity in the field of education, especially around the idea of education for all. The contextual roots of this explosion can be traced to several factors. Perhaps foremost among them, the basic assumption on which many earlier forms of non-governmental cooperation in the field of education had been founded—the idea that education is an entitlement of citizenship, properly provided by a state whose capacity as service provider was expected to expand—was steadily eroded by a worldwide economic crisis, as well as by the rise of a new set of ideas about public policy in Western welfare states.

For many countries in the South, the 1980s was a lost decade in which primary enrolment rates declined and school systems fell into disarray. Meanwhile, in the North, questions about the ongoing capacity of governments to continue to expand both domestic social services, such as education, and international development assistance were met with an increasingly popular blend of neo-conservative and hyperliberal ideas. From the mid-1980s, debates about education across countries belonging to the OECD were increasingly characterised by a new interest in such issues as privatisation, public choice, decentralisation, the use of national testing, and cost recovery and efficiency, each linked to this new policy agenda. Similar ideas were promulgated by the major multilateral and bilateral development organisations involved in the field of educational cooperation. In the late 1980s, four major international organisations (UNICEF, UNESCO, the World Bank, and the United Nations Development Programme (UNDP) decided to host a World Conference on Education for All (WCEFA).

Held in Jomtien in 1990, the WCEFA harnessed together a relatively uncoordinated group of education specialists across these agencies in an effort to expose the deterioration of worldwide access to education in the poorest of the developing countries. Its formal goal was to get governments in both the North and the South to sign on to a program of action aimed at solving this crisis. But the motivation for the WCEFA also calve from the practical recognition among senior managers in UNESCO, UNICEF, and the World Bank that education might be an issue capable of revitalising and legitimating their organisations in the face of mounting rich country reluctance to expand North-South development assistance.

In turn, the WCEFA popularised the notion of a crisis in educational access at a time when a new wave of world conferences and transnational non-governmental advocacy networks was emerging, including a network of NGOs focused on the right of children. Beginning with the Rio Conference on the Environment in 1992, "education for all" (EFA) was taken up as a major theme in a series of United Nations-sponsored world conferences and summits, as well as by NGO networks on human rights, women, and child survival. Following Jomtien, an interagency Education for All Commission was established, with a secretariat in Unesco and a steering committee formed of representatives from intergovernmental and bilateral aid organisations.

The EFA marked the beginning of a new era of awareness and interest in non-governmental organisations among intergovernmental organisations, which officially recognised a role for non-governmental actors in the provision of educational services. In light of this recognition, a remarkable number of non-governmental participants were invited to attend the Jomtien conference. Non-governmental organisations were involved in preconference regional consultations; 125 were invited to be formal conference participants, and art NGO representative was invited to sit on the WCEFA steering committee.

While the WCEFA declaration, and the "education for all" activities that followed it, officially promoted the idea that non-governmental actors were fundamental to the achievement of EFA, it also seems clear that the official thinking about NGO participation was focused primarily on the role of NGOs as flexible collaborators in the provision of educational services. This was made clear in preparations for Jomtien. Here, NGOs were given little opportunity to participate in the selection of NGO participants.

Instead, sponsoring intergovernmental organisations and national delegations contended for control of invitations, with the result that some Western-based development and relief NGOs were invited, while many of the literacy and adult education NGOs officially affiliated with Unesco through its Collective Consultation on Literacy were ignored. Even though the WCEFA secretariat hosted an, NGO meeting one day ahead of the WCEFA, this selection process "ensured that the NGO contingent at EFA would not, unlike many of the governmental donor organisations, form a preexisting group."

Many NGO delegates were critical of the WCEFA conference, comparing it with the grassroots NGO organisation that preceded preparations for the Unesco sponsored International Literacy Year (ILY) conference in 1990. They argued that the WCEFA was dominated by an interagency agenda, was predominantly staffed by Western education development professionals, and embodied a Western-led set of solutions for developing country problems that emphasised a traditional North to South delivery of education that virtually ignored the issue of adult literacy.

Jomtien follow-up activities, likewise, suggested a peripheral role for non-governmental actors: no clear structures for NGO participation in post-Jomtien activities were established, and there was no NGO representative on the EFA Interagency Steering Commission until 1997. Unesco's Collective Consultation on Literacy, a NGO body that might have been expected to play a strong role vis-a-vis the new EFA secretariat at Unesco, instead remained quite marginalised in the EFA structures.

This remained the case even after the Unesco NGO Collective Consultation became the first NGO coalition invited to appoint a representative to the interagency Education for All Steering Committee in 1997, in part because intergovernmental organisations provided little financial support to help the body develop the participation of its membership and, in part, because the earlier focus of its membership on literacy and non-formal education had been supplanted by the jomtien focus on formal schooling. Thus, despite heroic efforts on the part of its co-chairs in 1998 and 1999, the Unesco Collective Consultation proved unable to generate a common mobilising frame or set of mobilising strategies for non-governmental actors in relation to the promises of education for all.

The WCEFA and its follow-up activities acted as all important catalyst for the development of new transnational linkages among non-governmental educational actors in two ways. First, WCEFA set the stage for an expanding pool of funding for non-governmentally implemented educational projects. Second, WCEFA put out a set of formal commitments among governments to which non-governmental actors could later hold governments and international organisations accountable.

At least five important trends in non-governmental activity emerged after jomtien, each marking a considerable expansion in the education-related networking and advocacy efforts of non-governmental organisations. A wide number of international non-governmental organisations involved in development and relief had begun to open or expand their programs in basic education and girls' education, by the mid-1990s. These are Northern based and vary considerably in the quality of their relationships to Southern non-governmental actors including various national branches of Save the Children, World Vision, and Care launched educational advocacy initiatives in the 1990s. For the most part, these advocacy initiatives are not linked to the more radical demands for global governance and global transformation that have characterised the new wave of INGO activism in fields like gender, development, or debt relief.

The energies of these organisations have remained by and large focused on developing their own capacities for service provision in the field of education. Their repertoires for contention focus primarily on expanding their individual representation within intergovernmental and non-governmental organisations. They attend international conferences and adopt the broad framing of educational problems established at them, especially where these frame the problem of education for all within the notion of children's rights.

In the late 1990s, education became a prim theme in the advocacy work of these networks. Two examples are illustrative here. "Reality of Aid" is an initiative, first launched by the International Council on Voluntary Action and Eurostep in 1993, which is aimed at providing independent reports on official development aid. In 1997, 1998, and 1999, its reports focused on donor performance in basic education. Similarly, Social Watch, an initiative sponsored by a broad coalition of Southern. NGOs, has published reports that draw attention to governmental commitments to basic education made at the WCEFA and the World Summit for Social Development.

In fall 1999, three non-governmental actors launched independent advocacy campaigns that targeted the education for ail commitment made by governments and international organisations at Jomtien. Two of these, Oxfam and ActionAid, are large, multi-branched Northern development NGOs with successful policies of fostering Southern non-governmental organisational partnerships and experience in developing highly publicised campaigns for fund-raising in the North. The third campaign was launched by Education International, an international association of teachers' unions formed in 1993. In 1999, these organisations joined their campaigns to launch a Global Campaign for Education, targeting both the end-of-decade review of Jomtien education for all efforts, the UN follow-up conference of the Social Summit, and the spring meetings of the Group of Seven.

EVOLUTION OF GLOBAL CAMPAIGN FOR EDUCATION

Role of Oxfam International

The Oxfam International is the orgaisation which has palyed the major role in forging the Global Campaign for Education. In 1995, convinced that processes of globalisation required Oxfam to augment its influence and involvement in an emerging global political arena, the federation of Oxfams created Oxfam International, a network organisation designed to increase Oxfam's influence on donor and Southern governments and international organisations, especially on such issues as debt relief, International Monetary Fund (IMF) structural adjustment programs, and intergovernmental commitments to development assistance and global social welfare.

Discussion within Oxfam international turned to the idea of launching a global campaign in 1997, when the organisation felt a need to revitalise its debt and structural adjustment campaigns. The federated Oxfams launched their joint campaign "Education Now" in March 1999. Initially, the campaign appeared squarely focused on establishing Oxfam's own agenda *vis a vis* international organisations, the public, and the interagency EFA network. Oxfam sought, and received, the endorsement of one of Britain's largest newspapers, *the Guardian*. It approached both the World Bank and UNICEF with a global action plan in December 1998, proposing that they adopt the Global Action Plan as the financial mechanism for meeting EFA goals.

The Global Action Plan called for specific financial commitments for meeting the Jomtien Education for All tar gets; the establishment of an independent facility for delivering resources to education debt relief for impoverished countries; reform of the IMF, World Bank, and other intergovernmental organisations whose policies have impeded spending on basic education and other social services; increases in levels of bilateral foreign aid; and the use of debt relief and policy reforms to encourage Southern governments to spend more on education.

To quote from Oxfam's *Education Now*:

> "Various polite formulations can be found to explain away the collective failure of governments. But the hard fact is that the rights of the world's children are being violated by the world's governments—the same governments that have reneged on the promises made at Jomtien."

Oxfam also made a clear statement that education must be free and properly delivered by the state-both issues that were sidestepped in the final declaration of the Jomtien conference.

Oxfam was quickly invited to join the interagency committee overseeing post Jomtien efforts, as an NGO representative on the EFA steering committee. Media coverage of the campaign was also significant. However, by summer 1999, Oxfam's call for a Global Action Plan had been modified by the steering committee, whose members ruled out the idea of a special funding facility for education.

At the July 1999 Group of 8 (G8) summit, Oxfam joined with Education International to conduct a high-level lobbying campaign, and it also participated in the Jubilee 2000 direct action. One outcome of this lobbying was a statement by the G7 and GS ministers promising a new debt relief initiative that placed considerable emphasis on access to education; the G7 ministers also promised to include civil society in the preparation and implementation of World Bank and IMF projects. Education International later joined Oxfam in meetings with the heads of the IMF and the World Bank. Oxfam International also launched efforts to engage its national chapters in local advocacy around the Education Now campaign. This proved somewhat problematic, however, because Oxfam affiliates often have a limited background in education and few links to other educational actors. Oxfam sought to overcome this handicap by developing a broader coalition of non-governmental actors involved in education at the international level.

Role of Education International

During 1999, Education International, the association of teachers trade unions emerged as Oxfam's chief partner in global educational advocacy. It later became the coordinator and headquarter organisation for the Global Campaign for Education. Education International's participation marks two novel events in the field of non-governmental activism in education. First, it suggests a renewed solidarity and internationalism among teachers unions, which have for decades been sharply divided into rival international associations. Second, it marks the beginning of a new era of cooperation between international trade union associations and other international non-governmental actors around a common agenda for global change.

The Education International, is a worldwide trade union organisation of education personnel that is committed to both the expansion of trade unionism among teachers and the development of a unified, professional vision of global educational issues. It has 23 million individual members, drawn from 294 national trade unions and associations in 152 countries and territories. It is governed by policy resolutions made at triennial World Congresses, and it has an elected executive board.

Education International's new mobilising frame is captured well in the address of Fred Van Leeuwen, the organisation's general secretary, at Education International's founding congress. He promised that Education International would wage a battle with neo-liberalism, step up efforts to influence the IMF and the World Bank, and target the international education crisis by austerity measures in the South and by neoliberal schemes in the North, put forth to destroy free compulsory education and replace it with some form of fragmented semi-public or private system.

Alongside its more traditional advocacy of the right of teachers to collective bargaining, Education International, like Oxfam, has become engaged in broader debates about economic globalisation. Indicative of this, it has expanded its activities to include research and lobbying related to the World Trade Organisation. Education International is also active in the defence of children's rights and the promotion of human rights more generally. It has played an active role in the child labour movement and is a founding member and international convener of the Global March against Child Labour, the fourth INGO to join the Global Campaign on Education.

The Education International officially launched a campaign calling for 'Quality Public Education for All', in 1999 after it was given the mandate to do so by resolution of its 1998 World Congress. The ideological centrepiece of its mobilising frame is an unequivocal commitment to the notion of publicly funded and provided free education. In the view of Education International, public education is a necessary safeguard against the growth of economic and social inequality. It argues that public education is also more likely to encompass a humanistic, plural, and democratically oriented curriculum. The Education International campaign has also argued for the right of teachers to participate in national and international educational policy-making arenas.

The Education International campaign takes up specific policy issues related to what it describes its the it neoliberal policy agenda in education; it questions existing approaches to national standardised testing, decentralisation, privatisation, and civil service reform. Each of these issues is taken tap in the newsletters and journals Education International circulates to its membership, and in research and policy documents it posts on its popular web site. Education International's decision to help launch the Global Campaign for Education in fall 1999 brought to new non-governmental advocacy in education both a distinctive mobilising frame and a new and extensive repertoire for contention.

Role of ActionAid

ActionAid, is a famous British NGO, is not only among the largest UK development NGOs, but also a member of a family of NGOs having affiliates in Ireland, France, Italy, and Greece. It emphasises community development and partnership with Southern NGOs and citizens organisations. Since 1990, it has engaged in advocacy work, with current campaigns on the issues of education for all, ending the sex trade, and the threat to Third World agriculture posed by genetically engineered seeds. Unlike Oxfam, ActionAid has worked extensively in the field of education in developing countries, and it is well known for its development of community-based methods for teaching adult literacy and for its early involvement in non-formal and non-governmental educational initiatives.

Role of Global March against Child Labour

Global March against Child Labour is a Southern-based coalition of NGOs. It views itself as the world's largest social movement in defence of exploited children, also joined the leadership of the Global Campaign in 1999. Launched in 1997, the Global March was initially organised around a highly publicised series of national demonstrations and a worldwide march in which both national policies and international agreements related to child labour were the lobbying target. The campaign appears to have played an important role in getting governments to agree to the development of the new international Convention on the Worst Forms of Child Labour. The Global March coalition placed education high on its agenda, going so far as to argue that free education is the best way of ending child labour.

The ActionAid's Elimu campaign and the Global March Colation brought to the Global Campaign for Education a unique opportunity for partnetrship with a large number of souther NGOs. Several Southern coalitions subsequently joined the campaign, some of which include the South African NGO Coalition; the Campaign for Popular Education; the Brazilian National Campaign for the Right to Education; the Citizen's Education Initiative in India; the Ghana National Education Campaign Coalition; the Civil Society Action Committee on EFA, Nigeria; Association du Sahel d'Aide a la Femme et al. Enfance. Mali; Cadre de Concertation en Basic Education, Burkina Faso; Consultation of Adult Education in Latin America, Mexico; Forum for African Women Educationalists, Mozambique; and Tanzania Education Network.

The campaign's eight-person steering committee reflects this widening membership: four positions are held by representatives of Action Aid, Oxfam, Education International, and the Global March against Child Labour. The other four are held by four Southern NGO coalitions, including a representative from CAMPS, Bangladesh; Education International, Togo; the Brazilian National Campaign for the Right to Education; and the South African National NGO Coalition. With these partnersthe Global Campaign for Education promised to mobilise public pressure on governments to fulfil their promises to provide free, qulaity education for all people, in particlar for our children and for women. Each of the campaign's sponsoring organisations continued to develop its own independent campaign, while joining in a series of joint efforts leading up to the Dakar world forum. These included a "millennium appeal" letter sent to heads of states calling for high-level participation in the EFA review and commitment to the goal of education for all; and a "Global Week of Action" in April 2000 to engage NGOs and teachers unions around the world in advocacy activities the week prior to the Dakar meeting. Campaigners also joined UNESCO in hosting an NGO parallel conference at the Africa regional EFA preconference meetings in 1999.

The campaigners' preparations for the Dakar meeting suggested a new kind of coherence and mobilisation among non-governmental actors in the field of education.

In November 1999, they began a heated and contentious exchange with the intergovernmental agencies sponsoring the EFA review. Campaign sponsors sent a strongly worded letter to World Bank president James Wolfensohn signalling their intention to make the Dakar forum a key event in their campaign. The letter described the interagency EFA forum as "failing to galvanise governments and build a constituency around the EFA project," and it demanded "evidence of a concrete global plan of action through which the resources needed to achieve the goal of education for all can be mobilised; and through which civil society and local communities are given a greater voice in the development of education policies."

In February 2000, Oxfam announced that it would leave the EFA Forum Steering Committee in protest of its failure to organise an effective EFA effort with concrete targets and commitments, a new kind of international financial mechanism for delivering educational assistance, and a better organised and more democratic EFA secretariat. Just before the Dakar meeting, a clear, nine-point platform was adopted and widely circulated among campaign members, which they planned to use as the basis for lobbying at the Dakar declaration. Press conferences were held in Tokyo and Washington, D.G. Meetings with members of national delegations and other important actors such. as the European Union were held. Throughout the week before the Dakar conference, electronic messages were shared among Global Campaign participants as they tried to identify which high-level leaders would be attending Dakar and which delegations would meet with them in Dakar. All of these efforts took place in the face of the relative disorganisation of the World Forum organisers, who both attempted to keep a tight limit on NGO invitations to Dakar and failed to establish explicit procedures or mechanisms for the amendment of the Dakar declaration.

THE WORLD EDUCATION FORUM

At the Dakar 2000 World Education Forum was the most recent in a long line of international meetings held to discuss global educational problems and the culminating meeting of the United Nations Education for All decade. The Dakar meeting was somewhat different from the Jomtien conference, where non-governmental actors participated alongside other delegates; and where only a small, UNESCO-hosted NGO preconference was held. Dakar was also much smaller in scale than the major UN conferences of the 1990s, with fewer than 800 issued invitations and no formal United Nations oversight. Members of the conference's interagency steering committee hoped to channel NGO participation into regional preparatory conferences, and thus they kept tight control over a highly limited number of invitations to the World Forum. These were primarily given to national delegations. As a result, non-governmental participants formally invited to participate in the World Education Forum numbered only 55. Less than 300 invitations were issued to the Dakar NGO preconference.

The World Education Forum was, nonetheless, similar to many other UN conferences in that it included both an officially sponsored preconference for non-governmental actors and a series of drafting and round table meetings intended to produce a new frame work for action as well as a set of intergovernmental commitments on the theme of "education for all."

Non-governmental actors took their participation in Dakar very seriously, and they used the event as an occasion to develop their advocacy networks, as well as their repertoires for contention. Dakar, therefore, provides an important opportunity to consider the nature and extent of the "civility," "democracy," and "contention" exhibited in the new educational advocacy efforts among non-governmental organisations.

Non-governmental participation at Dakar and the kinds of non-governmental activism leading up to it suggest a growing density of transnational nongovernment activities around the theme of "education for all," indicative of the kind of civility that Anne Marie Clark, Elisabeth Friedman, and Kathryn Hochstelder describe in their account of NGO activism at other major United Nations Conferences during the 1990s.

The Dakar conference saw the participation of a slightly larger number of non-governmental actors than did the WCEFA in 1989. Continuing the shift begun at jomtien, large development and relief organisations, as well as a few non-profit consulting groups, held a disproportionate number of invitations, while members of literacy and adult education groups participated in smaller numbers and with less coherence. But the real change between the two conferences can primarily be found in the development of a highly cohesive strategy for coordination among Non-governmental participants.

Focused primarily around the leadership of the Global Campaign for Education, non-governmental actors held preconference strategy sessions, met daily for debriefings, huddled around the campaign's media table, argued over the content of their formal report to the World Education Forum, and held meetings to elect non-governmental representatives to the two key committees formed for the conference, the Declaration Drafting Committee and the Futures Committee.

Even though many points of disagreement between campaigners and non-campaigners emerged, the nine-point "Bottom Line" platform prepared by the Global Campaigners became the recognised mobilising frame for infra-NGO discussions and for general lobbying efforts. The coherence of the campaign's mobilising frank is suggested in the fact that Global Campaign members were elected for the large majority of NGO seats on the Drafting and Futures Committees. Among the NGOs participating in the campaign, Dakar saw a high degree of frame alignment and the development of widely shared understandings about the "rules of the game" each suggestive of a widening civility.

Initial efforts to limit the numbers of non-governmental organisations attending the preconference and the formal proceedings of the World Education Forum were ultimately reversed in a last-minute decision by the UNESCO director general on the eve of the first day of the forum. At the forum itself, non-governmental actors were also integrated in various ways into the conference proceedings: they read a statement of their demands at the opening of the forum, addressed several of the plenary sessions, elected a total of 10 representatives to the Steering and Futures Committees, and had a plenary and strategy session devoted to the sole issue of future EFA; participation with civil society. Southern NGOs were invited to special meetings with national delegates from Britain and the Netherlands. Speeches by officials from intergovernmental organisations all governments formally endorsed the Global Campaign and recognised a new role for what was commonly referred to as "civil society" in achieving education for all.

Official recognition of the Global Campaign was carried further when several high level officials held individual meetings with the campaigners. The character of this civility, however, varied. Among intergovernmental bodies, for example, the World Bank showed the strongest interest in working with campaigners. Unesco, on the other hand, did not formally endorse the campaign or hold a separate meeting with the campaigners, at least partly because its EFA secretariat was criticised by many of the participating non-governmental organisations.

All of these factors suggest a more formalised recognition of non-governmental actors at Dakar than at Jomtien, a new acceptance of their role as policy level interlocutors, and new degrees of coordination and coalition building among NGOs themselves. Of course this new civility was not "complete," and below we discuss some of the rivalries and uncivil behaviour which did occur. Potential threats to the campaign's contributions to global civility can be seen in competition among campaign sponsors and the possibility of serious disputes over their various visions of education. For example, there would seem to be a likely tension between Action Aid's emphasis on local community control of education and the assumption by Education International and its teachers unions that educational decision making is properly concentrated at the national level.

The patterns of civility initiated by the campaign at Dakar are continuing to widen. In Dakar, both non-governmental participants and some officials were quick to criticise the dominant role played by the Global Campaign at the conference, pointing out in particular that the campaign is led by a few Northern-based organisations, several with limited experience in the field of education and with less than altruistic motives. Some Southern NGO participants, as well as members of the Global Campaign itself, questioned whether this dominance had led to too great a campaign focus on Northern governments and international organisations at the expense of building self-sufficient Southern coalitions. Reflecting this, Southern organisations voiced less satisfaction than others about the accomplishments of the campaigners at Dakar, because these did not include serious targets for Southern government expenditure on education.

Leaders from Save the Children Alliance, Care, and World Vision faulted the campaign's overemphasis on resource mobilisation and its narrow definition of schooling. Others regretted the loss of real discussion about education-specific matters and criticised the campaigners for importing a slick lobbying machinery into the EFA process.

Dakar followed a common UN model for international meetings that is structured around the goal of achieving consensus among governmental delegations and that is only gradually developing a common approach to the integration of non-governmental actors in the process. At Dakar, this model was evidenced in efforts to control NGO invitations and in the absence of transparent and preestablished processes for amending the declaration. The official intergovernmental community provided no direct funding for NGO participation, and official organisers felt very limited responsibility for ensuring that a wide, or representative, sample of NGOs participated. In this context, what happened at Dakar is not surprising the loudest voices among the non-governmental participants became recognised as the common voice for civil society at the conference.

The issue ofNGO participation was so openly debated might be seen as an indication that a certain criterion of democratic practice was achieved at Dakar. However, the overall pattern of relationships among NGOs at Dakar tended to mimic the structure of center-periphery relations in the world system, in which Northern actors play leadership and coordination roles. Furthermore, NGO criticisms of the EFA structure and their efforts to formalise their role in future EFA activities seem to have been sidetracked. According to the July 2000 newsletter of ActionAid's Elimu Campaign,

> "no concrete alterative to existing EFA structures was agreed . . . UNESCO Director Generaoool Matsuura made a change to the Framework after it had been adopted by the plenary, giving a negative message as to Unesco's intentions to become more transparent and accountable . . . . No explicit steps were proposed to increase coordination and cooperation by the international community."

Ultimately the test of democracy lies in the realisation of NGO commitments to collaborate with a broader range of partners and to engage Southern and smaller NGOs in educational advocacy. Even if this should occur, however, careful empirical study will be needed to ascertain whether a greater representation of ideas from the grassroots occurs. Increased levels of interaction might also cause rising levels, of disagreement and competition in ways that will test the formal commitment to "democratising" relationships among actors, or it could produce a top-down socialisation of new and weaker partners in which authentic participation is lost.

REFERENCES

Connie McNeely and Yun-Kyung Cha, "Worldwide Education Convergence through International Organisations: Avenues for Research", *Education Policy Analysis Archives*, 2, n. 14, (1994).

Global Campaign for Education, *The Global Action Plan for Education*, Brussels: Global Campaign for Education/ Education International, 2000.

International Consultation of NGOs, *NGO Declaration on Education For All*, (Dakar: International Consultation on Education or all 2000), p.4.

Miriam Henry, Bob, Lingard, Fazal Rizvi, and Sandra Taylor, *The OECD, Globalisation and Eduction Policy*, Oxford: Pergamon, 2000.

Philips Jones, "UNESCO and the Political Global Literacy", *Comparative Education Review*, 34, no. 1, 1988.

Appendix

Resolutions Adopted by the Third World Congress of Education International Meeting in Jomeitin (Thailand) from 25 to 29 July, 2001

Meeting in Jomtien (Thailand) in July, 2001

EDUCATING IN A GLOBAL ECONOMY

Preamble

1. Education is the key to participation in the global economy of the 21st century, based on technological revolutions in communications and transfer of information, as well as major changes in production, transport and distribution, and the economic value of knowledge. This global economy is based upon levels of mobility unprecedented in human history— mobility of information, of finance, of goods and services, and of people, but also mobility of disease, of crime, of arms and instruments of repression. Extremes of wealth and poverty within and among countries are greater than ever. In this new era with its opportunities and threats, each of the principal aims of Education International is more relevant than ever in seeking to build societies that are fair and just for all their citizens, that respect universal values of democracy and human rights, and whose development—social as well as economic—will be equitable and sustainable. In every country, this global

economy seeks to permanently reduce the labour cost, and questions the right to education, and to qualification.

The development of quality higher education systems in developing countries (alongside the expansion of primary, secondary and vocational education) is an essential precondition for the training of the specialists needed for economic and social development, as well as for capacity-building within the education sector as a whole;

2. Education has always reflected and been influenced by changes in economy and society, while at the same time acting upon those changes. The relationship between education, economy and society is interactive. At a time of rapid and even fundamental changes in economy and society, there are great new challenges for education:

   — achieving Education for All;
   — making life-long learning a reality for all;
   — reaffirming the values of education in relation to personal development, the world of work and the rights and responsibilities of citizenship in democratic societies;
   — rethinking educational content and methods, taking into account the potential and the consequences of new technologies;
   — recruiting enough qualified people to work in the education sector;
   — defining the key role of the teacher as a specialist in the provision and management of learning opportunities;
   — interacting with a broader spectrum of partners, parents and local communities, trade unions and enterprises, and non-governmental organisations;

3. There are also threats to education arising out of the global economy:

— commercialisation of educational services, with consequent risks of inequity, discrimination and deepening of the digital divide;
— non-respect for diversity of culture, traditions and languages;
— introduction, under the guise of 'reform', of a 'culture of enterprise' based on self-interest, with the consequent risk of undermining the ethical values of education and of the teaching profession;
— decreasing attention to the values underlying democracy, and increasing attention to the values of competition and the market;
— short-sighted solutions to the new challenges, such as hiring unqualified people or draining teachers from the south towards the north;
— changes in the role of the State, with more emphasis on regulation and less on guarantees of equity and non-discrimination;

4. Huge public funds are being released to encourage the development of on-line education, and the promise of an education via new technologies is being used as an excuse to deny legitimate claims regarding the building or the upgrading of schools and the recruitment of new teachers and personnel of all categories.

   More and more students are deprived of their right to study, as they are compelled to follow electronic courses and watch video-conferences instead of following regular courses. University institutions are trying to seize teachers' intellectual property rights and plan to sell their courses to other universities, to business and to individual buyers. This leads to the privatisation of schools and to the emergence of specialised firms;

The Third World Congress of Education International, meeting in Jomtien, Thailand, from 25 to 29 July, 2001:

Calls on all Governments:

— *to draw up* national action plans by December 2002 for Education For All, using transparent and democratic processes based on the development and improvement of a public education service, involving the various partners, particularly education unions, parents, students and NGOs active in the education sector;

— *ratify and implement* the ILO Convention adopted in June 1999 forbidding the worst forms of child labour, for the purpose of bringing a definitive end to all forms of exploitation of children;

— *endeavour* to concretely implement the decisions of the Jomtien and Dakar conferences on Education For All;

— *to establish* consultative processes with partners in educational reform;

— *to take steps*, in close consultation with education unions, for the recruitment of sufficient qualified teachers and other educational personnel;

— *to enter* into negotiations with education unions in order to upgrade the status of the teaching profession;

— *to take* the necessary political decisions to ensure adequate funding of education at all levels, with a minimum allocation of 6 percent of Gross National Product (GNP);

— *to establish* a tax on financial transactions (Tobin tax) in order to fight against financial speculation and instability while finding new funds for the education systems in developing countries;

Calls on member countries of the OECD:

— *to implement* the proposals of the G8 Summits and complete them in order to obtain the writing off of the debt of the least developed countries, on the understanding that resources so saved will be re-allocated by those countries to education and health;

— *to raise* levels of official development assistance to 0.7 percent of GNP, and to give priority to assistance in achieving the goals of the education for all campaign, as well as basic health measures for all families;

— *to give* special attention to cooperative teacher education programs in developing countries, and to respect the interests of those countries when recruiting teachers;

Calls on the United Nations, its specialised agencies and programs , and other intergovernmental agencies:

— *to coordinate* their efforts towards achievement of the goals of the Declaration of Dakar - Education For All before the year 2015;

— *to take* advantage of the World Summit on Sustainable Development (Rio + 10, Johannesburg 2002) to emphasise basic education as the main tool for confronting worldwide problems such as environmental degradation, demographic growth and "consumerist" waste;

— *to act* in order to take, as quickly as possible, within the Kyoto protocol framework, concrete and constraining measures submitted to effective monitoring mechanisms;

— *to mobilise* the efforts of the international community so as to raise the resources necessary for the attainment of these goals;

— *to respect*, throughout the UN systems and other intergovernmental agencies, the ILO Declaration on Fundamental Principles and Rights at Work;

— *to work* with the trade union movement, business and organisations of civil society on issues arising from the erosion of national tax bases and new approaches to financing global needs in a global economy;

— *to give* priority to balanced investment in all levels of education without resort to redistribution of funds from one educational sector to another;

Congress recommends that EI and its member organisations:

— *maintain* the campaign for quality public education for all, in cooperation with its non-governmental and inter-governmental partners, and the campaign against child labour;

— *take* all the initiatives at the national, regional and international levels to defend and improve the public education system, thereby guaranteeing the pedagogical freedom of the teacher according to the 1966 UNESCO/ILO Recommendation and the rights of the young and adults to a basic and lifelong quality education, and that they be interlocutors recognised by the political leadership in the field of education;

— *advocate* through interventions to intergovernmental agencies and national governments, and campaigns directed at public opinion, a concept of education based on quality provision for all by qualified and motivated educators, and the personal development of free men and women able to contribute to society, not merely units of production;

— *oppose* in principle the commodification of education and research services by the WTO and the General Agreement on Trade in Services (GATS) and monitor closely any moves to apply the GATS to education and research services and mobilise against such moves in appropriate ways, including campaigns directed at public opinion;

— *give* particular attention to the issue of teacher recruitment and related issues of the status of the teaching profession;

— *share* research and information on conditions and trends in education and teaching;

— *undertake* an analysis of the impact of the global economy on copyright and related issues of intellectual property affecting teachers, as well as standards of educational materials, including educational software, and respect for cultural diversity;

— *promote* continuing solidarity among the member organisations of Education International, through development and emergency assistance, mobilisation against violations of human and trade union rights, and the extension of information and communication technology;

— *give* high priority to enhancing the activism of member organisations to enable them to respond to the threats to public education posed by neo-liberal economic and education policies being pursued by global institutions such as the World Bank, IMF and WTO. New programs are urgently needed for development with human and labour rights and the public provision of high quality community services such as education.

— *develop* the key role which EI can play in assisting member organisations to campaign more effectively through activities which educate and mobilise members and which support them in building alliances with NGOs and other community movements which share the objectives of EI;

— *focus* attention on the key demand to exclude education and other basic social services from agreements which national governments may reach in the framework of the General Agreement on Trade in Services (GATS), or bilateral and regional trade agreements.

PARTNERSHIP TO ACHIEVE EDUCATION FOR ALL

The Third World Congress of Education International, meeting in Jomtien, Thailand, from 25 to 29 July, 2001:

Notes that:

1. Over 115 million primary-school-age children do not attend school and large numbers of children drop out before they have reached grade 5;

2. Of the 882 million illiterates in the world, 63.7 per cent are women;
3. More than two thirds of the governments in the world allocate less than the minimum of 6 per cent of their Gross National Product (GNP) to education as recommended by the Delors Commission;
4. The majority of industrialised countries do not allocate 0.7 per cent of their GNP to development as recommended by the UN General Assembly, and only a small part of the funds provided for development is allocated to basic education;
5. The ambitions and objectives determined by world organizations and forums are constantly revised downwards, and they are not respected;

Believes that:

6. All governments have a responsibility to fulfil their human rights obligation to provide, free and compulsory basic education of good quality for all children, especially girls, youth, immigrants, indigenous students, children with special needs or in difficult circumstances and those belonging to ethnic minorities, in accordance with the commitment made in the Dakar Framework for Action by 2015. In today's world, the mission of quality public schooling is not limited to the basic years of education, but includes secondary school and the acquisition of vocational qualifications;
7. It is not sufficient to improve enrolment figures without considering the quality of education;
8. Partnership is a key concept for the achievement of education for all. The objective of the different parties must be the common interest. Proposals and activities must be implemented respecting the responsibilities of the different partners, and financing must preserve the public character of education;

Recommends that:

9. Teacher trade unions approach ministries of education and form partnerships where possible, with the shared objective of achieving education for all;
10. The ministries put in place a mechanism for information, consultations and negotiations aimed at improving teachers' salaries and working conditions, the resources, learning materials and equipment in schools, teacher education and the training of educational personnel;
11. Teacher unions take initiatives which will support improvements in the quality of education;
12. Schools be based on democratic participation, and accountability to civil society, a partnership to elaborate new ways of co-operation between school and parents, a partnership between schools, and trade unions and different sectors of the community, and a shared commitment to combat child labour;
13. Without putting into question the priority role of public formal education, new forms of cooperation and broad national alliances be sought, particularly with NGOs, in order to develop complementary forms of education in the context of the objectives of education for all;
14. A universal commitment to education for all must include reforms of International Monetary Fund and World Bank structural adjustment policies; a programme for debt cancellation; increased allocations to free public education at all levels in the development co-operation budgets of the industrialised countries; and further examination of the possibilities for developing international agreements on investment, financial transactions and taxation that will prevent situations where countries are not able to levy or collect the taxes needed to improve education systems;
15. Teacher unions, other unions and trade union centres form alliances around shared objectives to achieve education for all;

EI should:

16. Prepare a detailed plan of action as part of the Global Campaign for Education in co-operation with other organisations, to pressure governments to meet their obligation to provide free public quality education for all.

EDUCATION AND NEW TECHNOLOGY

The Third World Congress of Education International, meeting in Jomtien, Thailand, from 25 to 29 July, 2001:

1. *Considers* that the use of new information and communication technologies (ICT) in education and training will develop further, as is already the case in most other professional sectors;
2. *Considers* that their use may create opportunities for more widespread and diversified access to knowledge, but will pose at the same time major challenges for education personnel and their unions. ICT must be the means of improving education and strenghthening union rights by facilitating access to information, and democracy;
3. *Notes* that currently, the use of new information and communication technologies (ICT) in traditional systems of education and training, or outside these systems, generates inequality in terms of access, not only between industrialised and developing countries, but also between the privileged and the disadvantaged in all countries;
4. *Stresses* that it is in the nature of the trade union movement to take these challenges into consideration and to define appropriate strategies so that new information and communication technologies (ICT) become an instrument of democratisation providing access to "quality public education for all". Teachers must keep the key role in the learning processwhich will consist in knowledge and education for citizenship. This new

learning needs a development of research in education to explore and analyse the different pedagogical ways of using ICT. Teachers must be associated with this research so they can take advantage of its results;

5. *Stresses* that the virtual marketing and export of education, particularly at the level of higher education, has resulted in the opening of a huge market to ambitious investors taking advantage of the current political and economic environment;
6. *Stresses* that the huge financial stakes inherent in the commercialisation of knowledge pose a problem of intellectual property rights and of the qualitative design, production and dissemination of software, along with the risk of the existence of e-learning monopolies to the detriment of the cultural diversity, conservation of ethnic identity, values and history of our societies;
7. *Stresses* that the increasingly substantial and diversified supply of courses on the Internet raises the question of their quality and of the accreditation of diplomas obtained by those who follow these courses;
8. *Stresses* that effective digital learning will require more teachers with higher skills than ever before with subsequent implications for the provision of training and support;
9. *Stresses* that public education must play its part to give teachers professional tools (producing and circulating software) inspired by true educational and pedagogical choices.

The Third World Congress of Education International:

10. *Demands* that all teachers and education personnel receive adequate training in the use of new information and communication technologies (ICT) and that gradually all schools be connected to the Internet free of charge, with the necessary access restrictions and security

protocols (filters, firewall, etc.) to guarantee strictly pedagogical usage.The collective dimension through ICT and the role of team work of teachers must be taken in account in this training;

11. *Mandates* the Executive Board to carry on the necessary discussions with UNESCO, other relevant bodies, the OECD and governments to ensure that the design, production and dissemination of education software will be organised appropriately to guarantee the cultural diversity, conservation of ethnic identity, values and history required for international understanding;
12. *Mandates* the Executive Board to carry on the necessary discussions with UNESCO, other relevant bodies, the OECD and governments so that education will not be considered as a commodity, and intergovernmental cultural agreements and principles of UNESCO will prevail over the commercial rules of WTO in the exchanges of education services;
13. *Mandates* the Executive Board to vigorously advocate the provisions and use of learning software and to pursue means of providing software at prices affordable to developing countries, and to encourage a better distribution of knowledge to all;
14. *Mandates* the Executive Board to defend the interests of education personnel with respect to working conditions, career opportunities and intellectual property rights and to develop codes of good practice on these and related issues;
15. *Mandates* the Executive Board to take the necessary action to determine the impact of technology, in particular the potential hazards to children's health and safety but also its effects on young children's learning environment;
16. *Mandates* EI and member organisations to support national and international research into the educational, social and economic impacts of technological

developments affecting education and the working conditions of teachers;

17. *Mandates* the Executive Board to undertake the necessary action so that public authorities can take advantage of the technological revolution to guarantee the fair distribution of information and knowledge, and to carry on the necessary consciousness-raising activities with civil society organisations on the great opportunities presented by this revolution but also on the challenges it poses to "quality public education for all" in the Third Millenium.

GLOBALISATION AND THE RIGHT [illegible] CONDIITONS OF TEACHERS [illegible] PERSONNEL

The Third World Congress of Education International, meeting in Jomtien, Thailand, from 25 to 29 July, 2001:

1. *Recognising* the reality of globalisation brings both challenges and opportunities but that in terms of impact current patterns of globalisation, driven by powerful economic forces, governments and international institutions, threaten the working conditions of education personnel by introducing a neo-liberal model to dismantle the welfare state and move to a competitive state by privatising education;
2. *Concerned* at attempts to change education from a human right provided through public service for the collective good to a commodity to be acquired for private advantage;
3. *Recognising* that pressure is required at the national and international levels to oppose the inclusion of education in the General Agreement of Trade in Services (GATS) and to ensure that the policies of the World Trade Organisation(WTO), the World Bank and the International Monetary Fund (IMF) acknowledge public education as a human right;

4. *Noting* that the 2001 report of the Committee of Experts on the application of the ILO/UNESCO Recommendation on the Status of Teachers (CEART) states There has been a tremendous expansion of education against a background of pauperisation of teaching and learning conditions creating an environment unattractive to potential recruits and to teachers currently in service.
5. *Acknowledging* that demands for predictability, accountability, flexibility, and efficiency have led to new forms of management in education and have resulted in a deterioration of working conditions and relationships in education;

S AND EMPLOYMENT
AND EDUCATION

tional ... y for patterns of globalisation that is ... based, people-oriented and based on mutual help and solidarity;

7. *Concerned* at the levels of stress and burnout in education workers;
8. Congress recommends that EI and its member organisations shall;
   a) Extend union membership to include all education personnel if appropriate;
   b) Organise education personnel on part-time and temporary contracts as well as those working in the non-formal education system if appropriate;
   c) Demand the trade union rights guaranteed in international human rights instruments for all education personnel;
   d) Promote and pilot new patterns of organisation in education to provide more job satisfaction through empowerment of education personnel;
   e) Negotiate for the support services necessary to provide quality education;
   f) Shape the use of new technology as a tool to help with the learning process to educate people;

g) Negotiate the right to and the terms for participation in decision making at all levels of education;

h) Explore collegial approaches to team work that give team members different responsibilities;

i) Negotiate terms of employment that reward those who choose to continue working directly with students instead of opting for management positions;

j) Challenge the time-consuming bureaucratic tasks that are required of educators;

k) Negotiate time for preparation, planning and team consultation for staff;

l) Negotiate salaries, entitlements and conditions of work commensurate with those with similar qualifications and responsibilities in other sectors and that are sufficient to fully accomplish their professional responsibilities;

m) Ensure quality training programmes, both initial and in-service, are available to all education personnel at times that make it possible for all education personnel to take advantage of the programmes.

n) Lower the number of students per class to improve the success of students;

o) Improve the working environment of education personnel through provision of functional institutions with modern equipment and improved, relevant pedagogical materials;

p) Make teaching a more attractive profession by reversing the trend to lower the status and recognise the increasing difficulty of the work:

q) Support teacher exchange among countries but avoid the brain drain of qualified teachers by wealthier countries;

r) Promote equality of rights between men and women, particularly concerning salary, working conditions and entitlements;

s) Oppose the fragmentation and disintegration of formal collective bargaining and the resulting variation in conditions of service;

t) Demand the establishment of appropriate collective bargaining and dispute resolution mechanisms for all education employees.

GENDER PERSPECTIVE IN DEVELOPMENT COOPERATION

The Third World Congress of Education International, meeting in Jomtien, Thailand, from 25 to 29 July, 2001:

1. *Recalls* that the constitution commits EI "to combat all forms of racism and of bias or discrimination in education and society due to gender, marital status, sexual orientation, age, religion, political opinion, social or economic status or national or ethnic origin";
2. *Recognises* EI's commitment to promoting the equality of men and women, of boys and girls in society, in education and in the trade union movement and supports the efforts of EI in reinforcing the participation of women in EI's activities through, among other strategies, the use of quotas for women's participation;
3. *Notes* that while the majority of members of EI member organizations are women, fewer women than men hold positions of responsibility in teacher unions;
4. *Recognises* that the economic conditions of women are lower than those of men, and that structural adjustment policies applied through neoliberalism have worsened the status of women, who are today more vulnerable;
5. *Recognises* also that women do not truly benefit from the same opportunities as men in any part of the world and that they continue to struggle for equality, respect, dignity, development and peace, equity in healthcare, social security, well-being needed to recover self-esteem;

6. *Recalls* the UNICEF report on the State of the World's Children, 1999 and the Beijing Platform highlight the lack of educational opportunities for women and girls;
7. *Notes* that the Second World Congress of Education International determined that EI and member organizations shall establish a work programme in each region to, among other things, ensure that a gender analysis is an integral part of all research and analysis done by EI .
8. *Recalls* the EI development cooperation policy adopted by the 2nd World Congress which notes that development cooperation draws on the concepts of independence, promotion of democracy, of quality public education services for all, increasing autonomy, gender equity, sustainable development, long-term planning and mutual respect;
9. *Recognises* the importance of the current EI and member organisations' development cooperation programmes in increasing the participation of women in education unions and in their employment as educators;
10. *Recognises* that while development projects improve conditions and leadership opportunities for women in the teacher unions and education communities, more programmes are needed to ensure effective gender equality over the long term;
11. *Recognises* further that successful gender projects and other projects that are oriented towards the improvement of women's rights in development cooperation enable women to share among themselves but also enable them to represent their interests in the mainstream of the union, the community and their country;
12. *Recognises* the extreme importance of promoting sustainability of women's programmes;
13. *Acknowledges* that in regard to gender projects in development cooperation, training for the union leadership as well as the grassroots is required in order to

achieve sustainability and to mainstream not marginalised women's issues;

14. The Congress determines that EI and its member organizations must, in monitoring the work on gender and development cooperation, commit to:

— Support the continuing need for projects and programmes on gender issues, targeted at women and other projects and programmes, aimed at improving the rights and the role of women, and not only targeted at them;

— Lobby towards governments in order to improve the economic, social and educational conditions of women and girls;

— Provide gender awareness training and training on other issues of concern to women for union leaders, union staff and women at continental, national, regional and local levels and contribute to the increasing participation of women in positions of responsibility by looking for means to reconcile trade union responsibilities and family life;

— Develop a gender analysis instrument to assess the overall impact of proposed programmes and projects and ensure that such analysis is undertaken for all development cooperation project proposals;

— Incorporate an analysis of the current situation of the union to provide a basis for evaluation of the project outcomes, in particular, sustainability;

— Include indicators of quality and sustainability as well as quantifying measures in project evaluation and measures of project effectiveness;

— Carry on the campaigns for full protection of maternity, breast-feeding, and care of pre-school children;

— Include on the negotiation agendas of EI member organisations, issues of concern specifically to women;

— Stimulate the development of curricula that promote non sexist education;
— Dedicate larger ressources to the development of projects for women;
— Strengthen and consolidate the networks of women educators per region, and move on with regional plans to ensure that experiences are shared, both in instances where gender and development has made progress and where it is only just starting to boost initiatives in each organisation.

TRANSNATIONAL PROVISON OF HIGHER EDUCATION

The Third World Congress of Education International meeting in Jomtien, Thailand, from 25 to 29 July 2001:

A. Notes:

1. The growth of provision of higher education across national borders, utilizing mainly internet-based technologies, by traditional universities as well as by solely on-line providers;
2. The participation by a number of universities in joint ventures with for-profit corporations and other higher education institutions for the provision of higher education relying on internet-based materials and technologies;
3. Growing concern among higher education personnel, students and the communities they work with regarding the lack of clear and unambiguous information available in relation to governance structures, quality assurance and accreditation procedures, and employment practices within such joint ventures;

B. Believes that:

4. Predominantly on-line higher education providers should be subject to rigorous quality assurance mechanisms to

ensure a curriculum developed, taught and under academic control of faculty who have tenure and academic freedom , and this principle should be reflected in international accreditation procedures;

5. It is the responsibility of national governments, international organisations and higher education providers to ensure that the expansion of web-based transnational higher education provision is informed by public interest concerns and objectives, and not solely by profit motives or market forces;

Accordingly, EI should:

6. Encourage higher education trade unions to develop strategies for actively organising members across national boundaries to ensure that the employment rights of personnel employed by transnational providers are protected;
7. In conjunction with higher education unions that have already undertaken significant work in this area, develop guidelines for best practice in relation to the provision of transnational education and actively pursue their endorsement and implementation by UNESCO, the ILO, the World Trade Organisation and international accreditation bodies, such implementation to be pursed in conjonction with EI.

   Such guidelines should address, among other issues, governance structures, quality assurance, the importance of culturally relevant content and modes of delivery, accreditation, intellectual property management and academic freedom.

STATUS OF HIGHER EDUCATION PERSONNEL

The Third World Congress of Education International, meeting in Jomtien, Thailand, from 25 to 29 July, 2001:

A. Education International affirms:

1. The rights and freedoms of higher education teaching personnel as defined in the UNESCO Recommendation concerning the Status of Higher Education Teaching Personnel;
2. The important role all higher education personnel play in contributing, through their work, to the dissemination of knowledge, the furthering of social and economic goals, and the pursuit of innovation and new ideas;
3. The responsibility of personnel working in higher education institutions to work towards making the benefits of higher education available to all;

B. However, Education International notes:

4. An erosion in academic freedom, particularly in terms of academics' right to engage in teaching, research and scholarship without interference, and their responsibility to promote the work of the university as critic and conscience of society;

C. Education International believes that this is the product of a number of converging factors, including:

5. The increasing reliance of universities around the world on corporate and other forms of private funding;
6. The erosion of tenure and other forms of oNGOing employment;
7. The failure of national governments to observe and give substance to the rights and freedoms of higher education personnel as endorsed in the UNESCO Recommandation;
8. The absence to date of a report from the Director General on the world situation with regard to academic freedom, as required by Article 75 of the UNESCO Recommandation;

D. Therefore, Education International should:

9. Continue to engage in discussions with the ILO as to how the rights and freedoms expressed in the UNESCO

Recommandation concerning the Status of Higher Education Teaching Personnel might be promoted and protected in international agreements, and to protect the rights and freedoms of all higher education personnel;

10. Organise a conference involving representatives of EI affiliates, national governments, and NGO's (including UNESCO) to review implementation of the document (including the publication of reports on academic freedom from Member States) and formulate a strategy to ensure that it has wider efficacy.

SITUATION OF COLOMBIAN EDUCATORS

The Third World Congress of Education International, meeting in Jomtien, Thailand, from 25 to 29 July, 2001:

1. Recalls that, as set out in Article 2(b) of the Constitution of Education International, one of the organisation's objectives is to promote peace, democracy, social justice and equality among all peoples and nations, and to promote the implementation of the Universal Declaration of Human Rights through the development of education and the collective strength of teachers and education workers;
2. Notes the Vienna Declaration and the Action Programme adopted following the UN Conference on Human Rights, which state that human rights and fundamental civil liberties are inherent in all human beings and that protecting and promoting these rights and freedoms is the first responsibility of governments;
3. Highlights and denounces the fact that since 1987 Colombian educators have been subjected to all manner of political persecution and attacks against their trade unions, and have been the victims of numerous "disappearances" and murders; more specifically, that to date 433 teachers have been murdered or have

disappeared and more than 1,000 have had to leave their homes under threat of death, and that in the first few months of 2001 seven of our colleagues have already fallen victim to the wave of violence unleashed against teachers in Colombia;

4. Denounces and rejects the repressive policies—aimed at quashing social protest—which the Colombian government under the leadership of the President of the Republic, Andrés Pastrana AraNGO, has been implementing against Colombian workers in general and teachers in particular;

In view of the above, the Congress recommends that Education International and its member organisations:

5. Uphold the human rights of all teachers;
6. Convey to Colombia's leaders their condemnation of the wave of persecution and assassinations;
7. Urge the Colombian government to condemn and reject the persecution and murder of Colombian educators and to take effective measures to guarantee the free exercise of the teaching profession and of trade union activity.

SITUATION IN THE FORMER YUGOSLOVIAN REPUBLIC OF MACEDONA

The Third World Congress of Education International, meeting in Jomtien, Thailand, from 25 to 29 July, 2001:

1. Cannot condone demands for political rights through the use of force and terror. Therefore, the Congress strongly supports the legal authorities of FYR Macedonia in their attempt at settling all open issues through dialogue. In this respect, the Congress also urges international institutions, such as the UN, the Council of Europe, the EU and NATO, to continue giving the necessary support to

the democratically elected leadership of FYR Macedonia so that it can find a quick solution to the current crisis;

2. Bearing in mind that these unwanted events have an extremely negative influence on the development of FYR Macedonia, particularly on the development of and reforms in the education sector and the living conditions of workers and all citizens, pledges that the Education International will undertake all necessary measures and activities, including calling upon international financial organisations and EI affiliates worldwide to extend material and financial assistance and other forms of benefits to their colleagues in FYR Macedonia so that they can overcome the current crisis more quickly and easily;
3. Calls on the Macedonian government to recognise and accept the rights of indigenous Albanian Macedonians to learn in their mother tongue in schools and to participate in public administration in Macedonia;
4. Encourages the EI affiliate in the country to continue its activities before the competent state bodies for re-establishing normal conditions for continuation of education in all the schools located in the affected regions.

RESOULTION ON TRAFFLICKING IN WOMEN GIRLS AND BOYS

The Third World Congress of Education International, meeting in Jomtien, Thailand, from 25 to 29 July, 2001:

1. *Noting* that trafficking in women and girls has become one of the fastest growing criminal enterprises in the world affecting all nations;
2. *Further* noting that an estimated two million women and girls are trafficked annually around the world, for the purpose of forced labor, domestic servitude or sexual exploitation;

3. *Concerned* that traffickers in women and girls, like narcotic traffickers, operate boldly across international borders, using modern means of communication and trade to lure victims with false promises as well as using force, deception, and coercion to enslave victims;
4. *Outraged* that well-established criminal organizations traffic in women, girls and boys capitalising on increased poverty, rising unemployment and disintegrating social networks in developing countries;
5. *Noting* that Europe, North America, the Gulf States, India and Asia are important destination points for trafficking victims;
6. *Appalled* that increasingly very young children are being trafficked because of fear of contracting HIV/AIDS;

The Third World Congress of Education International calls on governments to:

7. *combat* trafficking in women, girls and boys through public awareness campaigns that provide information on the means traffickers use to lure young women, girls and boys who are then forced into prostitution;
8. *ensure* that sufficient funds are available to provide law enforcement agencies with the means necessary to combat trafficking and to prosecute traffickers to the full extent of the law;
9. *enact* "long reach laws' that will allow for the trial in the country of origin of any person charged with soliciting an underage child;
10. *treat* women, girls and boys who are victims of trafficking as victims and to provide support, counselling and training to them to be able to leave prostitution and to support themselves;
11. *provide* free compulsory education for children and to provide the necessary transitional services for

children to be able to attend school and support themselves.

RESOULION ON BURMA

The Third World Congress of Education International, meeting in Jomtien, Thailand, from 25 to 29 July, 2001:

1. *Notes* with concern the systematic and increasingly severe violations of civil, political, economic, social and cultural rights in Burma;
2. *Condemns* the military government for not convening the National Convention since 1996 in order to implement its commitment to the international community to take the steps necessary to recognise the democratically elected government headed by Aung San Suu Kyi;
3. *Notes* the increased repression of any form of public political activity along with the systematic surveillance of those exercising their rights to freedom of thought, expression, assembly and association as well as the harassment of their families;
4. *Deplores* the fact that multinational companies support dictatorship in Burma through their activities in the country;
5. *Deplores* the continued extra-judicial, summary and arbitrary executions, torture and abuse of women and children by government agents;
6. *Further deplores* the imposition of oppressive measures directed at ethnic and religious minorities;
7. *Condemns* the violations of human rights including systematic programmes of forced relocation directed against ethnic minorities as well as the use of forced labour, trafficking, sexual violence and exploitation, committed by military personnel and especially directed at women who are returning refugees, the internally displaced, members of ethnic minorities or members of

the political opposition;

8. *Equally condemns* the severe restrictions on all forms of domestic media and international publications;
9. *Deeply concerned* at violations of the rights of children and youth including lack of access to schools and the closure for over three years of most higher education institutions;

The Third World Congress of Education International:

10. *Calls* on the United Nations to insist that the military government of Burma implement the recommendations of the UN Special Rapporteur on Burma, as well as encouraging UN Member States to implement the resolution on Burma adopted by the 2001 ILO General Conference;
11. *Requests* the Economic and Social Council of the United Nations to hold a special session to outline the steps to be taken to get the military government of Burma to conform to UN resolutions;
12. *Urges* EI member organisations to lobby their government and the WTO to insist that WTO procedures cannot be used to stop countries wishing to impose sanctions on Burma because of its human rights violations;
13. *Urges* EI member organisations to ask their governments to support activities that will assist Burmese refugees and in particular to provide opportunities for education for Burmese students;
14. *Encourages* EI member organisations to include programmes to assist the refugees on the Thai/ Burmese border in the provision of education programmes;
15. *Calls* on EI member organisations to undertake a programme at the national level to raise awareness of the plight of Burmese citizens and to support initiatives, including unrestricted communication and access to

Aung San Suu Kyi and other leaders of the National League for Democracy, to ensure respect for the ILO Convention on Forced Labour, UN Convention on the Rights of the Child and other human rights instruments.

SITUATION IN NEPAL

The Third World Congress of Education International, meeting in Jomtien, Thailand, from 25 to 29 July, 2001:

1. *Expresses* solidarity with the affiliated trade unions (NNTA and NTA) and the Nepalese people following the assassination of the royal family;
2. *Regrets* having been forced to transfer the venue of the present World Congress from Kathmandu to Jomtien for obvious security reasons, which continue to apply, and having thus missed the opportunity of showing to the global community of trade union educators the economic, social and cultural reality of a country seeking development;
3. *Stresses* that contemporary history shows that development always goes hand in hand with the democratic and transparent functioning of governmental institutions, to which the population and democratic organisations of civil society must adhere, and that guerilla practices most often delay any possibility of development, owing to the hesitations of potential investors, amongst others;
4. *Recognises* the struggle against poverty which prevents many Nepalese children from participating in formal schooling;

The Third Education International World Congress:

5. *Requests* that the Nepalese government and the organisations part of or supporting the guerilla find a

political solution to the present conflict, so that the country returns to peace and stability, which are prerequisites to any development;

6. *Requests* that NNTA and NTA promote an education in favour of civil peace and democracy in a context of social justice. Only political and democratic stability can protect the rights of Nepalese teachers including their personal safety, ensure freedom for Nepalese communities, improve the economic conditions for the citizens of Nepal and promote unity and social justice;
7. *Requests* the Executive Board to take the appropriate initiatives by the next Congress, in collaboration with the Nepalese authorities, international institutions and organisations of the Nepalese society, to promote education for all and to campaign against illiteracy in the framework of the Global Campaign for Education, in order to help reduce poverty.

RESOLUTION ON THE SITUATION IN AFGHANISTAN

The Third World Congress of Education International, meeting in Jomtien, Thailand, from 25 to 29 July, 2001:

1. *Whereas*, in 1996, after nearly 20 years of invasion, internal strife and civil war, the political and military force known as the Taliban took control of the government of Afghanistan. At the time, many Afghanis welcomed the Taliban in the hope that the new government would bring stability, security and economic relief to Afghanistan. However, in the intervening years the Taliban has failed to meet these aspirations and has established an authoritarian state that has deprived Afghans of their basic human rights;
2. *Whereas*, the 56th session of the year 2000 United Nations Commission on Human Rights "condemned the

widespread violations and abuses of human rights and humanitarian law and the continuing grave violations of the human rights of women and girls, including all forms of discrimination against them;"

3. *Whereas*, human rights organizations report that the Taliban has deliberately and systematically killed thousands of people. Additionally, under Taliban edicts women in Afghanistan have been made virtual prisoners in their own homes; and girls have been prohibited from attending school;
4. *Whereas*, on May 22, 2001 the Taliban ordered Hindu men in Afghanistan to wear yellow cloth badges pinned to their shirt pockets, and Hindu and Sikh women to veil themselves in public as Muslin women are required to do;
5. *Resolved,* that the Education International most stongly condemns the continuing violations of human and political rights carried out by the Taliban movement in Afghanistan. We especially note the actions by the Taliban that have virtually eliminated any rights, including the right to education, for women and girls in Afghanistan;
6. *Resolved,* that the Education International strongly condemns the action by the Taliban to require Hindu men to wear yellow badges. This is an extreme example of racism and human rights violation reminiscent of Nazi Germany. Historically, such actions have been part of systematic actions to expel or eliminate entire categories of national minorities;
7. *Resolved,* that the Education International calls on the United Nations and other appropriate governmental and non-governmental institutions and organizations to expose all continuing violations of human rights on the part of the Taliban and to take all possible actions to end these extreme violations of human rights by the Taliban against the people of Afghanistan.

RESOLUTION ON THE SITUATION IN PALESTINE

The Third World Congress of Education International, meeting in Jomtien, Thailand, from 25 to 29 July, 2001:

1. *Notes* with concern the dangerous escalation of the Israelo-Palestinian conflict, the principal victims of which are children, owing to the non-application of the UN resolutions and to the non-respect of the peace agreements signed between the two parties;
2. *Considers* the appeals for peace launched by the international community;
3. *Acknowledges* the wish of the Israeli teacher trade union (ITU) to open a dialogue with the Palestinian trade union leaders;
4. *Acknowledges* the role played by the Palestinian teacher trade union (GUPT) to support peace and justice;
5. *Calls for*
   a) the ending of all violence and the immediate application of the ceasefire without preconditions;
   b) the end of colony settlements on Palestinian territories;
   c) the resumption of the negociations in search of a global, equitable and sustainable peace on the basis of the agreements reached and the recognition of the legitimate rights of the two people recognised by the UN;
   d) all pupils and students to be able to attend school and university safely;
6. *Decides* to send an EI delegation to investigate the conditions of teachers and students in the Palestinian territories and in Israel;
7. *Decides* to organise an international conference of the Arab teacher trade unions affiliated to EI;

8. *Decides* to continue to organise, as shortly as possible, the conference, including peace and justice, entitled Learning to Live Together.

THE REVISION OF THE DISTORTION OF HISTORY IN JAPANESE TEXTBOOKS

The Third World Congress of Education International, meeting in Jomtien, Thailand, from 25 to 29 July, 2001:

1. *Concerned* that some Japanese history textbooks for middle schools edited under the initiative of Japanese right-wing groups were authorised by the Japanese government. Such outcome would damage the friendly relations among countries of the Asia-Pacific area and, moreover, have a negative influence on history that they promote and other inappropriate contents such as the glorification of the Japanese colonial rule and history of aggression. Therefore, we wish to declare the following;
2. *Reminds* the Japanese government that these days the international trend is to reflect on one's own history of wars and violence and make efforts to create a new peaceful age, as demonstrated by Germany, for example, which has made a grave reflection of its history and given good apologies and compensations to war victims. We further urge the government to (1) immediately correct such history textbooks that glorify its wars and colonial rule while distorting the historical truth and (2) positively participate in the international trend to bring about peace;
3. *Urges* the Japanese government to faithfully implement the UNESCO Recommendations (Education for International Understanding, Cooperation, and Peace and that for Liberty of Human and Fundamental Rights. Nov 19, 1974) stating that education should contribute to respect for the fundamental liberty and human rights,

establishment of social justice, and promotion of international understanding and world peace and also objection activities against all kinds of neo-colonialism, all forms of racism and fascism, and other ideologies arousing ethnical and racial hatred;

4. *Urges* the Japanese government to alter the procedure of selecting and adopting textbooks so as to allow reflection of reasonable opinions gathered from teachers and their associations, who are the subject of education;
5. *Demands* that the Japanese government settle complications arising with associated countries and develop cooperative relationships through immediate truthful history education based on the universal values pursued by mankind.

RESOLUTION ON THE SITUATION IN ALGERIA

The Third World Congress of Education International, meeting in Jomtien, Thailand, from 25 to 29 July, 2001:

1. *Alarmed* by the serious political and social situation in Algeria where the denial of civic liberties and democratic rights has been accompanied in the last few weeks by organised violence against young people and teachers, resulting in the deaths of more than 100 people. So far the government has ignored the social, political and cultural demands claims voiced in mass demonstrations;
2. *Noting* that this dramatic situation is fuelled by the incapacity of the government of using the country's wealth in the development, education and training of young people;
3. *Urges* the Algerian authorities to:
   a) Put an end to repression, which can only aggravate the crisis;
   b) Make every effort to bring about a democratic solution based on free debate, the rule of law, respect

for cultural diversity, and the right to education and health care;

c) Enable the free exercise of basic civic liberties (freedom of association and expression and freedom to organise demonstrations);

d) Facilitate, without any restrictions, the activities of national and international human rights and trade union organisations;

4. *Urges* the international community to help Algeria overcome this serious crisis;
5. *Wishes* to express its solidarity with, and support for its member union in Algeria, the SATEF, which should be allowed to freely express its views, act and negotiate with the authorities everywhere in the country.

RESOLUTION ON VIOLENCE, EDUCATION AND THE PEACE PROCESS IN SRI LANKA

The Third World Congress of Education International, meeting in Jomtien, Thailand, from 25 to 29 July, 2001:

1. *Noting* that the international airport of Sri Lanka was been on fire on 24th July 2001, having being attacked by rebels with knowledge and skills;
2. *Further noting* that Sri Lanka has a literacy record of about 92 per cent but recalling that education for all cannot be achieved successfully without wisdom and peace, i.e what is happening to Sri Lanka today may happen to any other country;
3. *Requests* the Sri Lankan government to expedite the peace process mediated by Norway with the support of the International community especially by the United States of America, the United Kingdom and India to find out a political solution to the ethnic issue in Sri Lanka;

4. *Requests* EI to pay more attention to the subject of loving kindness to inject mindfulness and wisdom to the future humanity to live in peace and prosperity.

RESOLUTION ON THE IMPRISONMENT OF EDUCATION TRADE UNION LEADERS IN KOREA

The Third World Congress of Education International, meeting in Jomtien, Thailand, from 25 to 29 July, 2001:

1. *Noting* that in Korea, only private school owners can decide on budget matters and the settlement of accounts, although teachers' salaries and expenses related to the management of schools are paid for by the national treasury. As a result, the work of some schools has been disrupted. The Ministry of Education does not pay attention to any of these matters;
2. *Further noting* that KTU organized a mass rally and its leaders went on a hunger strike in the month of June, during which two KTU leaders were detained;
3. *Demands* the release of those two detained teachers who were arrested during the demonstration against the corrupted private schools and also urges the Korean government to revise the private school laws.

RESOLUTION ON SOLIDARITY WITH THE TEACHERS AFFECTED BY THE EARTHQUAKE IN SOUTH PERU

The Third World Congress of Education International, meeting in Jomtien, Thailand, from 25 to 29 July, 2001:

Considering:

1. That, on Saturday 23 June 2001, the villages in the South of Peru were hit by an earthquake of a magnitude of 7° on the Richter scale. The earthquake has caused the death, ruin and despair of the inhabitants of this part of the country;

2. That this fact is far worse for the villages in the centre of the country, whose road infrastructure has been seriously damaged, preventing help from being given appropriately. Dozens of villages are isolated, families have lost their houses and homes, their crops have been ruined;
3. That the teachers in the South of Peru have lost their houses, and their schools have been seriously affected;

The Third World Congress of Education International wishes to:

4. *Express* its solidarity with the Peruvian people and with the teachers in particular;
5. *Request* that all the teachers in the world join the world campaign to support the people and in particular the teachers in Peru;
6. *Seek* the immediate attention of the Peruvian Government as well as the rehabilitation of the villages affected by the earthquake.

RESOLUTION ON THE SOLIDARITY WITH SUTEP AND THE PERUVIAN PEOPLE FOR HAVING DEFEATED THE DICTATORSHIP OF FUJIMORI AND MONTESINOS

The Third World Congress of Education International, meeting in Jomtien, Thailand, from 25 to 29 July, 2001:

Considering:

1. That, since the beginning of the 1990s, Peru has been victimised by one of the dictatorships in South America, to apply the neoliberal model most unconditionally. In fact, the Fujimori regime restructured society, applied economic reforms and modified the legislation in direct favour of transnational capital, rendering the teachers, the workers, and the people defenseless and poor;

2. That, since April 1992, this regime was in power following a coup disrupting the Republican Congress, Public Authority, Judicial Authority and the means of communication, and installed with the complicity of the leaders of the armed forces a fierce dictatorship persecuting the opposition and the democratic sectors such as SUTEP;
3. That, the regime, in its intent to seize power for two or more presidential terms, changed into an officially democratic regime, but in reality became a corrupt dictatorship. The Fujimori and Montesinos criminals killed while remaining unpunished, plundered the country's resources, and overexploited its workers. And as if that was not enough, they repressed the people mercilessly, and from their position of power engaged in arms and drugs trafficking;
4. That the dictatorship had as one of its objectives the privatisation of public education and imposed the "recommendations" of the International Monetary Fund and the World Bank, which in the long run have accelerated the deterioration of public education. At this point SUTEP, representing 285,000 teachers, had to defend firmly quality public education as well as the necessity to develop a national plan on education, which would put education back on its tracks.
5. That, especially in the last two years, the main fighting strategy of the Peruvians has been the utmost unity of action to defeat the dictatorship. In this process, SUTEP has played a crucial and decisive role. At the end of 2000, the corrupt regime was thrown out by the people. Today, Vladimiro Montesinos is imprisoned, and Alberto Fujimori, the other major criminal, is protected by the Japanese Government;
6. That the actions of the dictatorship not only have affected the economy, the productive structure and the agriculture, resulting in the fact that an unprecedented

50.7 per cent of the population now lives in poverty; but the dictatorship has also institutionalised corruption, blackmail and immorality, affecting the whole society;

In conclusion, the Third Education International World Congress Wishes:

7. To express its solidarity with SUTEP and the Peruvian people in their democratic and antidictatorial fight which has defeated the dictatorship of Fujimori and Montesinos and restored the democracy in Peru;
8. To urge the elected Government to implement from 28 July of this year, the readjustment of its political economy so as to help respond to the needs of the country;
9. The respect and validation of quality public education, converting it into a state affair with the fundamental strategic aim of developing the country;
10. The just punishment of the accused Vladimir Montesinos and the just extradition judgement and conviction of Alberto Fujimori;
11. Support for and solidarity with SUTEP's fight to achieve professional, economic, social, cultural and labour rights, towards the success of a National Education Project.

RESOLUTION ON THE INTERNATIONAL LABOUR ORGANISATION, THE WORLD TRADE ORGANISATION AND THE GLOBALISATION OF THE ECONOMY

The Third World Congress of Education International, meeting in Jomtien, Thailand, from 25 to 29 July, 2001:

1. *Recognising* the dramatic increase in world trade and foreign investment and the impact on citizens resulting from the globalisation of the world economy;
2. *Noting* the intensification of the liberalisation of trade since the establishment of the World Trade Organisation;

3. *Concerned* at the impact on workers' jobs, pay, conditions of employment and the pressures to limit the bargaining strength of trade unions by powerful transnational financial institutions prepared to increase the disparity within societies by forcing down wages and worsening employment conditions;
4. *Concerned* also at the pressures on governments to privatise education, healthcare and other public services;
5. *Supporting* the expansion of trade and investment, provided that the objective is to stimulate growth, to help end world poverty, to raise the living standards of all peoples and to ensure environmentally sustainable development;
6. *Welcomes* the existence of, and recognises the need for, international economic and financial institutions. However, Congress calls upon governments, especially those constituting the G8 Group, to require these institutions to be more open and democratic in their procedures, in setting their aims and in establishing their priorities;
7. *Believes* that greater public awareness and a more informed debate would prove beneficial to all the interests concerned;
8. *Convinced* that the right of access to markets confers the responsibility to ensure that the workers' basic rights are universally respected, that the State's capacity to develop public services such as education is not impeded, that production and distribution of cultural works are especially protected and that protection of the environment is respected;
9. *Welcomes* the consensus reached at the UN World Summit for Social Development, including the specific reference to the importance of respect for the seven basic international labour standards, to make progress in the reduction of poverty and unemployment;

10. *Supports* the work done by ICFTU and ITSs to find ways to ensure observance of international labour standards within international trade agreements and notes, with appreciation, the work of TUAC on the Multilateral Agreement on Investment (MAI) while stating principled opposition to this agreement;
11. *Calls* on the World Trade Organisation to take into account the efforts of governments, trade unions, employers and international organisations like the ILO to raise standards by implementing the ILO Conventions;
12. *Urges* the WTO and the ILO to establish a joint working group on Trade and Labour Standards to examine how core labour standards can be integrated into trade agreements, to determine operating mechanisms and means of co-operation between the WTO and the ILO;
13. *Believes* that the free market model, which underpins the WTO's trade liberalisation program, is inappropriate for education;
14. Congress calls on EI and its member organisations to:

— *Work* with the ICFTU and the ITSs to encourage the governments and employers on the Working Party of the ILO Governing Body on the Social Dimensions of the Liberalisation of International Trade to enter into dialogue with the Worker's Group to consider how the procedures of the WTO can be adapted to promote the observance of core ILO Conventions;

— *Publicise* among member organisations information to raise awareness of violations of standards by companies, particularly when child labour or forced or bonded labour are involved, or where workers are refused the right to organise;

— *Promote*—through the trade unions in different parts of the world—a new approach to the processes of regional integration. We must devise new organisational strategies for Mercosur, NAFTA, the European Union, the Central American Market, the Organisation of African Unity, and the various regional organisations in Asia;

— *Oppose*, through strategically planned actions, WTO plans which result in increasing poverty, concentrating wealth in the hands of a minority, and preventing the emergence of genuine programmes for health, education and scientific and technological development, geared to creating a more responsible and caring world;

— *Promote* the creation of negotiating bodies in each country to enable the trade unions to discuss the new framework which all these changes as a whole imply for working conditions and education;

— *Encourage* member organisations and their members to support companies that respect core labour standards in the production of their products and support initiatives to promote social labelling;

— *Participate* in the trade and labour standards discussions with the ICFTU, at the ILO and through TUAC atthe OECD;

— *Focus* specific attention on encouraging EI member organisations to lobby their governments to support strengthening the mandate of the ILO to deal with countries that consistently violate the core labour standards;

— *Continue* to work to promote the inclusion of core labour standards in trade agreements;

15. Congress also calls on EI and its member organisations to campaign for education, health care, and social services generally to be excluded from the scope of the WTO's General Agreement on Trade in Services (GATS). Consistent with this objective, EI and its member organisations should:

— *Demand* full openness and transparency of GATS negotiations e.g. publication of government mandates, consultation with national and international union organisations, publication of reports and projects on trade in services discussed within the OECD and regional trade groupings;

— *Oppose* proposals to transform GATS into a comprehensive top-down agreement, thereby placing the onus on countries to secure exemptions for particular services;

— *Support* the right of national governments to regulate the provision of education, such as culturally appropriate content for courses and qualifications, the licensing of schools and universities, and the supply of tertiary places in particular discipline areas and the number of corresponding schools or faculties where viability is a consideration;

— *Collect* information on the consequences of GATS to date, and establish links with campaigns by non-government organisations concerned about the GATS;

— *Oppose* the development of new GATS disciplines that would allow for WTO dispute-panels to judge whether technical standards and licensing and qualification requirements and procedures affecting education and other social services are too 'trade-restrictive';

— *Oppose* the development of new GATS disciplines that limit the rights of national governments to determine the allocation of government subsidies to education and social service providers.

HIGHER EDUCATION AND RESEARCH POLICY

The Third World Congress of Education International meeting in Jomtien, Thailand, from 25 to 29 July 2001:

A. Affirms EI's commitment to the continuing development of higher education and research noting that:

1. Higher education institutions play a central educational, economic and employment role in society, in scientific, technological and applied research and through the production of skilled graduates (including primary and secondary teachers);
2. Strong higher education and research institutions underpin a vibrant and pluralistic civil society, and enrich social and cultural life by generating new knowledge and by continuously enhancing humanity's intellectual and cultural heritage;
3. Higher education is often an important focus of resistance to authoritarian regimes, and plays a significant role in promoting human rights, democracy and cultural and intellectual tolerance;

B. Considers that the development of higher education and research should be guided by the following principles and priorities:

4. The importance of a strong, public higher education sector to ensure that access to lifelong learning is available to all citizens;
5. Access to and participation in higher education should be available to all that meet relevant entry criteria and should not be limited by the financial means or social origins of students. This means that higher education, as well as other education sectors, should be free of charge, and that the State should ensure that adequately funded student support schemes are available. Where fees do apply, they should not exceed 20 per cent of total course costs and appropriate subsidies, grants and options for deferred repayment must be available;
6. Funding for universities, colleges and research institutions is primarily the responsibility of the State,

and the State should maintain its overriding responsibility for ensuring that higher education and research institutions serve the public interest. Where private institutions exist and receive State support, they should be required to adhere to the same standards and levels of accountability as public institutions;

7. While the State has a right and an obligation to insist on public accountability from higher education and research institutions for the expenditure of public funds such accountability should not undermine institutional autonomy in relation to academic policies, curriculum, staff appointments and internal management. Institutional autonomy, in these spheres, is a precondition for the existence of academic freedom. This in turn guarantees that independent research, teaching and scholarship can flourish;

8. An essential element of academic freedom is the right of staff to be directly represented on all key decision-making bodies within universities, colleges and research institutions and for decision-making to reflect collegial principles. Collective decision-making must guarantee and develop individual staff rights such as the freedom to determine teaching style or the right to intellectual property;

9. Research and scholarship is guaranteed and underwritten by the existence of academic tenure or job security. Universities and colleges should provide tenured opportunities through appropriate policies or collective agreements. Member States of UNESCO should be encouraged to adhere to the terms of the UNESCO Recommendation Concerning the Status of Higher Education Teaching Personnel and to adopt positive measures for its speedy implementation. Where staff are not employed in tenured posts but on shorter term contracts, their industrial and professional rights should be equivalent to those of tenured colleagues;

C. Welcomes the progress made in the higher education and research sector since the Harare Congress, particularly in the following areas:

10. the significant increase in affiliations by unions representing higher education and research staff;
11. the major Conference organised jointly with UNESCO in Paris in March 1997;
12. the substantial work done on the UNESCO Recommendation Concerning the Status of Higher Education Teaching Personnel;

D. Considers that this work should be continued with a particular focus on:

— international cooperation in the areas of higher education and research;
— the democratisation of access to higher education in conjunction with the trend toward mass
— provision of higher education;
— the promotion of students' social status;
— the professionalisation of higher education;
— the world-wide financial crisis in higher education (particularly in the developing world);
— the threats to the academic freedom and working conditions of higher education and research staff;

Expanded EI work should aim to:

13. *Strengthen* EI's membership base in the higher education and research sector, and build networks in the sector globally and regionally;
14. *Achieve* and promote the adoption and implementation by National Governments of the UNESCO Recommendation Concerning the Status of Higher Education Teaching

Personnel, and develop an effective monitoring process for its implementation;

15. *Defend* higher education budgets from domestic and international threats in the context of a broader international defence of all education sectors. Opposition to international institutions' attempts to deregulate and privatise education is a central element of this defence;
16. *Develop* EI's policies on the role of universities and colleges in teacher education, on lifelong learning, on the implications of new technology and on the links between education and the economy;
17. *Support* academic freedom and the right to collective bargaining including the protection of intellectual property rights and the defence of contract and part-time staff;
18. *Promote* open and accountable institutional governance and management systems and the appropriate involvement of staff unions;
19. *Strengthen* the input of developing countries into the higher education and research work of EI including its regional structures;
20. *Develop* formally structured higher education and research forums as part of regular EI Regional Conferences and prior to the convening of World Congress Meetings;
21. *Ensure* that EI's higher education and research policies are fully covered in EI's dialogue, co-operative work and advocacy with the relevant international and regional bodies and institutions, to ensure that EI's influence within the higher education and research sector is maximised.

Bibliography

Aggarwal, J.C., *Education Policy in India, 1992, Retrospect and Prospect,* New Delhi, Shipra Publications, 1992.

Arora, G.L., *Child Centred Education for Learning without Burden,* Gurgaon, Haryana, Krishana Publishing Company, 1995.

Arjun Dev, et.al., 1996, *Human Rights: A Source Book,* National Council of Educational Research and Training (NCERT), New Delhi.

Arora, G.L., and Yadav S.K, 1995, 'Curriculum for Human Rights' *Progressive Educational Herald*, Vol, 10, No.1, Hyderabad, pp. 47-50.

Astin, A., 1977, *Four critical years.* San Francisco: Jossey-Bass.

Aries, P., 1962, *Centuries of childhood*, New York: Vintage.

Belanger, P., 1999, *Conference on Education for Democratic Citizenship: Methods, Practices and Strategies*, Warsaw, 4-8 December *1999 : Final report*, Council of Europe, UNESCO, European Commission.

Bergmann, B.R., 1991, Bloated administration, blighted campuses. Academe 77 (6). 12-16.

Blau, P.M., 1973, The organisation of academic work. New York: Wiley.

Bicego, C.T., & Boerma, J.T., 1993, Maternal education and child survival: A comparative study of survey data from 17 countries. *Social Science and Medicine,* 36, 207-228.

Birzea, C., 1996, Education in a World in Transition: between Post-communism and Post-modernism. In *Prospects, vol 26, no. 4,1996.* p. 673-681.

Clark, B.R. (1993). The problem of complexity in modern higher education. In S. Rothblatt & B. Witttrock (Eds.), *The European and American university since* 1800. New York: Cambridge University Press.

Chaurasia Gulab, *Teacher Education and Professional Organisations,* Authorspress, New Delhi, 2000.

Clark, B.R., & Neave, G., Eds. 1992, The encyclopedia of higher education, Volume 4: Academic disciplines and indexes. Oxford: Pergamon.

Dakar Framework for Action: Education for All: *Meeting Our Collective Commitments.* Text adopted by the World Education forum, Dakar, Senegal, 26-28 April 2000.

Danish Ministry of Education, National Education Authority, 2001, *UNESCO Permanent* System of Reporting for Peace, Human rights, Democracy, International understanding and Tolerance : National report *from Denmark.* Copenhagen: Danish Ministry of Education.

Dreeben, Robert, and Adam Gamoran, 1986, "Race, Instruction and Learning." *American Sociological Review* 51:660-69.

Dohmen, G., 1998, *The future of continuing education* in Europe: Lifelong learning for all in *changed learning environments*, Bonn: Federal Ministry of Education and Research.

Education and Development, National Commission on Education 1966, Government of India, New Delhi, 1968.

Education for All: Achieving the goal : The Amman Affirmation. Mid-Decade Meeting of the International Consultative Forum on Education for All, Amman, Jordan, 1996.

Education and Development, 1968, National Commission on Education 1966, Government of India, New Delhi.

Education for All Year 2000 Assessment:*Statistical Document* (2000). Paris: UNESCO, International Consultative Forumon Education for All.

EFA 2000 Assessment (2000) *Draft Country Report*: Japan http://www2.unesco.org/wef/countryreports/japan/contents.html.

EFA 2000 Assessment (2000) *Country report* :Namibia.

Education for All Year 2000 Assessment:*Statistical Document* (2000). Paris: UNESCO, International Consultative Forumon Education for All.

Eichberg, H., 1997, Otherness in encounter thinking folk identity, democracy and civil society with the help of Martin Buber. In

Adult learning and the challenge of the 21st century. Ove Korsgaard (ed.). Copenhagen: Association for World Education.

Framework for Action—Meeting Basic Learning Needs: Guidelines for Implementing the World Declaration on Education for All. Jomtien, Thailand, 5-9. March 1990.

Fulgini, Andrew, J., 1997, "The Academic Achievement of Adolescents from Immigrant Families: The Roles of Family Background, Attitudes, and Behaviour." *Child Development* 68:351-63.

Frank, D.J., Wong, S., Meyer, J. W. & Ramirez, F.O., 2000, What Counts as history: A cross-national and longitudinal study of university curricula. *Comparative Education Review*, 44, 29-53.

Government of India, 1966, Report on the Education Commission 1964-66, Education and National Development, GOI, New Delhi.

_______________, 1992, Programme of Action, National Policy on Education, 1986, GOI, Reprinted by UGC, New Delhi.

_______________, 1985, Ministry of Human Resource Development, Challenge of Education—A Policy Perspective, New Delhi.

Gumport, P.J., 2000, Academic restructuring: Organisational change and institutional imperatives. Higher Education: The International Journal of Higher Education and Educational Planning, 39, 67-91.

Himes. J., Colbert, V., and Mendez, R.G., 1994, *Child Labour and Basic Education in Latin America and the Caribbean: A Proposed UNICEF Initiative, Florence,* United nations Children's Fund Innocenti Research Centre.

Haggis, S.M. (1991) *Education For All :Purpose and context.* Roundtable themes I. Paris: UNESCO.

Hayashi, Shin-ichi (1999) *The History and Activities of Osaka Prefectural High School. Dowa* Education Research Associationhttp://www.erc.hrea.org/Library/curriculum_methodology/HRE_in_Asia2/chapter3.html#Dowa.

International Commission on Education for the Twenty-first Century (1996) *Learning : Thetreasure within : Report to UNESCO* / Jacques Delors (Chairman of the Commission). Paris:UNESCO.

Jain, A., & Nag, M., 1986, Importance of female primary education for fertility reduction in India. *Economic and Political Weekly*, 21, 1602-1608.

Jan Prucha and Eliska Walterova, *Education in a Changing Society*: Czechoslovakia (Prague: Charles University, 1992).

Jangira, N.K., Singh, Ajit and Yadav, S.K., *Training Needs and Motivation of Primary Teachers,* New Delhi, NCERT, 1994.

Jarvis, P., 2001, Globalisation, citizenship and the education of adults in contemporary society. In *Journal of world Education, vol 31, no. 1, 2001,* 21-26.

Kolucki, Barbara, New Focus for A Safe and Enhanced Learning Environment Report for United Nations Children's Fund, 1999.

Krogh, T. (1999) *Feasibility study on the creation* of an International Academy for Education *and Democracy.* Copenhagen: Ministry of Education.

Korsgaard, O., 2001, The battle regarding citizenship : From social citizenship to active citizenship, From adult education to life long learning. In *Journal of World Education, vol.31, no. 1, 2001,* 14-20.

Kalous; OECD, *Reviews of National Policies for Education.*

LeVine, R.A., 1980, Influence of women schooling on maternal behaviour in the Third World. *Comparative Education Review,* 24 (Suppl.), 78-105.

Ministry of Human Resource Development, *National Policy on Education*, New Delhi, Government of India, 1986.

Monbusho, 1996, *Promotion of DowaEducationhttp://www.monbu.go.jp/hakusyo/eng/2_c03.html#2.03.7*

_______________ , 2000, *The Educational Reform Plan* for the 21st Century : The Rainbow Plan (The Seven Priority Strategies)http://www.mext.go.jp/english/topics/21plan/010301.htm.

Ministry of Human Resource Development, *National Policy on Education*, New Delhi, Government of India, 1986.

Meyer. J., & Rowan, B., 1978, The structure of educational organisations, In Meyer (Ed,), Environments and organisations. San Francisco: Jossey-Bass.

National Advisory Committee, Ministry of Human Resource Development, *Learning with Burden,* New Delhi, Government of India 1993.

National Institute for Educational Research (1999) *Teacher Education for Peace and International Understanding.* - Tokyo: NIER.

NCTE, 1996, Human Rights and National Values, National Council for Teacher Education, New Delhi.

NCERT, *Concept of Evaluation in Education*, New Delhi, 1963.

O'Gara, Chloe et al, *Qualities of Caring: Good Practices in Infact and Toddier Group Care*, Washington, D.C., Education Section, World Bank/Academy for Education Development, 1999.

Pradhan, B., Subramanian, A., *Structural Adjustment, Education and Poor Households in India, Analysis of a Sample Survey*. Paper presented at World Bank Workshop on Poverty Reduction and Social Progress: New Trends and Emerging Lessons, April 1999, Dhaka.

Planning Commission, *Working Group on Early Childhood Education*, New Delhi, 1992.

Paul Beresford-Hill, "Markets and Education in Eastern Europe and the Baltic Republics," *in Education and Privatisation in Eastern Europe and the Baltic Republics,* Oxford Studies in Comparative Education (Wallingford: Triangle, 1998).

Pitha, P. (1996) Building up a new citizen in a post-totalitarian society: an educational approach in the Czech Republic. In Prospects, vol *26, no. 4, 1996,* p. 749-755.

Pike, Grham, Selby, David, 1998, in the Global Classroom, Books 1 and 2, Toronto, Pippin Publishing.

Rumberger, Russell W. and J. Douglas Wilms, 1992, "The Impact of Racial and Ethnic Segregation on the Achievement Gap in California High Schools." *Educational Evaluation and Policy Analysis.*

Report of the Committee set up by the Ministry of Human Resources Development, Govt. of India, on *Minimum Levels of Learning at Primary Stage,* NCERT, New Delhi, 1991.

Sixth All India Educational Survey / NCERT.

Towards education for all (1993) The Ministry of Education for Namibia.

UNICEF/EAPRO, *Education: Enrolment and Completion, Quality, Governance and Girls Education.* Fourth East Asia Pacific Ministerial Consultation—Goals and Strategies, Bangkok, United Nations Children's Fund East Asia and Pacific Regional Office, 1998.

UNICEF, 1999, *Progress, Challenges and Future Strategies in Basic Education.*

UNO, *Children and Juveniles in Detention: Application of Human Rights and Standards.* Vienna, Crime Prevention in Latin America, Presentation for Managers, n.d.

UNO, 1994, *Children and Juveniles in Detention: Application of Human Rights and Standards.* Vienna, Crime Prevention and Criminal Justice Branch, United Nations Organisation.

UNESCO/ICE-EFA, 1999, Assessing Learning Achievement, Paris, United Nations Educational, Scientific and Cultural Organisation.

Vasantha R. Patri, *Education in India: Programmes and Policies,* Authorspress, New Delhi, 2000.

Veldhuis, R., 1997, *Dimensions of citizenship, core* competences, variables and international activities. Speech given at the Council of Europe seminar, Strasbourg, 11-12 December 1997: Education to Democratic Citizenship: Basic concepts and core competences. http://culture.coe.fr/postsummit/citizenship/concepts/erap97_23.htm.

Wilson, Franklin, 1985, "The Impact of School Desegregation Programmes on While Public School Enrolment." *Sociology of Education.*

Wright, S., Morley, D., 1989, Learning Works: Searching for Organisational Futures. York University, Toronto, ABL Group, Faculty of Educational Studies.

World Bank, n.d., *The Wolrd Bank and Girl's Education,* Wahington, D.C., World Bank Human Development Network, Education Advisory Service.

World Declaration on Education for All: *Meeting Basic learning needs*, World Conference for Education for All, Jomtien, Thailand, 5-9 March 1990.

WHO, 1999, Child-Friendly Schools: A Mental Helath Promotion Initiative, Geneva, World Health Organisation.

WHO, 1998a, *Healthy Nutrition*, Geneva, World Health Organisation.

Zandstra, H., et al, Caqueza, 1979, Living Rural Development, Ottawa, International Development Research Centre.

Index

Sociocultural background, 3

Worldwide integration, 1